EVERYTHING
HE HASN'T TOLD YOU YET

For Scheherazade, who wove so many intricate and entertaining stories over one thousand and one nights, and for Shahriya, who learned to love her for her wisdom, creativity, and understanding.

Burton Silver & Martin O'Connor

EVERYTHING
HE HASN'T TOLD YOU YET

*A New Way to Get Men Talking
about Stuff That Matters*

TEN SPEED PRESS
Berkeley | Toronto

1➂

TEN SPEED PRESS
P.O. Box 7123
Berkeley, California 94707
www.tenspeed.com

Distributed in Canada by Ten Speed Press Canada.

The moral right of Burton Silver and Martin O'Connor to be identified
as the creators and writers of this work has been asserted by them in
accordance with the Copyright, Designs, and Patents Act, 1988.

Cover design by Katy Brown and Sacha Lees
Text design by Kevin Casey

Library of Congress Cataloging-in-Publication Data

Silver, Burton.
   Everything he hasn't told you yet : a new way to get men talking about
stuff that matters / by Burton Silver and Martin O'Connor.
      p. cm.
   Includes index
   ISBN 978-1-58008-886-2
   1. Men—Psychology. 2. Interpersonal communication. 3. Man-woman
relationships. I. O'Connor, Martin (Martin Peter) II. Title.
   HQ1090.S535 2007
   155.6'32—dc22
                                        2007017371

Printed and bound in China
First USA printing, 2007

1 2 3 4 5 6 7 8 9 10 — 11 10 09 08 07

ACKNOWLEDGMENTS

We wish to acknowledge the tumult and joy of our relationships past and present and the many kind folk who've willingly, and sometimes unwittingly, allowed us to try out the scenarios on them. For their valuable advice and suggestions, we would especially like to thank Jamie, Kevin, Ginny, Frances and Rick, Selma, Graham and Sarah, Neil, Ant and Mish, Rob and Michelle, Anna and Ross, David, Rick, Garry, Steve H., John, Andy and Michelle, Clive and Phyll, Ginny H., Kristen, Carla, Kyle, Dominic and Sasha, Avind and Jane, Biddy and Hugh, Ulli, Penny and Howard, Andrew, Ray, Sebastian and Julian, Pauline and Gareth, Daniella, Suzie, Lily, Ron, Ned, Pip, Caroline and Duncan, Frankie, Dale, Paul, Ben, and particularly Tiuta, who pulled us through when the going got tough.

For my family there is no thank-you big enough. My deepest gratitude to my wife, Melissa, for her love and guidance throughout the creation of this book, and to my children, Harry, Sarah, Francesca, and Dominic, who have endured four years of kitchen table conversations about male-female communication. Their patience, enthusiasm, and youthful insights have made an invaluable contribution to this book.

Burton Silver

Everyone is a product of their past, and this past is influenced in no small measure by the people who we love, and who love us in return. The people from my life I'd particularly like to acknowledge are my mother, Les, my sister Clare, my old friends Steve and Grace and their daughters Monique and Sarah, my dear mates, Ian, Tony, Ron, Rick, and Neil, and my saviors in a bad patch, Erin, Pauline, and their pal, Grant Burge.

Martin O'Connor

CONTENTS

We welcome your feedback.
Please visit the website for more scenarios and to share your
thoughts and experiences with other readers:

www.everythinghehasnttoldyouyet.com

INTRODUCTION

The genesis of any book is seldom straightforward. It usually has a certain serendipitous quality to it. *Everything He Hasn't Told You Yet* was no exception. One day, four years ago, a friend—we'll call her Ruth—asked us for advice. She had a new boyfriend who she thought might be "the one," but he wasn't very communicative, even about his passions. He loved golf, for instance, but when she tried to talk to him about it, he wasn't forthcoming. She'd asked all the standard questions, such as where he played, how long he'd been into golf, what his handicap was, etc., but only received the most basic responses. Surely if he was passionate about it he would want to share his enthusiasm.

But even though we were both involved in golf we couldn't think of any questions that might open him up, other than to ask him how often he cleaned his balls. Ruth was not amused, and stormed off saying: "Why can't you be serious? I just want to know him better."

We were left to contemplate what she had just said. Okay, it was fine that she wanted some depth, but if she only asked him closed questions, what did she expect? To compound matters, she was asking informational questions that treated him like a statistic rather than a person. Even if she had asked him how he felt about golf, it would have been too broad. He could have answered: "Fine yesterday, horrible today." We thought she needed to be more open-ended with her questioning. Were we right? If women want to connect with men on a deeper level, would they get better results by asking questions that men didn't already know the answer to and really had to think about?

Then and there we set ourselves the task of trying out on our golfing friends more personal questions that went beyond the superficial. We asked them things such as: How do you think your playing style reflects you as a person? Are you proud of your ability and why? Think back to the first time you ever stepped onto a golf course, can you remember how you felt? Were you in awe? Were you feeling intimidated or underwhelmed? Excited or frightened? Why?

> **How can you expect to connect with a man on a deeper level if you only ask him questions he already knows the answers to and doesn't really have to think about?**

We found that despite the more personal nature of these questions guys were enthusiastic and willing to share their thoughts and feelings. Why was this? It seemed to us that instead of asking for information, we were now asking questions that clearly respected the depth of their interest in the sport. We also deduced that by moving beyond small talk they felt an expectation to deliver. What surprised us was that we formed momentary but rewarding connections with guys who we'd been acquainted with for years but had not known well. These connections changed the way we talked with them because our questions showed them that we were interested in them as individuals, and not just in their golfing achievements, skill, or knowledge.

One of these conversations was at a mixed social gathering. We'd asked a friend—we'll call him Richard—how he'd become interested in golf. It turned out that his father had taught him. So we asked him whether it had been much fun. Had he enjoyed playing golf with his dad? He told us that while his dad had taught him the basics, he'd mostly left him to his own devices. Richard's dad didn't know how to act like a father because he'd never really had one himself—*his* dad had died when he was very young. As Richard explained, "It's probably why I spend so much time with my son at the club. I'm still not sure how much he likes golf, but I want to be there for him. I guess I want him to have what I didn't." At this point Richard's wife said, "You've never told me that before." To which Richard replied, "Well, you never really asked."

Like many of the other guys we'd talked to, Richard said he hadn't been hiding information from his wife. In fact, until we asked him our questions, his replies had been as big a secret to him as it had been to us, or her. We wondered how many other couples were out there who had "secrets" between each other that were just lying there because neither of them had the right language code to unearth them. So we shifted our attention from the male friends in our lives to the women, and we asked them directly about communicating with the men in their lives. Their responses were almost unanimous—like Ruth, they just couldn't seem to get their men to talk about more personal things. Now there could be all sorts of reasons why men withhold this sort of information, but one reason could be that their women ask the wrong questions, or ask the right ones in the wrong way.

We're not psychologists or counselors or self-proclaimed relationship experts. But we are writers, so contemplating whether our theory would translate into a useful resource was irresistible. We quickly succumbed to the idea and decided on a light, quirky approach, partly because it came naturally to us, but mostly because we felt that it best allowed the material to be absorbed, especially given the topic— couples gaining a closer connection within their relationships. Testing our theory on our friends had shown us that men would be far more willing to participate if the tone was light, engaging, and challenging.

We set about creating groups of questions that we thought would open guys up and allow them to talk more freely. But initial feedback was not good, and the reason soon became obvious. When we had asked our friends more involving questions, we were present to pick up on what they said and advance the dialogue. But with isolated questions printed in a book, there was no way of knowing what different men would say. Therefore, there was no means of feeding off their replies or gauging their interest in order to take the conversation to a deeper level. We were stumped.

Several months later we still had no solution and were ready to give up, when luck intervened. One evening a friend told us about an incident he'd had with his five-year-old nephew. He was looking after the little tyke one Saturday afternoon in his garage. He was working on his car, and the nephew was playing with a toy carpentry set. The boy soon became bored, and after a few fruitless attempts to get his uncle's attention, he locked himself in the car and started up the engine. A bunch of us were listening to this anecdote, and as the story unfolded, we noticed all the men were rapt, and began suggesting what they'd do in a similar situation. And of course, they all wanted to know what actually happened. It was then that we realized how we could make our book work. If we could extend men's involvement beyond the first question by creating a context that they could immerse themselves in, they might reciprocate with in-depth answers without specific guidance. How could we do that? Simple. We needed stories and we needed to put the men into them.

As writers we should have realized this a lot earlier. The first rule of a good story is that you have to have the reader identify with the protagonist. Then, when the story places the protagonist in challenging situations, the reader immediately becomes involved, takes on the problems as his own and wants to resolve them. We wrote up a few scenarios (including *Gordie in the Garage, #205*) and once again headed back to test our hypothesis. Results were immediate. Not only did the guys become involved, but also it seemed that the degree of separation from reality afforded by the scenarios allowed them to role-play with enthusiasm. This in turn gave them permission to talk more freely and candidly.

As our writing and testing continued, we realized that the interpretations at the end of each scenario were as eagerly anticipated as the scenarios themselves. This seemed to be part of the challenge, especially for men who want to know where they stand in the world. They were keen to know how they'd done. Were they bathed in glory or drenched in shame? Well, the truth is that we never intended the interpretations to be judgmental. They were designed as an initial guide to help couples sort through all the information that may have been revealed, and like the scenarios, they were merely kick starts to further discussion and closer connection.

When you put a man into a scenario that's involving and challenging, yet nonthreatening, you'll find he suddenly has plenty to say and begins to communicate on a much deeper level.

As to the subject matter of each scenario, we felt that if our objective was to help couples connect on a more intimate level, the themes had to be ones of substance but not too demanding initially. So we structured the book in seven levels and reintroduced the reader to a man as if she were meeting him for the first time. Opinions on women, status, physical appearance, family, and relationships in general may have seemed as if we were going over well-trodden and familiar territory, but we found that the gaps in our subjects' knowledge here were immense. As we stated earlier, these gaps or secrets weren't intentional omissions, they were merely gems waiting to be unearthed. The knowledge gained in the first levels then gave much more sense and context to the themes explored in the later chapters—namely, character traits such as honesty, commitment, and consideration. It's through these themes that couples really began to explore their respective stances from a united front and learned how to connect with mutual respect and understanding. Four years on and many trials later, we now have over 100 scenarios that can act as an invaluable tool for promoting meaningful, rich, and intriguing dialogue. That's because while the scenarios are involving and challenging, they're mostly not directly about him, which means he becomes absorbed in them as he does in a movie or novel and feels free to show his emotions and communicate on a much deeper level.

These scenarios can also approach sensitive themes from an oblique angle, and so lead into discussion more easily. For instance, a frivolous exercise on sports is directed at the delicate area of personal space, while a lighthearted exploration of fantasy is designed to encourage you both to share your feelings about honesty.

So who is this book for? If you are in a long-term relationship that you feel needs enriching, or if you're just getting to know a new man in your life, then the material in this book will be helpful. You may be single but want to use these scenarios as a barometer by trying them out on male friends, relatives, or coworkers. Alternatively, you may just want to use it for yourself to gain some personal insights and have a little fun. But essentially, if you are like most of the women we've talked to over the last few years who felt as if they were slamming their heads against an impenetrable wall, *Everything He Hasn't Told You Yet* will give you a unique way of communicating with men, and almost certainly lead to a closer connection.

Some of you have expressed concern about how to decode his answers. Don't try too hard. Let things unfold naturally. In the beginning you should simply be looking for gaps in your knowledge of him, clues as to why he's become the way he is, and opportunities to direct your conversations that will allow both of you to understand each other better. Most of the scenarios are reversible, which means that you can also reveal yourself to him. This may uncover some fascinating differences in your respective takes on the world, and again, it will be up to both of you to decide whether they represent hurdles to be negotiated, or differences to be celebrated.

It might be very tempting to use this book as a series of tests in order to support an unflattering take on your man, or ex-boyfriend or boss, by focusing on perceived negative interpretations, to the exclusion of all else. We can't stop you from doing this, but it's not what the book is about, and it would be a waste of a golden opportunity to form a more intimate connection with your man. Equally, you could fall into the trap of not honoring the information you receive by sharing it indiscriminately with your friends. If a man is to open up and reveal his "secrets"—his fears, dreams, and ambitions—he will need to know he can trust you with this new knowledge, and that you won't use it as ammunition to condemn him now or at some later date. Far from it. It should provide you both with the basis for an enduring friendship.

When your man is laughing, opening up, and revealing his secrets through these scenarios, somehow he will need to know that he can trust you with this new information.

And here lies the cornerstone of *Everything He Hasn't Told You Yet*. By asking him challenging yet hypothetical questions—ones that excite him and ask for solutions—you will engage him. You're saying to him that you know he has depth and that you're interested in this side of him. Your main concern is not how old he is, what his job is, what car he drives, or any other question that treats him like a commodity. You're treating him as a man of substance because you are a woman of substance, and if you knew him on a deeper level you'd be a great support to him, as he would be to you.

This approach works with men and women who want a partner to know them and all their faults, and still love them. The biggest truth we've discovered while writing *Everything He Hasn't Told You Yet* is that successful relationships are based on true friendship. For this to happen, there must be implicit trust. Men are used to being questioned by women in order to find out if they really are "the one." But how much perception and understanding you're able to show him through the course of these scenarios will determine whether he thinks *you're* "the one."

Time and time again in our testing, men told us that what a woman looked like, or how good she was in bed, was not the deciding factor when it came to choosing a life partner. In the end what they wanted was a woman who could see right through them and not fall for all the games they used to keep people from getting too close. They wanted a woman they could respect for the depth of her perception—a woman who understood them and still loved them. Not surprisingly, we found that women were looking for exactly the same thing in men.

What can make understanding difficult is our different communication styles. Women seek connection while men tend to be competitive and want to problem-solve. We know that drives you crazy. But now, instead of fighting it or giving up, you can use the nonthreatening scenarios in this book to encourage his natural inclination to analyze situations and provide solutions. In the process you'll find him opening up and conversing on a deeper, more connecting level.

Above all, we want you to have fun with this book. True friendship, while based on mutual trust, respect, and admiration, also needs levity to act as much as a release valve as a catalyst. With this in mind, we've given the scenarios a quirky, sometimes whimsical flavor to ensure that things don't become too heavy. Getting to know each other shouldn't be a serious chore. It should flow naturally with plenty of lighthearted moments. We all know that interesting and amusing conversations keep relationships alive. In this respect, you can play your part too. If you're able to stay relaxed, and translate this into your delivery, it will significantly raise the chances that your partner will respond in the same light manner, and give you back far more than you've ever received before.

INSTRUCTIONS

The Basic Approach

1. Choose a scenario that you want to try out on your man and choose the right time.

2. Read the preamble and scenario to yourself.

3. Read through the "What Did He Tell You?" section at the end of the scenario. However, don't read this section if you want him to try the exercise on you.

4. Having acquainted yourself with the setup, read the scenario to your man, starting from the words: "Ask Him This."

5. Read the "What Did He Tell You?" section to your man.

6. Be prepared to discuss anything that ensues from the completed scenario.

What's the Right Scenario and the Right Time?

Everything He Hasn't Told You Yet is a progressive course, which means that the book gradually moves from simple, fun scenarios to more demanding and challenging material. For instance, in Levels One and Two we explore personality, interests, skills, status perception, and stereotyping. These early chapters are, in essence, a kind of reacquainting exercise. They will give you a sense of the tangible absolutes that men carry with them.

From here we move to Level Three—the family. This is a pivotal chapter because it's from his early experiences that so much of his behavior has been formed and shaped. In the next two levels we explore how this background has affected his attitudes and behavior toward women and relationships.

In the last two levels we broaden our focus to include subjects such as integrity, consideration, tolerance, values, and all the other ingredients of character that impact on both his relationships and his place in the world.

As a consequence, we would recommend that your first forays into the book with your man should start at the beginning. Apart from the fact that the book has a certain order to it, the early levels are much more fun oriented and deal with less threatening issues. It's the ideal starting point.

As for the right time? Well, that's a judgment call. Use your intuition. But remember that some men may find these types of exercises threatening until they learn that it's safe to take part and their disclosures will be honored. So choose your moment wisely. Catch him when he's relaxed, and when time isn't going to be an issue—but not when he's zoning out in front of the television. Car journeys, as long as they're not stressful, can be a good time. Many of these scenarios can also be done over the phone or even online, one question at a time.

Why Should You Read the Preamble?

The preamble is the paragraph written in capital letters immediately under the title of each scenario. It is for your eyes only. Don't read it out aloud. It will give you helpful hints about how to approach each scenario, including what to look out for and how to style your delivery.

For example, we might ask you to keep a fast pace, thus promoting one-word replies that will limit the chance for him to screen his answers. In other scenarios, however, the content may be more complicated, and your man may need to be drawn out by you adding your own questions and by giving him more time.

What Did He Tell You?

This is the interpretation of your man's answers. Except when told otherwise in the preamble, you should read this section before you begin the scenario because it will give you a clear idea of what he's actually revealing to you as he replies to each question.

At the conclusion of the scenario you should then share this analysis with him. But remember, there are no right or wrong answers, so try not to be judgmental. The purpose of this book is to promote a deeper dialogue between both of you, and for you therefore to have a better understanding of each other.

It's also important to honor what he's revealed. He may be sharing some pretty personal stuff with you, and he'll only continue to do so if he feels you're being loyal. Therefore, we would suggest that you don't share his answers with your friends, and that for the most part, you should only deliver these scenarios privately. There are some scenarios that could be used in a group setting, but the majority of the book is intended for confidential sharing between you and the people you try them on.

Many of the scenarios are reversible, which means that you could get your man to ask you the questions. In this case it would be better for you not to read the "What Did He Tell You?" section first. That way, your answers will be as unguarded as his.

Your Delivery and His Responses

When reading the scenario, stick to any instructions from the preamble and try to keep your delivery light.

It's essential for you to treat the entire exercise with fun and lightheartedness. The last thing you want to do is make him clam up. So it'll be up to you to convince him that the scenario you've chosen is both entertaining and challenging. But if he shows signs of discomfort such as fidgeting or interrupting, either choose another scenario or just drop it altogether and pick it up again when you feel he'll be more comfortable.

Remain as impassive as you can. A positive or negative reaction on your part might preempt him and lead him off on a tangent that won't reflect what he's really thinking or feeling.

Many men feel uncomfortable talking about their emotions due mainly to the structure of the male brain. In fact, neural studies show that men take up to seven times longer than women to process emotional data. So try to keep the sessions relatively short at first, and make sure he's having fun. Work on the less-is-more theory. If you do more than one or two scenarios in one sitting they will gradually merge into each other, and you'll both retain little. The idea of this book, as we've said previously, is to promote discussion. So allow time for this to happen. Even if nothing immediately ensues, some of the issues raised will stay with him and he may bring them up later.

It's worth noting that men sometimes enjoy making fun of the scenarios by giving ridiculous replies. They can be surprisingly quick-witted with their answers and women have often admitted to us, somewhat guiltily, that they've been so helpless with laughter they couldn't steer their men back on course. In reality, this is no bad thing. Indeed, rather than trying to curtail your man's levity and make him take things seriously, we think you should let his humor take flight and even spur it on with a little disapproval. This is sure to encourage the "naughty boy" in him and drive him on to new comedic heights. When you finally crack, he'll feel his wit has been rewarded by your laughter, which in turn will flood your system with plenty of stress-reducing endorphins. Playfulness is a wonderful thing in a relationship and if these scenarios promote mutual hilarity, welcome it with open arms. After all, you can always come back to the exercise another time and do it "seriously."

Of course you need to be aware that making light of something is an effective way of providing a distraction in order to avoid a sensitive area. So his humor could in fact be signaling that he's not comfortable with the topic and letting you know that it may be a good idea to shelve it for a later time.

How to Use the Scenario Index

While we recommend that in the early stages of using this book you do the scenarios in the order that they appear, you will reach a stage in which your man is enjoying the experience and regards the book as an entertaining challenge, rather than a threat. At this point you may want to dip and dive through the later chapters. The best way to do this is to use the scenario index.

In the scenario index we've listed all the character traits and themes that are examined in the book. After each entry there are numbers that will direct you to relevant scenarios.

In Summary

- Stick to the early levels until you're both ready to advance.

- Keep your delivery light.

- Try to remain impassive.

- Before you start a scenario read the preamble, but only to yourself.

- Pick your moment, and don't let the time drag.

- Don't force the issue—if he appears at all unwilling, drop it for a later time.

- If he hams it up, enjoy his humor and laugh along.

- Respect his participation and he'll stay interested.

- There are no right or wrong answers.

Remember, *Everything He Hasn't Told You Yet* is about promoting deeper dialogue, having fun, and staying connected. It is not a book of tests. The only way your man can fail is to be too frightened to take part in the exercises. He succeeds by showing you he's not scared to reveal himself and when he does, your respect and understanding will be the reward. If he feels he doesn't stack up so well in a particular exercise, there is still a simple route to success by acknowledging his shortcoming—the bravest act of all.

LEVEL 1

What Floats His Boat?

What Floats His Boat? is the lightest series of scenarios designed to provide you and your man with hours of stimulating talk and laughter. It will also give you an idea of your man's interests, his reasoning ability, and a few of his basic values. If you are just beginning a new relationship, the information you get will be helpful in gauging whether he has a sense of fun and just how compatible you are with him. The facts you get from this level will be much like scanning his music and book collection to see where he's at. You'll learn what some of his priorities and core beliefs are, and gain insight into his self-image.

If you are already in a long-term relationship, these exercises will still be useful as warm-ups and allow him to answer basic questions that are nonthreatening. But note that even at this early stage you should be asking him feeling questions. When he's interested in something or someone, he'll appreciate a feeling question. In *#101 Who Does He Know?*, for instance, don't just sit on his answers. Prompt him to give more information later by asking him how he *felt* about a particular person, and why he *felt* this. Don't just ask him man-type questions that require information.

The second half of *What Floats His Boat?* examines his views on physical appearance and status, some of his basic values, and his self-awareness. You'll also get an early hint of his personality traits and his thinking patterns.

When two people are attracted to each other, the initial appeal may be strictly superficial. This appeal will be very strong, of course, because it will be based on personal preferences, many of which may have been shaped by experience. For instance, the early female role models in your man's life may have had a certain look, and may have behaved in a certain way. If he had positive experiences with these women, they will tend to act as a blueprint for future attraction.

Similarly, your man may have formed a blueprint of the ideal man based on the men in his past. This will have a big impact on the way he sees himself and the way he thinks others perceive him. It's where his views on status, career, and personality come into play.

The information you get from *What Floats His Boat?* will give you insights into your man's true sense of self, especially if you are patient, gentle, and thoughtful in the way you approach these exercises and the way you prompt him into more detail. Above all, you need to remember that what you'll hear from your man needs to be treated with respect, and not used as ammunition to hurt him or to support a position of yours. After all, the purpose of this book is to allow him to open up and stay connected. While the insights you gain from this chapter may be revealing, it will be the ensuing discussions that will ultimately enable both of you to see how this information has shaped your stances and behavior.

Remember, while you're discovering just how clever, cool, adventurous, and altruistic your man really is, he'll be taking careful note of just how perceptive and understanding *you* really are.

101.

WHO DOES HE KNOW?

THIS IS A GREAT EXERCISE TO BEGIN WITH. NAMES JUST POP UP OUT OF NOWHERE AND LEAD TO ENDLESS CONVERSATIONS. TRY IT YOURSELF AND SEE WHAT YOU COME UP WITH. BECAUSE OF THE WAY WORD ASSOCIATION WORKS, YOU'LL NEED TO READ THE NAMES QUITE QUICKLY. IF HE STRUGGLES WITH A NAME, JUST MOVE ON.

ASK HIM THIS: "Who are your favorites from the world of music, movies, television, the arts, and politics? I'm going to read you a list of first names and I want you to give the first surname that comes to mind."

Hugh…	Uncle…	Mickey…	Walt…
Gary…	Walter…	Margot…	Rita…
Lucy…	Margaret…	Doctor…	Harry…
Judge…	Ben…	Julia…	Emily…
Julie…	Will…	William…	Ronald…
Ruth…	Venus…	Lily…	Dorothy…

Martha...	Donald...	Peggy...	Elizabeth...
Liz...	Marilyn...	Carol...	Susan...
Frank...	Woody...	Hank...	Henry...
Tom...	Billy...	Sally...	Charlotte...
John...	Johnny...	Mary...	Richard...
Dick...	Howard...	Emma...	Alice...
Lou...	Louis...	Minnie...	Betty...
Bob...	Joan...	Shirley...	Claire...
Don...	Jane...	Danny...	Douglas...
Stephen...	Steve...	George...	Ted...
Daniel...	Helen...	Max...	Michael...
Ken...	Martin...	Barbara...	Amy...
Joe...	Rachel...	Debbie...	Carmen...
Faye...	Arthur...	Sylvia...	Gloria...
Kelly...	Arnold...	Linda...	Mark...

WHAT DID HE TELL YOU?

This exercise will reveal much about his general knowledge, his interests, his past influences, and very possibly his age—or at least the era that he may feel most comfortable in.* Can you detect a pattern in his answers? For instance, how many of the people he mentioned are athletes? Or actors? Or writers? Or politicians? And what about you? Did it bring up people and interests in your life that he was curious about?

Of course you will probably already know about each other's current social networks and primary interests, but it's surprising how some of the more latent influences in one's life can be revealed in this exercise. All sorts of surnames will pop up out of nowhere and catch you unawares. There'll be people who seem to be of no particular consequence at all, or folk who've had a significant influence on your lives in the past or now. By asking each other about these people, you'll be able to bring back memories that can tell you both a great deal about your upbringing and the people who've shaped you.

As we mentioned earlier, the patterns are what you should be looking for. If your man's answers to Ronald, Mickey, Donald, Tom, Woody, George, and Howard were Ronald McDonald, Mickey Mouse, Donald Duck, Tom and Jerry, Woody Woodpecker, George of the Jungle, and Howard the Duck, then maybe he's too young for you. Too young at heart anyway. And if you picked Lily Langtree, Don Ameche, Mary Pickford, and Walter Pigeon, you may possibly be too old for him!

It's fun to return to this exercise and do it again at a later date because the names you pick the second time around will more than likely be different. Of course you can always add your own selection of names to the list to give it more scope.

* Also note that some of his answers may be influenced by topical events being played out in the media, and he may give names of people he wouldn't normally be interested in.

TWENTY THINGS YOU NEED TO KNOW WHEN HE'S WATCHING SPORTS

SO WHAT IS IT WITH HIM AND SPORTS? READ THE ANALYSIS AT THE END AND YOU MIGHT EVEN FEEL SORRY FOR HIM.

ASK HIM THIS: "So, what do I need to know when you're watching sports? I'm going to read you a series of statements and I want you to complete them as quickly as possible."

> Rule 1: When you have friends over to watch the game, time is put aside before the start to…
>
> Rule 2: When the guys come over, it's okay for me to say hello but…
>
> Rule 3: The only possible reasons you would stop watching a live sports event are…
>
> Rule 4: If you're watching a recorded game, I should never, ever…
>
> Rule 5: If I want to watch the game with you, I should never…
>
> Rule 6: When you're watching sports, children are…

Rule 7: While watching sports, the remote control is...

Rule 8: If the phone rings during a game, the standard rule is...

Rule 9: When there's an injury or commercial break in the broadcast, it doesn't mean that I can...

Rule 10: Food during the game is great, but it should always be...

Rule 11: When the opposing team scores, you reserve the right to...

Rule 12: When your team scores, it's not unreasonable for you to...

Rule 13: Watching sports is important to you because...

Rule 14: Keeping abreast of sports by watching shows such as SportsCenter enables you to...

Rule 15: Sports gives you an insight into...

Rule 16: Watching sports makes you feel...

Rule 17: If your team loses, you often need to...

Rule 18: When your team wins, there is an almost compulsive urge to...

Rule 19: After the game, time is set aside to...

Rule 20: Watching sports is much more than voyeurism. Essentially, it's...

What Did He Tell You?

Okay, we just thought he needed an opportunity to state his case on sports. None of this will be a surprise to him, and it probably won't be a surprise to you either. But maybe this exercise will show you how sacred and ritualized males' sports watching really is. According to evolutionary psychologists the reason is straightforward: sports are a means of displaying physical fitness in order to attract females and intimidate sexual rivals. Winning at sports necessitates being robust and aggressive—traits that show not only his ability to protect you, but also that he possesses the heritable fitness to sire healthy offspring. Sports such as skiing and golf that require expensive equipment and exotic venues also serve as indicators of wealth.

Watching sports, they say, is an indirect form of display. For men who are unable to participate at the top level, joining the crowd or tuning into the sportscast is an important way of demonstrating their continued involvement and an appreciation of the game. This also applies to long discussions about sports, usually held within earshot of women. So when your man is standing on the sofa screaming obscenities at the umpire on the tube, or enthusiastically engaged in interminable after-match postmortems, he's actually subtly letting you know how deeply concerned he is with the intricacies of physical competition—and that means he's going to be better at defending you. So cut him some slack; watching sports is his way of showing that he's worthy of your love. Believe us!*

There may be another more biological reason for all the countless hours of watching and reading that sports occupies in a man's life. Put simply, men still have the male hormone, testosterone, surging through their blood, which ensures they're aggressive enough to effectively extend and defend their realm. While women have hormones such as oxytocin, which point them toward empathy and nurturing, men are more spatially oriented and hormonally disposed to activities that require the construction, practice, and analysis of system hierarchies such as business and sports. So while women discuss who's having a tough time with their relationship, men are likely to be talking about how a rule change would improve the game.

Another viewpoint contends that women's changing roles over the last few decades have contributed to an upsurge in males watching sports. While women continue to reinvent their place in the world, men have been marking time. Technological and industrial development, as well as a growing competition from women, have left them somewhat rudderless. Traditionally, men were the hunters and defenders, and because of their different physical attributes, they were more suited to defending their families and communities. But things have changed. Traditional work requiring strength and stamina is gradually decreasing, and attempts to resolve major conflicts now lean toward tactical and strategic weapons systems rather than hand-to-hand combat. As a result, the search for a male identity has intensified and found expression in the physicality of sports.

And just for the record, we're reliably informed that men who are into solo sports such as mountain biking or surfing guard their independence and enjoy spending time alone. On the other hand, guys who are into established team sports such as football, baseball, and basketball tend to be competitive—on the field and off. Men who aren't into sports much tend to be independent thinkers and more sensitive than most.

* We feel it only fair to warn you that a recent study of two thousand British men showed they were nearly twice as loyal to their favorite soccer team as they were to their partners. In fact, fifty-two percent said they would ditch their partners if their relationship wasn't going well as opposed to ninety-four percent who said they'd never stop loving their team no matter how badly it was doing.

103.

MAKING SOME NOISE

THE MORE YOU CAN MAKE THIS EXERCISE SEEM LIKE A DARE, THE FUNNIER HE'LL COME ACROSS. TRY NOT TO BE JUDGMENTAL. MOVE ON QUICKLY TO EACH NEW SOUND.

ASK HIM THIS: "How many different noises can you make? I'm going to read you a list of situations or objects and I want you to imitate the sounds that they make."

- Make the sounds you hear at the Indy 500.

- Make the sound of a horse.

- Make the sound of a babbling brook.

- Make the sound of a raging storm.

- Make the sound of bubbles.

- Make the sound of a trombone.

- Make the sound of a helicopter approaching.

- Make the sound of an espresso coffee machine.

- Talk like Donald Duck.

- Talk like John Wayne.

- Make the sounds of a Jackie Chan fight scene.

- Make the sounds of two heavyweight boxers in a title fight.

- Make the sound of someone using a chain saw and accidently cutting off one of their legs.

- Make the sound of someone falling off a cliff while playing a banjo.

- Make the sound of a tomcat serenading another cat in heat.

- Make the sound of someone trying to start a car on a very cold morning.

- Make the sound of taking out an enemy tank by blasting it with a machine gun and then tossing a grenade at it. (If he spends more than five minutes on this, he could have an anger management problem.)

- Make the sound of a bullfrog serenading a female frog. (You could respond as a female frog to help him along.)

- Make the sound of a freight train coming toward you and then speeding off into the distance.

- Say the word "huh" fifty times, starting slowly and gradually building up speed.

- Lastly, do you have a signature noise that you could share with me now?

What Did He Tell You?

Does he have a sense of fun? Was he prepared to take a risk and let himself appear a bit foolish? Did he get so into the sounds that he even used physical actions to accompany them? If he did, it shows that he can laugh at himself and enjoy entertaining others.

But being able to imitate sounds also tells us about a man's ability to relate. You may have noticed that from the time boys are able to verbalize, many of them indulge in mimicking the sounds they hear around them. Whether they're real or imaginary, dogs or dragons, magpies or martians, every nuance of noise is subject to a constant round of practice and performance. These sound effects are inserted into their fantasy play, which is a necessary preparation for adulthood. The more realistic they can make these games with lifelike sounds, the more they can get into the role and the more intense the experience will be—and of course the more others will want to play with them.

For some, this practice continues into adulthood; at social gatherings from Rome to Reno, grown men take delight in competing with each other to reproduce complex sounds with nothing more than their hands, lips, and vocal chords. In earlier times, imitating bird song or animal mating sounds would have been useful in hunting, but nowadays such displays of skill serve another purpose.

Because it's often so unexpected, good mimicry can be surprisingly funny and immediately attract attention. For example, a man who can adopt a perfect foreign accent is able to make his stories far more entertaining and become the life and soul of the party. In so doing, he not only increases his chances of being noticed by potential mates, but also shows that he is good at relationships. That's because women intuitively know that good imitators have to be good listeners and observers, and that means they can empathize.

104.

ISLAND OF FIRE

MEN LOVE THIS BRAINTEASER. YOU MAY NEED TO REPEAT IT
A COUPLE OF TIMES TO MAKE SURE HE FULLY UNDERSTANDS
THE PROBLEM.

ASK HIM THIS: "You and your girlfriend have been dropped off
by helicopter at the southern end of an island in order to observe
an endangered species of bird. The island is very small. It's only a
hundred yards wide and a thousand yards long. It also has sheer cliffs
hundreds of feet high all around it. But finding the rare bird will be
difficult because the island is covered in thick brush that's five feet tall."

Unfortunately, even before you've started your search things
take a bad turn. You see smoke. As the helicopter took off over
the northern end of the island, the pilot flicked out a cigarette
butt and inadvertently started a fire that smoldered unobserved
for a while and then flared up. It's now being fanned by a
strong wind heading in your direction, and you have no way
of contacting the helicopter or calling for help. The fire will
reach you in half an hour. You don't have any tools with you,
so you try to dig a hole with your hands but the ground is too
hard. You look over the edge of the cliffs and realize that even
climbing down a few feet is impossible, and jumping would
mean certain death. Even from where you're standing you

can tell the heat of the fire is intense. Trying to run through it would be fatal. So, in order to survive, what do you and your girlfriend do?

What Did He Tell You?

Did he have a clue? What about you? Did you know? This is an exercise in logic and survival skills. How quickly was he able to think? How many different ideas did he manage to come up with?

Island of Fire is not about right or wrong. In fact, ninety percent of the men who've tried this exercise haven't been able to figure out the solution.* But that's not the point. Try to imagine his problem-solving abilities as a continuum, with one end representing an early surrender and the other end representing pigheaded stubbornness. Where does he fall on this continuum? Obviously, you don't want him to give up too easily, but you also don't want him to turn the exercise into some kind of mission to demonstrate his superiority. He needs to know when to give in having exhausted all his possibilities. And it would be great if he could do this with a little humility.

You might also like to consider whether he involved the girlfriend in his survival attempt or whether he tried to solve it alone. This could tell you whether he's a team player who's prepared to share his problems within a relationship or someone who feels that the big questions are the preserve of the male.

* The answer? You run forward to the fire with a long piece of scrub and set it alight. You take this burning scrub and start another fire a hundred yards from the southern end of the island. When this has burnt off, you can both stand in the burnt area and you will be safe from the advancing flames of the original fire. That's because when it gets to you there will be nothing left for it to burn. To avoid getting scorched when you go to light the piece of scrub, you can wrap your girlfriend's clothes over yours to provide additional protection.

105.

WAR ZONE

WHEN THE CHIPS ARE DOWN, AND ENEMY SOLDIERS ARE
SCOURING THE COUNTRYSIDE FOR YOU, HOW COOL, CALM,
AND COLLECTED WILL YOUR MAN BE WHEN IT COMES TO
MAKING SURE YOU'RE SAFE?

ASK HIM THIS: "Do you ever think about a war on your home turf? I'm going to read you a scenario and I want you to answer the questions as we go along."

It's wartime and your country has been invaded. Your wife, who is a photographer, has just taken pictures of the invading troop positions. These images will be crucial to a counter-attack planned by the resistance forces for the next day. You are having toast and coffee while looking at the images on her camera's digital display when you see an enemy vehicle approaching. You bundle her and her camera into a big old trunk in the loft. You just have time to lock it and hide the key in a jar of raspberry jam that's on the kitchen table before a female officer and two male soldiers rush in. The soldiers tie you to a chair and then search the house while the officer interrogates you. I'm going to play the part of the officer and while I'm questioning you I want you to hold your hands behind your back as if you're tied to the chair.

The officer says, "Were you the only person here before we arrived?"

You say...

She asks, "Is anybody hiding here?"

You say...

Then she says, "We've had reports that a woman was seen taking photographs of our troops. Do you know her?"

You say...

The officer says, "We've been told that your wife is a photographer. Is she here?"

Then she says, "When did you last see her?"

You say...

"What was she wearing at that time?"

Then she asks, "When do you expect her back?"

You say...

"Why are there two empty coffee cups here?"

"Why does this one have lipstick on the rim?"

"Are you telling the truth?"

"Then what is this empty camera case doing here?"

At this point one of the soldiers comes in and whispers in her ear.

"My men have told me that there is a heavy trunk in the loft. What is in this trunk?"

"The trunk is locked. Where is the key?"

"There are two pieces of toast here on two plates. Who was the second plate for?"

"You expect me to believe that?"

"I can tell from your body language that everything you've told me has been a lie. Do you know what we do to people who won't cooperate? We get rid of them. But if you confess now I'll go easy on you. So, where is your wife?"

"Look, I'm going to count to three and if you haven't told me where your wife is, I'm going to shoot you. Do you understand?"

"Alright! One........Two..........do you have a last request?"

"Interesting. One........Two..........Thinking about killing you is making me hungry. You wouldn't mind if I had a cup of coffee and some fresh toast, would you?"

"This raspberry jam, do you mind if I try some?"

At this point the two soldiers come back into the room and say that they haven't been able to break into the trunk.

She asks you, "Are you *sure* you don't know where the key to the trunk is?"

"Well, we're going to have to get into it because it's the only place my men haven't looked. We can either shoot the lock off, which may put holes into whatever is inside, or we can get you to help us drag it to the loft door and let it drop two stories so that it smashes open. You choose. Do we shoot the lock off or do you help us drop it?"

What do you say?

What Did He Tell You?

How did he do under pressure, and perhaps more importantly, how did you feel applying it? Some women tell us they were surprised at how much they enjoyed being the overbearing interrogator and were disappointed when the scenario came to an end. Others have reported hating being so heavy. How you felt may tell you whether you'd like to take a more dominant role in relationship interactions or whether you're more comfortable being submissive or neutral. And how did your man feel about being questioned in this way? Did he dislike you in this role or did he enjoy you playing the heavy with him? Did he feel weakened by having his hands behind his back?

Were you impressed with his efforts? How well do you think he'd be able to protect you with his verbal acuity? Did he answer the last question quickly so as not to draw attention to the importance of the trunk or did he make the mistake of deliberating too long. Or was he not really in role anyway? Did he see the jam problem coming up when you asked for toast? How did he answer the last question? Did he choose to help drag the trunk so that his hands would be untied and he'd have time to think of a physical strategy?

106.

THE TALKING CAMEL

This is a fun exercise that will activate your man's brain by placing him in unusual situations. His answers may surprise you.

Ask Him This: "How do you cope with the unexpected? I'm going to read you a series of scenarios, and I want you to answer the incomplete statement at the end of each story. But remember, there are no right or wrong answers. Just go with the first thing that comes to mind."

1. You are lost in the desert and meet up with a camel that can talk. If you could only ask it one question, this question would be…

2. You discover a man lying on the floor in a room. He has a knife stuck in his throat and he's near death. If you could only ask him one question, this question would be…

3. You've traveled thousands of miles to meet a guru who claims to know the meaning of life. But when you arrive at his camp, a terrorist is about to execute him. If you could only ask the guru one question, this would be…

4. A favorite relative of yours has suddenly died, and you are told by the executor of the estate that you are the sole beneficiary. But there is one condition. You can only claim your inheritance if you ask the executor the right question. This question would be…

5. Your girlfriend/wife/partner tells you that she's an alien and at this very moment is about to be transported back to her home planet. You don't believe her. But she shows you her special powers and you're convinced. She asks you to go with her. Time is running out, and you can only ask her one question. This question would be…

6. You meet the woman of your dreams. She says she can't have a relationship with you but she will spend the night with you, if you ask her the right question. This question would be…

7. You're at a seance and the spirit of someone who was really close to you makes contact. You can only ask this spirit one question. Firstly, this spirit's name is…And your question would be…

What Did He Tell You?

Which tack does he take in each scenario? For example, in the first scenario does he ask the camel how to get out of the desert, or does he ask it how come it can talk? Does he ask the guru how he can help him, or what the meaning of life is?

In everyday life it's normal or even instinctive to gravitate toward the safety of comfort zones where our responses are predictable. From here, though, we aren't particularly challenged, and we learn little about ourselves. However, the unfamiliar is an entirely different proposition. Being confronted by an alien girlfriend or the spirit of a loved one will tap into our subconscious, and expose our fears, our ability to be empathetic, our imagination, and our capacity to deal with change or difference.

His replies will also tell you whether he has an overview that goes beyond his own needs. Is he concerned for the welfare of others, or is he more self-centered?

These scenarios may bring up his past experiences and his priorities. You'll be able to find out more about them by asking him to elaborate on his questions. Does he justify them? Did these justifications make sense to you?

Many of the responses in this exercise could be treated lightly,* but if you go with the flow and add a few extra questions you might still discover a few things about your man's character that you didn't know before.

* As these are quite different situations they will elicit a myriad of different answers. But at this point in the book, rather than go into a deep interpretation of them we thought we'd share some of the answers that cropped up during testing.

In the first scenario, one guy must have come from a terribly formal background, because despite the fact that he was lost in the desert and could only ask one thing, he offered: "How are you?" to the camel.

In the fifth scenario, one man clearly wasn't interested in galactic travel and simply wanted to know if he could use his girlfriend's credit cards in her absence.

Another man, when referring to meeting the woman of his dreams in the sixth scenario, asked: "You won't tell my wife, will you?"

107.

SHAPING UP

BECAUSE THIS EXERCISE HAS A SUBTLE TWIST, READ IT THROUGH FIRST SO YOU CAN BETTER RECOGNIZE HOW HE SEES HIMSELF. WHAT HE THINKS AND WHAT HE SEES MAY BE TWO ENTIRELY DIFFERENT THINGS.

ASK HIM THIS: "How important is physical appearance to you? I'm going to read you a series of statements about men's physical appearance and I want you to finish these statements as quickly as possible."

- The ideal man's height should be…

- The ideal man's weight should be…

- The ideal man's hair should be…

- His chest should be…

- His stomach should be…

- His arms should be…

- His legs should be…

- His hands should be…

- His eyes should be…

- The ideal man's complexion should be…

- His walk should be…

- His handshake should be…

- His voice should be…

- His smile should be…

Now I want to ask about you.

- If you had to describe yourself physically, you'd say your height is…

- Your weight is…

- Your hair is…

- Your chest is…

- Your stomach is…

- Your arms are…

- Your legs are…

- Your hands are…

- Your eyes are…

- Your complexion is…

- Your walk is…

- Your handshake is…

- Your voice is…

- Your smile is…

Lastly, is there anything about your appearance that you would like to change by way of cosmetic surgery?

WHAT DID HE TELL YOU?

Every society has an ideal body type, largely dictated by the media. How quickly he answers the first set of questions will tell you how aware he is of these dimensions. So how close was he to his ideal man, and how comfortable was he with any differences? How close was his ideal man to how you perceive the ideal man?

You should be able to see whether he's comfortable in his own skin by the way he answers. A natural tone to his voice will show that he's okay about himself. Humor or awkwardness could reveal a different story. How do *you* feel about his body?

How accurate was his description of his own body? This will tell you how realistic he is. How comfortable are you with his body? Are there parts that you'd like to change? How different was his ideal man from your's? Does this matter, and if it does, have you told him?

It's possible he's not at all body conscious and so it's never occurred to him to look at the perfect male. Equally, he may genuinely feel that his body is just the way he likes it. Remember though, no one is perfect, and there won't be many men whose self-description will match the idealized model.

108.

GETTING HIS PRIORITIES STRAIGHT

SO JUST WHERE DO *YOU* FIT INTO THE PICTURE?

ASK HIM THIS: "How do you think things rate in the world?"

- What is likely to give you a higher status: an expensive car or an expensive house?

- A car or a yacht?

- A yacht or a house?

- A beautiful wife or a car?

- A beautiful wife or a yacht?

- A beautiful girlfriend or a beautiful wife?

- A beautiful girlfriend, or a beautiful wife and two lovely children?

- A beautiful wife plus a beautiful girlfriend or a yacht?

- A beautiful girlfriend, a car, and a yacht, or a house and a lovely wife and two lovely children?

WHAT DID HE TELL YOU?

We dread to think! Need to know more? See "status" in the index.

109.

FAME

MOST PEOPLE HARBOR A DESIRE TO BE IN THE LIMELIGHT.
HERE'S YOUR CHANCE TO SEE HOW TRUE THIS IS FOR YOUR
MAN, AND ALSO WHAT HE'D LIKE TO BE NOTED FOR.

ASK HIM THIS: "Have you ever thought about being famous? I'm going to ask you some questions about fame and I want you to answer them as quickly as you can."

You have become very famous and are now making headlines around the world. You're being interviewed on the phone by a *New York Times* reporter. This particular reporter has a reputation for asking personally invasive questions. However, if she asks a question that you consider too personal you can terminate the interview by simply saying, "This interview is now over."

To help you get into your role, you need to think of some field of endeavor for which you could possibly see yourself becoming famous. This field would be…

So now the interview.

The reporter from the *New York Times* says:

"We always write a short promotional piece the day before a featured interview, and we like to give the subject the chance to say how they'd like to be introduced. So, what would you like us to say about you?"

"So, now let's start the interview proper. How do you think this newfound fame will change you personally?"

"How will it change your family and your lifestyle?"

"How will this fame change your relationship with your friends and colleagues?"

"Can you tell us about any clues from your childhood that could have signaled the fame that's now befallen you?"

"You've become a household name. Did you ever imagine that you'd become this famous?"

"Which people have helped you along the way to achieving this remarkable high point?"

"How far can you see this success developing?"

"Now that you've reached this point, what's left?"

"What's been the reaction from your friends and relatives?"

"What TV shows have you been asked to appear on?"

"Any other special events, such as opening the World Series or whatever?"

"Clearly, this fame has made you very, very wealthy. Can you tell us what's on your shopping list?"

"You'll recall Andy Warhol's quote about everyone having fifteen minutes of fame—do you think that this is simply your quarter hour?"

"What about people who say you don't deserve such incredible recognition?"

"What would happen if you lost everything?"

"Fame and fortune have their pitfalls. What negative aspects have you experienced so far or can foresee?"

"Does it scare you at all that you've become so public?"

"Do you have any advice for anyone else who's suddenly thrust into the limelight like you?"

"Finally, I have to tell you that we've done a bit of digging and discovered that there's something in your past that could be used by less honorable sections of the media to embarrass you. Would you like to take this opportunity to preempt any bad publicity by putting the record straight?"

WHAT DID HE TELL YOU?

So what are his dreams? Does he harbor any secret or not so secret visions of glory? Is he ambitious?* And where do these wishes for fame stem from? Is it because he wants to be acknowledged or lauded? Is it because he's unhappy with what he's achieved in his life so far? Or is he simply enjoying a fantasy?

How realistic is he being? This should give you a clue as to his motives or his reasons for wanting fame in the first place.

Did he achieve his fame by dint of his own efforts or did it come about through luck? This should tell you whether he expects to work for what he gets or hopes that he'll get lucky one day.

Most importantly, what does he plan to do with his fame? Will he use it to do something useful in the community, or will he simply rest on his laurels and enjoy the applause?

None of the questions were particularly invasive except perhaps for the last one. But if he did react adversely and terminate the interview, it may suggest that he's a fairly private person or possibly highly defensive. It could also mean that he hasn't fantasized too much about becoming famous and therefore not considered the possible ramifications of being suddenly thrust into the limelight.

* The word *ambitious* often carries negative connotations, but having a goal in life is wonderful as long as it's considered. For instance, ambition can be a dirty word if it means trampling over anyone who gets in the way. It can also lead to tunnel vision or obsession. Ambition at the purest level is about having meaningful targets to aspire to, a love of the process that's required to get there, and a maturity to handle the failures and set new goals if you don't.

A LIGHTER SHADE OF MALE

IN THIS EXERCISE IT'S NOT SO MUCH WHAT HE ANSWERS AS
HOW HE ACTS THAT'S IMPORTANT. IT WORKS BEST IF YOU
DON'T TELL HIM WHEN HE'S WRONG BUT ENCOURAGE HIM TO
KEEP GOING BY TELLING HIM HIS EXPLANATIONS ARE GOOD.

ASK HIM THIS: "How worldly are you? I'm going to read a list of
things, and I want you to tell me what they are in as much detail as
possible."

- A bouquet is…
- Satin is…
- A cuticle is…
- Cellulite is…
- A pirouette is…
- Angora is…
- Brocade is…
- Chiffon is…

- A nosegay is…
- Tartan is…
- A follicle is…
- An arabesque is…
- An astrakhan is…
- Plaid is…
- Batik is…
- Gingham is…

- Epaulets are…
- A bodice is…
- Sequins are…
- A pleat is…
- Mohair is…
- A tiara is…
- A corsage is…
- Taffeta is…
- Seersucker is…
- A doily is…
- A chaise lounge is…
- A kilim is…

- A fedora is…
- Cross-stitch is…
- Spangles are…
- Chenille is…
- A brooch is…
- A futon is…
- A locket is…
- A negligee is…
- A sarong is…
- Mascara is …
- A valance is…
- A trousseau is…

WHAT DID HE TELL YOU?

Did he regale you with fascinating descriptions that included words such as tufted, sheer, and twilled, or did he become rather bleak and mumble things such as, "I think it could be a bra thing." If he drew a blank on about eighty-five percent of these, you're with a real man. Fifty percent or better may indicate a lighter shade of male. Either way, how does he react when you tell him? And how did you do? If you scored more than five percent incorrect, you're probably under thirty or have spent most of your life studying gorillas in the Congo.

We've come across another breed of men who hate to be beat and take the opportunity to detract from their ignorance of all things feminine by amusing you with more creative definitions. Here are some of them. Remember, all the experts agree that humor is the sign of a creative mind and an agile intellect. So, don't knock his attempts to be funny.

Nosegay: A man who likes smelling other men.

Crepe: A French bowel movement.

Locket: A chastity belt.

Kilim: A contract on a man's life.

Negligee: A man who omits to do something in bed.

Cuticle: A small testicle.

Cellulite: The L.E.D. display on a mobile phone.

Astrakhan: A receptacle for ashtrays.

Mohair: The fine hair on a woman's top lip.

Brocade: A police indentification parade.

Sequins: Five water babies.

Futon: A Scottish footstool.

Chenille: Didn't she sing "Muskrat Love"?

111.

WOMAN UP TREE

Is he Tarzan, Indiana Jones, MacGyver, or Sherlock Holmes? Here's your chance to find out.

Ask Him This: "Do you know how to handle a crisis? I'm going to read a scenario and I want you to answer the questions at the end."

You're walking through the African bush. You have a backpack containing a knife, a camera, a water bottle, two chicken rolls, a box of matches, a length of rope, and a copy of *Playboy*.

Suddenly you hear a cry for help, and looking ahead to a clearing, you can see a woman trapped high up in a tree. At the foot of the tree is a lion who seems very agitated and totally preoccupied with the woman. The lion hasn't seen you.

- What would be your main consideration?

- What would you do?

- How could you use the items in your backpack to help?

- What does the woman look like?

- How does it all turn out in the end?

What Did He Tell You?

What's your man like when it comes to logic? How clearheaded is he? We can only applaud his resourcefulness at finding ways to utilize the contents of his backpack, but in truth, the most sensible thing to do would be to go for help. The woman may be terrified but she is in no immediate danger, and the lion isn't aware of his presence. He can only hope that the woman doesn't try to get down before help arrives.

Most men say that their main consideration is the safety of the woman but almost always, the more resourceful the man is in attempting to save her, the more young and attractive he will describe her as being. For many men this is the classic fantasy. He uses great skill and bravery in attempting to rescue her and hopes in return that he will receive her favors. Certainly, in most cases, that's how he says it turns out.

So how did your man do? Did he succeed? If so, did he seem triumphant? And what really was his main consideration? He might say that it was to save the woman, but the more he concentrates on the articles in the backpack, the more he's actually thinking about how he can demonstrate his ingenuity. In this case, the woman is of secondary importance. And what about the lion? Did your man try to avoid harming it, or did it end up as a hearth rug?

What about you? Do you find heroic acts by men a turn-on? Men know that women rank firefighters as particularly sexy—being brave enough to pit themselves against one of nature's fiercest elements. This could be why men struggle valiantly with *#104 Island of Fire*. How do you rate other heroic acts by men? Is saving a cat that's stuck up a tree, delivering a baby, or saving a drowning child up there with letting you have the television remote?

112.

THE CONTINUUM

IF YOU LIKE SIMPLE, STRAIGHTFORWARD EXERCISES, THEN
THIS IS THE ONE FOR YOU. BY THE TIME HE'S FINISHED, YOU
SHOULD KNOW WHETHER, BEHIND HIS GLOSSY EXTERIOR,
THERE BEATS A HEART OF PURE PASSION OR PINSTRIPE.

ASK HIM THIS: "What are your favorite action words? I'm going
to read lists of action words, and I want you to pick the word that
describes what you'd most like to do. I'll read the lists forward and
then I'll reverse the order. Then I want you to choose what you'd like
to do the most. Here's the first list:

>   Sit, stand, walk, run, jump.
>   Jump, run, walk, stand, sit.
- The action you'd most like to do is...

>   Float, wade, paddle, swim, dive.
>   Dive, swim, paddle, wade, float.
- The action you'd most like to do is...

>   Nudge, push, shove, slap, punch.
>   Punch, slap, shove, push, nudge.
- The action you'd most like to do is...

Hop, step, skip, jump, leap.
Leap, jump, skip, step, hop.
• The action you'd most like to do is...

Touch, feel, hold, stroke, press.
Press, stroke, hold, feel, touch.
• The action you'd most like to do is...

Warm, heat, boil, burn, incinerate.
Incinerate, burn, boil, heat, warm.
• The action you'd most like to do is...

Drop, pass, toss, throw, chuck.
Chuck, throw, toss, pass, drop.
• The action you'd most like to do is...

Press, fold, crease, crumple, tear.
Tear, crumple, crease, fold, press.
• The action you'd most like to do is...

Scratch, cut, tear, rip, gouge.
Gouge, rip, tear, cut, scratch.
• The action you'd most like to do is...

Crack, break, shatter, smash, pulverize.
Pulverize, smash, shatter, break, crack.
• The action you'd most like to do is...

Whisper, talk, shout, holler, scream.
Scream, holler, shout, talk, whisper.
• The action you'd most like to do is...

What Did He Tell You?

Is he adventurous or passive? Does he go down the middle or does he prefer an extreme? To gain more clarity, you could go back and ask him why he picked each one. Perhaps he related each sequence to an activity. This would explain his choice. And what about you? What did you relate to?

The first word in the first line of each two lines of words begins with a passive verb and moves progressively through to more active words, finishing with the most extreme word. We think it's a fair bet that the word choices your man makes will point to how active or passive he is. But remember, if he's mainly one or the other you'll need to be aware of the possible extremes. If he wants to do the most active things, he could be irresponsible, impetuous, and reckless at worst, or exciting, proactive, and adventurous at best. At the other end of the scale he could be gentle, sensitive, and creative at best, or pessimistic, lazy, and slow at worst.

In the end maybe only you and your man will really know how accurate this exercise is. But you could try to get to the bottom of why he made his choices. If he picked active words, it doesn't necessarily mean that he's active himself. The same logic applies if he chose passive words. He may just like the sound of the words, and doesn't take into account their actual meaning or significance. But there should be a general trend between active and passive. You may also like to discuss what areas within a relationship he prefers to take an active or passive role in. What roles do you feel most comfortable with, and are there role conflicts you can identify?

113.

COPYWRITER OR COWBOY?

THIS IS A RELATIVELY SIMPLE EXERCISE NOT ONLY TO
DETERMINE WHETHER HE'S HAPPY IN HIS JOB, BUT ALSO TO
DEMONSTRATE WHERE HE SEES HIMSELF IN THE WORLD.

ASK HIM THIS: "Have you ever thought about changing your job? I'm going to read you alternative occupations, and I want you to tell me which one you'd prefer to have and why."

- A doctor or a lawyer?

- A computer programmer or a choreographer?

- A novelist or a navigator?

- A playwright or a politician?

- A journalist or a judge?

- An acrobat or an architect?

- A broadcaster or a biochemist?

- An attorney or an astrophysicist?

- A composer or a civil engineer?

- An astronaut or an accountant?

- A dentist or a designer?

- A gardener or a glass blower?

- A park ranger or a private investigator?

- A cartoonist or a cardiologist?

- An air traffic controller or an ambassador?

- A photographer or a pharmacist?

- A copywriter or a cowboy?

- A sculptor or a salesman?

- A waiter or a welder?

- A smuggler or a stockbroker?

- A magician or a masseuse?

- A teacher or a talent scout?

Now I'm going to read you the occupations again, and this time I want you to tell me which one you see as having a higher status in society.

WHAT DID HE TELL YOU?

Were his choices based on his perception of job satisfaction, lifestyle, salary, or security? Did his responses suggest he was in the right sort of job at the moment or that he'd be better off in some other field of endeavor?

Was he enthusiastic about taking on some of these occupations, pointing to a positive attitude, or did he dwell on the unlikelihood of them ever being career possibilities? Did the occupations he picked the second time match up with his choices the first time? If they did, then it would suggest that status is more important to him than job satisfaction. How important is status to you? What if you had a higher status job than your man? Would that worry you? And would it worry him?

This all begs the question: what exactly does status mean to you? Is it money, fame, relevance, or recognition? And how does that balance out with job satisfaction? Would you rather be rich or happy? And are the two mutually exclusive? It also begs the question: where did your opinions on status come from?

Our concept of status is often predetermined by the views of our parents, by role models, and to a major extent by our peers. We can also be hugely affected by the media, and we might erroneously latch on to the idea that short-term fame will translate into meaningful status, hence the popularity of reality television shows.

The idea that money equals status could be attributed to the people in our past, but more likely, it will have to do with our own experiences, particularly if we've gone through periods of financial hardship. For many people, having money means never having to bow to anyone or anything.

So where do you both fit?

114.

MEAN TO ME

THIS EXERCISE IS LIKE A PERSONAL SNAPSHOT. YOU'LL NEED
PEN AND PAPER TO NOTE DOWN HIS ANSWERS SO YOU CAN
REFER BACK TO THEM LATER AND GET HIM TO ELABORATE.
JUST DO THE ONES THAT INTEREST YOU AND HAVE HIM ASK
YOU THE ONES THAT INTEREST HIM. AND REMEMBER, THE
LENGTH OF HIS REPLIES WILL BE DICTATED BY THE SPEED
OF YOUR DELIVERY.

ASK HIM THIS: "What makes up your life? I'm going to read you a list, and I want you to tell me what these things mean to you. Your answers can be as long or as short as you want."

- An automobile means…
- Home means…
- Family means…
- Work means…
- Thanksgiving means…
- Christmas means…
- A vacation means…
- Sex means…
- Making love means…
- Having a fling means…
- Dating means…
- The boss means…

- Love means...

- Intimacy means...

- Government means...

- Music means...

- War means...

- Eating means...

- Children mean...

- Space means...

- Fashion means...

- Giving means...

- Secrecy means...

- Solitude means...

- Environment means...

- Fear means...

- Death means...

- Commitment means...

- Honesty means...

- God means...

- Art means...

- Peace means...

- Swearing means...

- Time means...

- Motion means...

- Fun means...

- Privacy means...

- Freedom means...

- Growth means...

- Worry means...

- Evil means...

- Goodness means...

WHAT DID HE TELL YOU?

What did he tell you that you didn't know before? Don't worry if his answers don't match up with yours. This is not a compatibility test, simply a way of sharing experiences, values, and perceptions.

As we stated at the beginning, your answers will give each of you a snapshot of your lives and provide a reflection of your current states of mind, rather than your overall opinion on the subjects in question.

The topics could also bring up strong emotional associations that may color your answers, revealing an ability to move past the semantic meanings of the words. For instance, if his response to *God* was abstract (such as pain, or betrayal, or love), then the meaning of the word will be less important than the feelings it evokes. It will also, of course, infer that some past event has shaped the way the person feels about God.

The study of semantics shows that while every word in the English language has a meaning, it also has a connotation that may be different for each person who hears it. This connotation is based on a set of variables such as experience, context, and outcome. Art, for example, could trigger a memory of a drawing class that first sparked someone's creative side. If this artistic pursuit was ultimately rewarding, then the word *art* will have a warm, uplifting association.

A word's connotation can also be triggered by the tone or inflection of the delivery. If the word *solitude* was spoken in a grave sort of way, the response will probably follow suit. But if it was spoken in a colorful tone, then the response could be entirely different. Solitude in this context could invoke feelings of relief and peace.

So to ensure that you gain an accurate snapshot, keep asking extra questions to get as much detail as you can, and keep the delivery of the words neutral. That way you'll be able to gauge whether your man is merely answering factually or tapping into his emotional side. Remember, you can always run this exercise again, each adding the words you'd like a response to.

115.

SHOW ME THE MONEY

WE'VE ALL FANTASIZED ABOUT BEING STINKING RICH, BUT IN THIS EXERCISE WE ASK HIM TO PUSH THE LIMITS OF HIS IMAGINATION AND ACTUALLY SPELL OUT WHAT HE'D DO WITH LIMITLESS MONEY. YOU MAY BE SURPRISED AT WHAT YOU LEARN. TRY GETTING HIM TO ASK YOU THE SAME QUESTIONS BEFORE YOU READ THE INTERPRETATION.

ASK HIM THIS: "What would you do with a fortune? Listen to the following story and complete the statements as quickly as possible."

- A wealthy benefactor gives you five million dollars. You use this money to…

- He then gives you another five million dollars. You use this money to…

- He then gives you another five million dollars. You use this money to…

- He then gives you ten million dollars. You use this money to…

(Keep giving him millions of dollars until he runs out of ideas.)

WHAT DID HE TELL YOU?

Beneath the surface this exercise is about his dreams, his visions for the future, his altruism, and his foresight. Five million dollars is usually enough money to more than cover any initial desires he might have, and the next few million will help to complete them by adding those little (and not so little) flourishes. But at some point, there will be nothing else to use the money for unless he's able to think past his desires, and begin to consider other people or causes. What should be interesting for you is how grand and therefore expensive his desires are, and just how quickly his altruistic side kicks in. Remember that an expensive dream doesn't have to infer indulgence. It could signify that he's ambitious. Equally, someone who bypasses personal wealth for the better good of mankind could simply lack imagination. It's up to you to decide.

Show Me the Money should also bring up a few extra questions. For instance, do you even care if a man has vision? Within a relationship, is it important that either of you have major aspirations? Should they match? And what are *your* aspirations?

116.

DON'T MOVE!

THIS IS A VERY PERSONAL EXERCISE THAT REQUIRES YOU TO GET QUITE CLOSE TO YOUR MAN AND SEARCH HIS FACE FOR THE MOST SUBTLE EXPRESSIONS. SO TRY TO TAKE THE INTIMIDATION FACTOR OUT OF THE SITUATION BY KEEPING YOUR APPROACH LIGHT AND FUN.

ASK HIM THIS: "What are your nonverbal communication skills like? I want you to imagine that you and I have been selected to appear on a TV show called *Super Couples*. In one segment we are tested on our nonverbal communication skills, so we need to practice telling each other how we feel without using words or hand gestures. We lose points for obvious signals, so I want you to communicate with as little bodily or facial movement as possible. You're going to have to try thinking yourself into your role so your emotions are expressed 'naturally.' You may need to take a minute or two to do this."

- Tell me that you like me.

- Tell me that you love me.

- Tell me that you want me.

- Tell me that you hate me.

- Tell me that you care about me.

- Tell me that you sympathize with me.

- Tell me that you're confused by me.

- Tell me that you're annoyed with me.

- Tell me that you're proud of me.

- Tell me that you're disappointed with me.

(You might like to reverse the exercise and show him how *you* would express these feelings nonverbally. You could also see if you can adopt an expression without telling him what it is, and see if he can decode it. And have him do the same with you.)

What Did He Tell You?

Did he have more than two expressions, and was he able to show these without using big gestures? Only you can judge how well he did in this exercise, but it's important to let him know just how much is conveyed by his facial expression.

We all hate being misunderstood, and therefore knowing your partner's expressions will give you better insight into what he's thinking or feeling. In fact, we tend to put more store in facial signals than words, and generally, the better we are at reading each other's expressions, the smoother our communication will be. Maybe your man isn't much of a talker, or at least not a particularly animated talker. But his face and body are telling you things whether he knows he's doing it or not.

Was he surprised at how much you picked up from the smallest expression or nuance? Numerous studies have shown that women are better than men at reading emotion in facial expressions, so it's natural that men aren't so aware of what their faces reveal.* They are therefore less likely to realize that they may be giving out mixed messages— saying one thing while their faces are quite clearly saying something else. Once they understand that they can't mask their emotions behind words, they're likely to become more honest about them, and save a lot of wasted time in denial. Of course, many men see themselves in the protective role and try to shield women from worry. But women are seldom fooled by this facade, and the downside is that they feel unloved and shut out by their partners' refusal to open up and be honest.

Don't Move! is worth repeating, partly because initially he may feel a little self-conscious or it may take him a while to get into the swing of it. But it also gives both of you a chance to look into each other's faces without having to speak. When you repeat the exercise, do three expressions and see if he can guess what they are.

An interesting thing to consider is whether either of you used images or situations from the past in order to conjure up the feelings you were trying to express.

If you've enjoyed this exercise you can take it further by picking out people in public places and seeing if you and your partner agree on what their faces are expressing.

* Men are better than women at reading *anger* in facial expressions, especially in other men. Researchers have also found that people of similar cultural backgrounds are more accurate in reading each other's emotional expressions. This research has shown that the better a person is at reading the emotional expressions of others, the more emotionally intelligent and socially adjusted he or she will be.

117.

ADJECTIVELY SPEAKING

JUST HOW CONVENTIONAL IS YOUR MAN'S VIEW OF MEN
AND WOMEN? THIS EXERCISE SHOULD GIVE YOU AN IDEA.
MAKE A NOTE OF THE WORDS HE ATTRIBUTES TO WOMEN.

ASK HIM THIS: "How do you describe males and females? I'm going to read a list of words, and I want you to tell me if they apply more to men or to women."

controlling   deceitful   boarish   unreasonable   belligerent

downtrodden   aggressive   passive   corrupt   meddling   cruel

scheming   pedantic   unstable   insensitive   complaining   selfish

brutal   dissatisfied   cunning   silly   untrustworthy   illogical

argumentative   stubborn   lazy   erratic   boastful   meek   stoic

insecure   narrow-minded   fearful   cowardly   neurotic   greedy

vulnerable   hypocritical   slovenly   sadistic   nagging   brash

fiery   reckless   hysterical   perverted   flighty   pugnacious

high-strung   ferocious   flustered   inhumane   spiteful

WHAT DID HE TELL YOU?

So how does he see women? Were the words he attributed to them mostly submissive, or did he occasionally give them a more powerful stance? Were most of his male words forceful, or did he sometimes attribute weaker qualities to men?

Unlike languages such as French or Italian, English is technically gender free. But through usage, experience, and circumstance, our words have gradually evolved with distinct connotations that suggest they belong to one sex or another. Obviously, there are no hard-and-fast rules about this, and it is highly subjective. But you only have to look at a word like *brutal* to see what we mean. How could *brutal* be anything but male? Equally, nine out of ten people would say the word *spiteful* was feminine.

But what about that one person out of ten who didn't agree? Essentially, that's what this exercise is about. We want you to look for those crossovers in your man's answers. Did he think that *sadistic* was feminine? Did he think that *meddling* was male?

These anomalies may well point to his past, to specific people with whom he's been involved. It may point to his family background. Either way, you will learn more by going back and asking him to explain some of his conclusions. You could also do the exercise again and get him to think in reference to his family. You might like to try it yourself and see how you rate men and women.

LEVEL 2

Scratching the Surface

Okay, we've explored the more obvious, tangible side of your man, and the way he initially scans his world. Hopefully, he will have felt elevated and celebrated for who he is. Level One was all about getting him to be receptive to conversation and encouraging a curiosity for knowledge.

Let's delve deeper now. In Level Two, we will look a little closer at his self-image. Does he treat himself with care and respect? Does this reflect his ability to respect and empathize with others? In *Scratching the Surface,* the exercises will indicate his sense of responsibility, teamwork, and fair play. We will also concentrate on his logic and his listening and communication skills.

While you're doing these exercises, you need to keep reminding yourself that the aim is not just to gain information. For many of you, especially those who are already in a long-term relationship, the things a man discloses may not be new to you. So the process is more about finding out why he is the way he is. By understanding this, you will be able to relate to him more effectively, and, in turn, engage him in more meaningful dialogue.

201.

TOSSING YOUR ROCKS OFF

HERE'S A SCENARIO THAT SUSPENDS HIM OVER THE RIVER OF LIFE AND THEN WATCHES AS HE CASTS HIMSELF IN.

ASK HIM THIS: "Do you like throwing stones? I'm going to read you a short scenario, and I want you to answer the questions at the end."

You are standing on a bridge above a river. You have three rocks lined up on the bridge railing in front of you. There's one large rock, one medium rock, and one small rock. You are going to toss them off and let them drop into the river below.

- Which one do you toss first, then second, and then third?

- Describe the rocks.

- Is the bridge old or new?

- What is the bridge made of?

- Describe the water below the bridge.

- How high is the bridge?

- Imagine you are observing yourself standing on the bridge from a distance. Describe what you see.

What Did He Tell You?

Okay, we know this is just a bit of fun, but you may be surprised at how the conversation unfolds when you ask him why he threw the stones in the order he did.

If he starts with the small one first, then the middle-sized one, and then the big one, we think he will tend to be more measured in his approach to life. He'll probably be prepared to hold off on the big splash and be high on emotional intelligence. He will likely be an attentive lover, though he may lack spontaneity.

If he starts with the large rock and works down, then he is likely to be more impulsive, less patient, and a seeker of instant gratification. He could be a less attentive lover but may make up for it by being more passionate.

We're guessing here but we figure men who toss the middle-sized rocks first tend to be less sure of themselves. But we do think you should beware the man who tosses all his rocks off at the same time!

If you'd like to delve a little more deeply and take a larger pinch of salt, you can look at how he describes the rocks. Was each one different? If so, it means he wants variety in his life. He'll choose a multiplicity of ideas, activities, and companions, which means he's not putting all his eggs in one basket. The man with rocks of the same type will seek peace of mind by going for what he knows he can rely on.

Were the rocks smooth or rough? Were they pleasant to pick up and hold, suggesting that he has a strong sensual and gentle side, or were they rough and jagged, meaning he may be a less sensitive and more rugged individual?

The age of the bridge represents his philosophic connection with the world. An old bridge means that his guiding principles gain their sustenance from ancient wisdom, while a modern bridge indicates a man whose drivers are more practical, independent, and contemporary.

The more permanent the materials that the bridge is made of, the more fixed he will be in his philosophic outlook on life.

What about the water? Was it deep and slow moving or was it a raging torrent? A quiet, deeper body of water below suggests a more profound thinker who takes time over decisions, while a fast-flowing current speaks of a man of action who is fond of excitement and has little time for theoretical niceties.

And how high was his bridge? We think the higher it is above the water, the more of a splash your man will want to make to let others know he's there, especially if he tells you that the rocks make a loud noise. The lower it is, the more the event is likely to be something personal—just for him, and maybe you, if he imagined you were there too. Most men see themselves standing alone on the bridge, but if you were there as well, we think it's a very good sign.

Don't be dismayed if your man points out a few inconsistencies in the interpretations.* He may tell you, for example, that the reason a guy wants his rock to fall into a deep, slow-moving river is so that it will make a bigger, more obvious splash, and that it's tenuous to suggest it has to do with deep thinking. If he can come up with this kind of observation it means he can think for himself, and that's another very good sign.

* Don't be surprised either if your man claims his motivation for tossing his rocks off was to test some physical law and that our rationale is therefore invalid. He might well be telling the truth. More men than women are interested in the way the world works, and they see rock tossing as an opportunity to confirm their knowledge of important things such as terminal velocity. For example, he may claim to have tossed all his rocks off at the same time as a way of proving Newton's Second Law of Motion—that all objects will fall with the same rate of acceleration, regardless of their mass. He's right, of course, but if he's this analytical, what's he trying to prove when he kisses you—the Natural Law of Suction? And then of course there's the Law of Penetrability!

202.

THEY'RE *YOUR* PARENTS

THIS EXERCISE WILL REVEAL A NUMBER OF THINGS ABOUT YOUR MAN, PARTICULARLY HIS ABILITY TO MAKE JUDGMENT CALLS AND HIS READINESS TO LAY BLAME.

ASK HIM THIS: "How are you at decision making? I'm going to read a story, and I want you to listen carefully and then answer a simple question at the end."

Josh has to pick up the kids from school and get them back home in time to see their grandparents who are only there a short time before going to the airport and flying off to Denver. But the traffic is terrible and by the time Josh gets to the school he's already running late. He has no cell phone.

Once he's got the kids, he heads home, but with a couple of miles to go the car steering feels a little heavy. He pulls over and discovers that one of the front tires has a slow leak but figures if he goes faster he'll make it home before it goes completely flat.

When he finally arrives, though, the grandparents have already taken their cab to the airport, the kids start crying, and Josh's wife, Kayla, is absolutely furious. She says, "Just this once,

couldn't you have been on time? You know how much they
wanted to see their grandparents! This is the third time in four
weeks you haven't gotten the kids somewhere on time!"

Not waiting for a reply, she storms outside, telling him that
he can look after the kids and cook dinner. He tries to warn
her about the flat tire, but she gets in the car, slams the door,
and races off. Five minutes later she calls the house, saying
she's had a flat tire and crashed the car. And what's worse is
that she'd forgotten to pay the car insurance, which was due
the week before. She's still really furious, but Josh says, "Well,
don't blame me! It's not my fault."

- So, is Josh at fault?

What Did He Tell You?

How fair and responsible is he? Does he side with Josh or Kayla? If
he sided with Josh, what were his arguments? Many men will side
with the husband purely because Kayla was being emotional and
generalizing ("Just this once, couldn't you…") She's also becoming
"historical" ("This is the third time…"), which is something men
find difficult to handle. There's also the matter of her failing in her
responsibility to pay the car insurance, but this will be nothing
compared to what men might perceive as "typical female hysteria."

So on the surface it would appear that Kayla was in the wrong. But
we think the question of responsibility goes back further than her
emotional outburst. Surely, Josh risked his kids' lives and his own by
driving on a tire that could have blown at any time. What happened
next is irrelevant. He was already late, so he could have cut his
losses, changed the tire, and tried to make it to the airport to see the
grandparents there.

203.

MARIA HASN'T FORGIVEN YOU YET

YOU KNOW WHAT IT'S LIKE TO JUGGLE A THOUSAND DIFFERENT SKILLS AND DUTIES IN ONE DAY. SO HERE'S YOUR CHANCE TO SEE HOW YOUR MAN STACKS UP. BUT CUT HIM A LITTLE SLACK. YOU'RE GOING TO BOMBARD HIM WITH INFORMATION, SO READ IT SLOWLY, AND BE PREPARED TO REPEAT SECTIONS IF HE ASKS.

ASK HIM THIS: "What are your organizational skills like? I'm going to read you a scenario, and I want you to answer some questions at the end."

I want you to imagine that you're a senior executive of a large manufacturing plant in a small town. Your wife calls you at 11 a.m. to tell you that she needs your help. She knows you have an important meeting at 2:30 p.m., but your three-year-old daughter has fallen on some broken glass and got a piece of it deeply embedded in her knee. She needs to be seen by a surgeon in the city, which is two hours away.

The local doctor has made an appointment for your daughter to see the surgeon in the city at 1:45 p.m. and your wife will drive her there. But it means she won't be able to pick up Jason, your six-year-old son, from school at 3 p.m.

Normally she'd arrange with her sister, Julie, to pick him up, but she can't get a hold of her. Your neighbors, Wendy and Maria, might be able to do this, but she thinks that Wendy is shopping because she's not answering her phone, and Maria could be visiting her mother, something she often does in the morning.

Wendy might drop into her husband's work so you could try to reach her there, or maybe you could get hold of Maria at her mother's.

Whoever you get to do the picking up needs to know that Jason has a piano lesson at 3:30 with Mrs. Tweedy, and he'll need a snack at 4:15 when it's over, before he goes to soccer practice in the gymnasium at 5:30. You'll have finished work at 5:30, so you can pick him up at 6:30 on your way home.

You need to remember that Wendy has to meet her daughter at the train station at 4:45 and that Julie's husband always has their car from 4:30 for his night shift, so she won't be able to pick him up from soccer practice.

And don't forget that Maria hasn't forgiven you yet for that comment you made about her mother's weight. And remember Jason is on a gluten-free diet.

Having given you all this information, your wife is now in a rush and really only has time for just one or two questions from you.

- What would you want to ask her?

- How would you handle things?

What Did He Tell You?

This scenario probably sounds very familiar to you. But for a guy it's likely to be information overload and he may feel totally swamped. So is he capable of dealing with these sorts of domestic organizational problems, or does it send him into a tailspin?

Does he get annoyed about being put upon? And how does he actually deal with the situation? Many men would simply get an employee to pick Jason up at school and bring him back to the plant where he'd stay until work was over for the day, reasoning that skipping piano and soccer for one day wouldn't be such a big deal.

How does that make you feel? Some women become irritated by the fact that when a man has to take care of the children it's usually just for a day or a short time, so he feels justified in throwing routines out the window and, instead, plans special activities. This makes him out to be the good guy and leaves the women feeling undermined and undervalued.

But the reason men often handle the situation this way is because they don't know what else to do. They're simply not aware of the range of possible options, and they look for the simplest and safest way out. What would you do, for instance, if you had to fill in for him at an important meeting and you knew only a few rudimentary facts about the people attending? Surely, you would postpone the meeting, or at least use delaying tactics until he got back. Should an important meeting take precedence over a child's soccer game and piano lesson?

That said, it does seem that women are more capable of (some would argue more used to) handling a variety of different situations at the same time because they're better equipped to retain a multiplicity of data. They also have better peripheral vision than men, who have a more focused way of viewing things.

204.

MEETING ELVIS

THIS EXERCISE CAN BE VERY REVEALING, SO BE GENTLE HERE. DON'T START UNTIL YOU'VE READ THE INTERPRETATION AT THE END AND DECIDED WHETHER YOU THINK IT'S FAIR. YOU'LL NEED PEN AND PAPER FOR THIS ONE. NUMBER A SHEET FROM 1 THROUGH 38 AND THEN NOTE DOWN HIS PERCENTAGE FIGURES FOR EACH QUESTION.

ASK HIM THIS: "What do you daydream about? We all fantasize about fame, wealth, sex, love, and much more. So what if a university research unit conducted a survey of fantasies that men between the ages of sixteen and sixty enjoy? How would the numbers stack up?

"I'm going to read you a series of subjects, and I want you to tell me the percentage of men who you think would have had these daydreams. Try to be as accurate as you can."

1. What percentage would fantasize about being an astronaut?...

2. A movie star?...

3. A ballet dancer?...

4. A rock star?...

5. A porn star?...

6. What about president of the United States?...

7. What about beating up their fathers?...

8. What percentage would fantasize about having sex with their sisters?...

9. Committing suicide?...

10. Murdering someone?...

11. Robbing a bank?...

12. Having a homosexual experience?...

13. What percentage would dream of being able to take off in a car and fly?...

14. Going insane?...

15. What percentage would fantasize about skinning a human being?...

16. Eating a human being by choice?...

17. Wearing women's clothing?...

18. Becoming a religious leader?...

19. What percentage would fantasize about being able to fly unassisted?...

20. Being another animal?...

21. Having group sex?...

22. Torturing someone?...

23. Being tortured by someone?...

24. Having a sex change?...

25. Having plastic surgery?...

26. Committing an act of terrorism?...

27. Moving to Canada?...

28. Setting someone on fire?...

29. What percentage would fantasize about burning down a building?...

30. Destroying the world?...

31. Faking their own disappearance?...

32. Having a limb amputated?...

33. Being an executioner?...

34. Having a better relationship with their family?...

35. What percentage would fantasize about going to heaven?...

36. Going to hell?...

37. Saving hundreds of people from death?...

38. Meeting Elvis?...

What Did He Tell You?

One of the key elements to fantasy is that it's hidden and very personal. But just as there can be a danger of fantasy taking over our sense of reality, we can also become confused as to what we should reveal to others and what we should keep to ourselves. For instance, daydreaming about meeting Elvis is probably something that wouldn't concern a loved one, so if this fantasy was kept secret it wouldn't be a big deal. But what if we had continual fantasies about dying? Should we reveal them to a loved one?

The problem is that, instinctively, we don't believe that others will look upon us in the same way if we do. This fear of being exposed and misjudged naturally leads us to hold back and results in a shallower connection with those who are close to us.

This exercise is an attempt to cut through some barriers and show that revealing personal information, whether a fantasy or a fear, will not expose your man as weak or flawed. Far from it. It should give you a better understanding of his imagination, his past, and his concerns. Hopefully, this will give you both a chance to share more openly. You might even have the same fantasies.

So, how does *Meeting Elvis* work? Most of us like to think that we're normal,* and this exercise certainly confirms the adage that there's safety in numbers. So if your man picks any percentage over fifty then he has probably thought about this particular subject.** For instance, if he says that seventy-five percent of the men dreamed about beating up their fathers, chances are pretty good that he has too. So is this something to worry about?

Opinion has been divided in the world of psychology. Sigmund Freud considered that daydreaming was the first nudge on that slippery slope to insanity. But in more recent times experts have developed the opposite view. They see fantasizing as a healthy way for individuals to experiment with their dreams in a guilt-free fashion. It's also seen as a survival device for either relieving stress or preempting future stressful situations. This, in turn, can enhance empathy.

But what happens when we fantasize about bad, angry, or even violent things? Again, experts see this as healthy. We all have what they often term a *shadow side*—a reservoir of repressed anger—and fantasizing can actually exorcise these demons. It's why actors often relish the opportunity to play a villain like Iago or Hannibal Lecter. It gives them a safe environment to express and release deep-seated rage.

* A recent study has revealed that on average we spend between ten to twenty percent of our day involved in daydreaming. While some of this fantasizing is simply to relieve boredom, it can also be a mechanism for escaping stress. Childhood loneliness or trauma often shape the depth or detail of these daydreams, and tend to forge a routine that survives into adulthood.

** Of course it's possible that he could base his percentages on a perception gained from the media. For example, he may not be interested in, let alone fantasize, about arson or skinning another human being, but its presence in the media may lead him to believe that quite a few men are into it. But even in this case he will seldom put the percentage above fifty.

205.

GORDIE IN THE GARAGE

GUYS LOVE THIS ONE. IT TESTS THEIR PATIENCE WITH
CHILDREN AND WILL GIVE YOU AN INSIGHT INTO HIS
PARENTING SKILLS. IT'S QUITE A LONG EXERCISE, SO YOU'LL
NEED TO KEEP YOUR DELIVERY UP TO ENSURE THAT THE
STORY SEEMS AS REAL AS POSSIBLE.

ASK HIM THIS: "What would you do if you had to look after a five-year-old boy? I'm going to read you a scenario, and I want you to complete the unfinished statements as quickly as possible."

It's a rainy Saturday. You're in the garage working on your car because your house is being fumigated and you can't go back inside for at least six hours. With you is a friend's son, five-year-old Gordon, who you're looking after for the afternoon. He's brought his carpentry set and is happily sawing away at some little scraps of wood you've given him.

Things go along smoothly for a while, but then Gordie decides that instead of little scraps of wood, he'd rather saw the legs of some outdoor furniture stacked in the garage. You say to him…

Gordie doesn't listen, so you take away the saw and say…

Gordie then gets his hammer out and begins banging away at the wood. But again he gets bored with this and he's just looking around the garage, hammer in hand, when you say…

Gordie watches you for a while, and then looks around for something else to do. He sees your golf bag and pulls out an iron. You say…

But he looks at you with defiance, kicks you on the shin, jumps in the car, locking all the doors, and then starts honking on the horn. You say…

At this moment the fumigator pops his head in and tells you that he's off, and that you shouldn't go into the house for at least five hours.

You search through your pockets for your car keys and then realize that they're in the ignition and that your spare set is in the house. Unfortunately, Gordie sees the keys at the same time as you do and starts fiddling with them. You say to him…

But Gordie isn't listening. He's managed to turn on the ignition and has started up the wipers. You say to him…

By this time, however, he's activated the car sound system, and he's also touched the button for the garage door, which is now slowly opening and letting rain pour in. You say to Gordie…

You close the garage door using the inside control and put a length of wooden beading on the bottom ledge and jam the other end to the ceiling, hoping that it will stop the door opening again. Then you go back to the driver's window in the car and say to Gordie…

Gordie presses the button again and the door tries to open.

You hadn't counted on the strength of the door motor and the beading starts to bend. You reach for it but it snaps just before you can get to it, and part of it hits you in the face. You're bleeding now from a cut to your nose, and you're angry. Very angry. Then you hear the unmistakable sound of the car being started. You say to Gordie…

But still Gordie won't budge, so finally you have no alternative but to smash one of the car windows. You reach in, take the keys out of the ignition, and then haul Gordie out of the car. You say to him…

And then you…

What Did He Tell You?

How patient was he? What negotiating skills did he show? How long did he manage to keep his cool and not resort to shaming, threats, name-calling, or obscenities? And was this point dictated by possible danger to him and the boy, or was it simply because he wanted to get the little brat?

Admittedly, little Gordon is the child from hell, and we've set up the scene so that the drama has to escalate and your man is not given the option of physically restraining the boy. But he can still acquit himself well if he manages to stay composed until near the end.

Things to look out for are his tone of voice, the volume, whether he's being kind but firm, and whether he's able to come up with ways of distracting the boy, even if they ultimately don't work. It's his intention and his style that's important. Is it punitive, rigid, or laissez-faire? You might like to ask him if things he said to Gordie were things his parents said to him.

How would you have handled the situation? Do you think you could have coped better? Do you think women in general can handle unruly boys better than men? Is it a boy's role to show that he's a man too and challenge authority? Does this carry on into adulthood? For instance, if your man had little respect for his mother's wishes, is he following the same course with you now?

What sort of understanding does he have of a five-year-old's behavior and reasoning ability? Does he have the ability to divert a head-on confrontation?

Parenting experts cite several causes for children's misbehavior, many of them relating directly to the adults' strategies. These causes include the escalation trap, where an adult uses a raised voice to get a message across. When the child ignores it, the volume level is turned up even more. Thus the child learns that he or she only needs to comply when Mom or Dad has become really, really angry.

Not setting clear boundaries or not following through with stated consequences are other causes. But above all, the experts claim, the best style of parenting is to be cool, calm, and collected, a style in which the adult asserts his or her position as the boss but in a nonpunitive way, so the child gets the message that it's the behavior being criticized and that the adult is still a loving and trustworthy person.

What were your mother's and father's parenting styles like? And what about *his* parents? Do you think they've affected the way you both take criticism within your relationship?

206.

JUMBLE GYM

MEN OFTEN SCOFF AT THE PHRASE "FEMALE INTUITION."
BUT IN THIS EXERCISE WE LET HIM IN ON A FEW SECRETS
AND SEE WHETHER HE CHANGES HIS MIND. BUT BECAUSE
YOU SHOULD ONLY READ THE SENTENCES OUT LOUD ONCE
TO AVOID UNINTENTIONAL CHEATING, YOU'LL NEED TO
READ SLOWLY AND VERY CLEARLY TO GIVE HIM A CHANCE.

ASK HIM THIS: "What are your listening skills like? I'm going to read
you two simple sentences that have been spliced together, and I want
you to try to tell me what they are."

For example, here are two sentences that have been spliced
together using consecutive words from each sentence to form a
third jumbled sentence that doesn't make sense:

The – she – cat – ate – ran – an – away – apple.

This nonsensical sentence was made up from:
"The cat ran away." And "She ate an apple."

Now try these. I'll read them out slowly word by word, but only
once. Just let your mind be open to all the words, and don't try
to make sense of anything until I've finished each sentence.

1. I – she – think – has – you – a – are – very – a – big – really – pair – nice – of – person – breasts. (I think you are a really nice person. She has a very big pair of breasts.)

2. I – would – am – you – falling – please – deeply – read – in – me – love – an – with – exciting – you – story. (I am falling deeply in love with you. Would you please read me an exciting story.)

3. Let's – I'll – go – fix – for – it – a – with – walk – my – in – electric – the – drill – park. (Let's go for a walk in the park. I'll fix it with my electric drill.)

4. My – I – new – saw – phone – her – can – in – text – the – automatically – nude. (My new phone can text automatically. I saw her in the nude.)

5. I – when – wish – I – you – turn – had – up – my – the – gift – bass – for – the – telling – house – jokes – shakes. (I wish you had my gift for telling jokes. When I turn up the bass the house shakes.)

6. It's – I – my – wish – best – I'd – round – met – of – you – golf – years – ever – ago. (It's my best round of golf ever. I wish I'd met you years ago.)

7. She – the – had – bear – ten – ate – beers – all – in – the – two – bananas – hours – in – and – the – passed – shop – out. (She had ten beers in two hours and passed out. The bear ate all the bananas in the shop.)

8. He – I – kissed – like – me – to – with – walk – such – on – passion – the – I – beach – thought – in – I'd – bare – die – feet. (He kissed me with such passion I thought I'd die. I like to walk on the beach in bare feet.)

9.   We – I – are – really – going – want – on – her – a – to – sailing – see – trip – Paris – for – in – our – the – honeymoon – springtime. (We are going on a sailing trip for our honeymoon. I really want her to see Paris in the springtime.)

What Did He Tell You?

How well he managed to untangle these sentences will tell you a whole lot about his intuitive ability. Was he able to sort the sentence into two or did he just look at you as if you were mad? (Remember he has to get both sentences because it's possible just to concentrate on the odd or even words in the sequence and get one sentence. For this reason you should only read him the jumbled sentence once.)

This exercise requires what we call unconcentrated concentration. We think it's as close as we can come to understanding a woman's intuition or playing a hunch. There's an old joke that says: "A woman's intuition is the result of millions of years of not thinking." It makes men roar with laughter and gets women pretty mad. But it's a very effective mode of perception and is exactly what you're trying to do— not think, but be alert and open. That's when things inexplicably come in. It's how we mostly listen to music—making sense of the whole composition rather than thinking about each note. If we were to break it down into its parts rather than letting all that complex information wash over us or surround us, we'd miss the overall effect.

When using intuition, you're unconsciously scanning a map of scattered fragments and "seeing" a pattern in a way that's not possible when you go from fragment to fragment. It's not simply overview that relies on gathering all the elements you can think of together and looking for a pattern. Overview is comparable to climbing a hill in order to look down on a battle unfolding below, whereas intuition somehow enables you to "see" the outcome peripherally without ever climbing the hill.

A woman will consistently score higher on this exercise than a man, which is hardly surprising given the structure of her brain and its hormone levels. Due to their larger corpus callosum, women are generally able to connect words with feelings more easily and can process language across a wider area of both hemispheres. Male brains respond better to action signals, while the female brain, with higher levels of serotonin and oxytocin, is more attuned to subtle aural cues. With these advantages, some women can even untangle the words when the sentences are read backwards!

If your man is having no luck with this exercise, get him to let all the words come in before he tries to make sense of them. Suggest he just sit there until something pops into his head. Or if you have an explanation of how you do it, let him try that too. If he succeeds, it may be the first step toward putting him in touch with his intuition. It could well be that he hasn't trusted his intuition in the past, and these jumbled sentences may start him on the road to being a whole lot more savvy.

You may find it interesting to note whether he was better able to sort out the sentences with sexual, athletic, automotive, or tool triggers first. Did he, for example, answer number 1 something like this: "I think she has really big breasts, and you are a nice person." In this case you could assume that the "trigger theme" for him was breasts. You will see in this example that he has come up with seventy-five percent of the words and the two messages are basically accurate. In this case he would be scored as correct. Once he's got the words *she, pair, breasts,* the other words suddenly form themselves into a familiar sequence. It's the same with *I, falling, love,* in number 2. The brain seizes on the emotional trigger words and will hold them while the other connecting words are automatically put into the most logical order. Perhaps this is the reason that quite a few men answer number 7 with "She had ten bears in two hours and passed out."

207.

THE MOTOR INN

THIS IS A MOTEL OWNER'S NIGHTMARE—GUESTS HAVING FUN AND CREATING HAVOC. *THE MOTOR INN* GIVES YOU A CHANCE TO SEE JUST HOW UPTIGHT OR CHILLED OUT HE REALLY IS.

ASK HIM THIS: "Have you ever worked in a motor inn? I'm going to read you a story, and I want you to stop me at various stages."

You've been asked to act as manager of a motor inn by the owner who is a friend of yours. It's a weeknight and there aren't likely to be many guests. Your friend fills you in on what you have to do and gives you a copy of the rules that are posted in every room.

The rules are as follows:

1. No visitors in rooms after 9 p.m.

2. No running anywhere in the motor inn.

3. No jumping into the Jacuzzi.

4. No visitors in the Jacuzzi after 10 p.m.

5. No food or drinks in the Jacuzzi.

6. No unaccompanied visitors at any time.

At about 5 p.m. two salesmen, Bob and John, check in and you give them each a room. They dine at a local restaurant and return around 8 p.m. with two young women, Vicki and Kate, whom they've invited over for a swim in the Jacuzzi.

As I outline the course of events that unfold, I want you to listen carefully and every time you hear that a rule is being broken, I want you to say, "Stop!" and point out which rule is being infringed. Remember the young women are visitors. To make it easier, I'm going to read the rules again before I start. (Repeat the rules.)

Bob and John and Vicki and Kate are getting along just fine in the Jacuzzi. Vicki has taken a shine to Bob, and John and Kate have found they have photography in common. John suggests to Kate that she might like to see some of his photos and they go off to his room wearing bathrobes. It's 9 p.m. Just as they get there John realizes he's left his room key by the Jacuzzi and he asks Kate to wait while he runs off to get it. About this time Vicki remembers that she has promised to call her mother and runs off to borrow Kate's cell phone. John runs back with the key. As he arrives, Vicki is talking on Kate's phone in the corridor and he lets Kate in to look at the photographs.

At 9:05 John gets a call from his brother. While he's talking to him, and Kate is looking at the photographs, Vicki comes in, gets some champagne from the minibar, and takes it down to John, who's waiting for her in the Jacuzzi. Vicki jumps into the pool with the unopened bottle of champagne. John grabs it, pops the cork, shakes it vigorously, and sprays it all over Vicki. They both scream with laughter. John decides that it would be more civilized to drink the rest out of glasses and runs off to get some from his room. He runs back with two glasses and some pretzels from the minibar to find that Bob and Kate have joined Vicki and finished off the bottle. Now he has to run off to get another bottle from his minibar, and Bob runs back to his room to get two more glasses and some nuts. They both arrive back together and jump into the pool just on the stroke of ten.

WHAT DID HE TELL YOU?

The point of this exercise is not so much to find out how many infringements he can pick these young revelers up on, but rather to determine how much he relishes the job and how fanatical he gets. Does he get a beady look in his eye and thump his fist on the table or wag his finger officiously in the air? Or is he laid back and not too concerned whether he misses a few? You could try asking him to guess how many individual rule breaks he thinks there were. We've found that the more controlling men are, the more likely they'll want to know and will often ask to read the passage to check that there are in fact twenty individual infringements. (Or are there?)

If he's a bit on the rigid side, he'll probably have his world well under control. But being a stickler for rules could make life around him a tad unpleasant when he's stressed or feeling insecure. On the other hand, if he isn't too concerned, he could be a very laid-back guy who's easy to be around but may lack a degree of firmness in his daily dealings with the world, and could let things slide.

What about you? Do you like clear rules, or would you rather people take responsibility for their own safety?

208.

IN IT UP TO YOUR SHOULDERS

THERE'S SOMETHING MOST PECULIAR GOING ON DOWN AT
THE FARM. WELL, THERE WOULD BE IF YOUR MAN HAD
ANYTHING TO DO WITH IT. HOW IS HE AT GETTING OUT OF
A TIGHT SPOT, OR INTO ONE, AS YOU WILL SOON DISCOVER?
READ AHEAD TO MAKE SURE YOU'RE COMFORTABLE WITH
THE QUESTIONS. HAVE FUN.

ASK HIM THIS: "What do you know about cows? I want you
to participate in a scenario with me and complete the unfinished
statements."

"You're about to be interviewed for an agricultural job that you
desperately need to support your family. You actually don't
have the academic qualifications necessary, but you're great
with animals and know if they ever find out, you'll already be
performing so well they'll keep you on anyway. I'm going to
play the part of the interviewer. The position is that of animal
husbandry technician and I should warn you that they won't
consider anyone over thirty, so you may have to lie about your
age."

"I'd like to welcome you to this interview and start by getting a
few basic questions out of the way."

"So first off, how old are you?"

"You graduated in animal husbandry last year, is that right?"

"And which college was that from?"

"I understand your top animal science subject was bovine fertility. What did you particularly enjoy about that?"

"Of course this job requires someone who can relate well to cows. So what are three things you really like about them?"

"Are there any particular breeds that you like working with?"

"I suppose you've milked cows by hand?"

"Tell me how many udders does a cow have?"

"And can you tell me what the purpose of a cow's tail is?"

"Now as you know this job mainly involves artificially inseminating cows. Of course I know you've done this before, but putting on those long rubber gloves and inserting a tube of bull's semen into the cow's vagina—do you think there's something perhaps unnatural or unethical about this?"

"In your opinion do cows enjoy being artificially inseminated?"

"Have you ever had any problems inseminating a cow?"

"What about tail clamp? How do you handle that?"

"Because we'll require you to train young inseminators from time to time, I'd like you to explain something to me about the process so I can get an idea of your communication skills.

As you know the normal method of artificially inseminating a cow is to push one hand holding the tube of semen into the cow's vagina, while the other hand goes right up into the cow's rectum. I'd like you to explain what this other hand is doing."

What Did He Tell You?

Was he a convincing liar or did he let the job description get to him and did he start laughing?* Did he surprise you with his ability to make things up off the cuff, or was he hopelessly honest or just plain incompetent? In the more spectacular situations of life and death, lying can be a risky business and often takes great courage. If it works it can protect your family from oppression. However, if it fails, it can plunge you into disaster. But is there a place for lying in more ordinary, day-to-day situations? What about at work, or within a relationship?

Now that you've heard him lying, does it worry you that he may have lied in a convincing manner to you in the past? Did he seem to enjoy lying or was he uncomfortable with it? Have you asked him how he felt about lying like that? How much would he lie to get a job? Should we always be totally honest with each other?

* Was he so thrown off guard during the exercise that he told you cows have four udders? It's actually one udder, four teats. Did he come up with a reasonable explanation for putting his arm right up inside the cow's rectum? The official reason is that you use this hand to feel through the rectal wall to position the tube correctly in the cervix before releasing the semen. Our two favorite replies to this question are: (1) Putting your arm up the rectum takes the cow's mind off what you're really doing, and (2) It's a way of giving the cow an orgasm, which ensures the insemination has a better chance of success.

209.

MULTI-ASKING

IF YOUR MAN INSISTS THAT HE CAN MULTITASK AS WELL AS YOU, TRY HIM ON THIS EXERCISE. YOU'LL BOTH FIND OUT IF HE'S RIGHT. TO GIVE HIM A FAIR CHANCE, YOU'LL NEED TO READ THIS CLEARLY AND AT A VERY EVEN TEMPO. HE'LL ALSO NEED PEN AND PAPER.

ASK HIM THIS: "How good are you at listening while you're doing something else? I'm going to ask you to add up a series of numbers while I read you a simple story. When I've finished reading the story, I'm going to ask you some questions about it. I want you to start with the number 3 and then add 4 to it to make 7 and then add another 4 to make 11 and then another 4 to make 15 and so on until I reach the end of the story. I want you to write down each number as you add 4 to it. So you'll write down 3, 7, 11, 15, and so on. Start at 3 now and I'll begin reading the story." (Repeat instructions if he has difficulty understanding them.)

John and Mary decided to vacation in New Zealand for three weeks during February. One day, while walking over a sheep farm beside a lake, they come across some people playing an unusual kind of golf game. John was surprised to hear the ball making a humming sound as it flew through the air, and when one landed close to him he saw that it was oval in shape, like a football rather than round. John, who played off a three handicap in his youth, stood by the ball and when a player came up to it he asked him to explain. The player told him that the game was called GolfCross and was invented in New Zealand. The idea was to hit the ball into a goal rather than into a hole. He told John that the oval ball was easier to control because it spun on two axes, which meant you couldn't slice or hook it unless you wanted to. Players used a special rubber cup that fitted over a normal golf tee, and this enabled them to angle the ball in the direction they wanted it to go. He explained that the skill was not in how you hit the ball but in knowing how to position it. John asked if he could hit the ball, and the player willingly teed it up for him in the vertical position. John used a nine iron and found that the ball went quite straight, hummed loudly, and stopped very quickly when it hit the ground.

That's the end of the story.

So first off, how many numbers did you get down? (His number sequence should look like this: 3, 7, 11, 15, 19, 23, 27, 31, 35, 39, 43, 47, 51, 55, 59, 63, 67, 71, 75, 79, 83, 87, 91, 95, 99, 103, 107, 111, 115, 119, and so on.)

Now I'm going to ask you some questions about the story.

- The country that John and Mary were vacationing in was…

- The shape of the golf ball was…

- In his youth John's handicap was…

- The oval golf ball is easier to control because…

- The club that John hit the ball with was a…

- The name of the golf game was…

- When John hit the ball it…

- John and Mary were walking over a…

- The oval ball is played into…

- The way to get the ball to go in a certain direction is…

What Did He Tell You?

What you've asked him to do here is to perform three distinct tasks at the same time: to calculate, to write, and to listen. Men are good at focusing on just one thing and find this multitasking a whole lot harder than women.

In this exercise they tend to concentrate on the math and will often get up to thirty numbers down accurately but will only be able to answer fifty percent of the questions. An above average multitasker will get twenty numbers down and be able to answer eight questions correctly. If your man is one of these, then he's likely to be able to handle complex daily household routines with ease. (See also #203.)

On the other hand, not being good at multitasking does have its benefits. Some complex problems can only be solved through blinkered vision—the kind of obsessive focus that would be impossible to achieve if he were open to outside stimuli.

If your man failed abysmally at this exercise, you may need to ensure that he's not doing something else when you ask him a question. Remember, lots of men have to turn their car radios down or off before they parallel park because they can't handle the noise distraction while performing a difficult physical task. *You* might be able to hear what your friend is telling you on the phone and listen to what he's asking you at the same time, but chances are he can't.

The whole area of multitasking is a much misunderstood phenomenon. In defense of our lack of multitasking ability, men will tend to quote psychologists who assert that no one can actually perform more than one thinking task at one time. This is true, but what we men often fail to grasp is that multitasking isn't necessarily concerned with thinking. For instance, women will contend that they can oversee cooking, talk to a friend on the phone, and supervise their children, all at the same time. But if you look closely at these activities, only the conversation with the friend requires thought. The other two are largely automatic tasks.

Experts in the field of psychology, education, and sociology use a term they call "automaticity"—or the ability to do something without thinking. Automaticity supports the cognitive process in order to free up attention for higher-level tasks. They claim that men and women are equally capable of doing this, but that women have a lot more practice at it. In childhood, boys tend to be nursed along, with parents doing basic tasks for them. The need for boys to expel physical energy seems to excuse them from performing chores such as making their own beds, tidying up, making their own school lunches, etc. Boys are given a much freer rein. Consequently, as adults they are conditioned to be more singularly focused.

Certain schools of thought believe that the optimum state of mind is to be openly attentive, in other words, to concentrate on the task at hand but also to be open to unforeseen influences. Having a mental peripheral vision allows us to grow and learn as individuals. But it takes practice.

Multitasking has its drawbacks. Recent studies have revealed that people not well practiced in multitasking actually become less efficient, increase their stress levels, and suffer short-term memory loss when they attempt it. So, our advice if you want to be better at multitasking is to take it slowly, and practice, practice, practice.

210.

SITUATIONS VACANT

THIS EXERCISE SHOULD TELL YOU WHERE HE SEES HIMSELF IN THE WORLD. IF YOU LOOK A LITTLE DEEPER, YOU MIGHT LEARN ABOUT HIS FEARS OR FRUSTRATIONS AND YOU MIGHT ALSO LEARN WHERE HE PLACES *YOU* IN THE WORLD.

ASK HIM THIS: "What comes to mind when you think about different places? I'm going to read you a series of statements, and I want you to answer the following questions as quickly as possible."

- You're in a church. What are you doing there?

- You're in a hospital. What are you doing there?

- You're on a battleship. What are you doing there?

- You're at a school. What are you doing there?

- You're at the United Nations. What are you doing there?

- You're in a motorcade. What are you doing there?

- You're at a casino. What are you doing there?

- You're on a film set. What are you doing there?

- You're in a prison. What are you doing there?

- You're in a theatrical production. What are you doing there?

- You're at a press conference. What are you doing there?

- You're in court. What are you doing there?

WHAT DID HE TELL YOU?

Where does he see himself in the world? Did he place himself in either a controlling, reactive, or submissive position? Or did he see himself as more of a bystander or server? For instance, at the press conference was he an integral part of the action (either the interviewer or the interviewee), or did he see himself in a subsidiary role (part of the support crew or a cameraman or even the venue management)?

Were you surprised at his choices? Was he being realistic or unrealistic about his position in the world? Of course, he might not necessarily be unrealistic. If he's a professional man but sees himself more in a role that lacks responsibility, then he might unconsciously be saying that he's unhappy with where he is at the moment, or that he needs a change or a break. Likewise, he might simply be a massive underachiever. If he is a cable guy or a janitor but always places himself in a position of authority, then he might need to ask himself what he's doing in that line of work. It might explain why he attacks his own job with a vigor that it doesn't deserve. His answers to *Situations Vacant* might also be displaying his hidden fears. Many of the situations in this exercise are potentially stressful, such as being in court, or a theatrical production, and while he may have given himself the role of prisoner or leading actor, he might be deliberately placing himself in danger as a way of testing himself. You may need to ask him to elaborate on his answers if you want to be certain of his motives. If you want to delve deeper, you could ask him to tell you what he thinks you'd be doing in these situations.

211.

ROW, ROW, ROW YOUR BOAT

How deep and thoughtful is your man? And what about you? This exercise is easily reversed, so have your man try it out on you before you look at the interpretation.

Ask Him This: Have you ever had to make a difficult decision about what to keep and what to throw away? I'm going to read you a scenario, and then I want you to make some choices.

You have decided to spend a whole year in a hut on an isolated island. You have stocked the hut with food and provisions, and there is nobody else on the island. You intend to spend your time there studying and thinking about your life so far. To this end you have decided to take with you the following very heavy boxes.

1. A box containing beautiful art books.

2. A box containing philosophy books.

3. A box containing novels, plays, and poetry.

4. A box containing your personal diaries.

5. A box containing love letters from your past loves.

6. A box containing a set of survival guides.

7. A box containing books of jokes.

You are about to make your final trip in a little row boat over to the island. Because the seven boxes are very heavy the boat sits rather low in the water, but as the sea is calm you figure there'll be no problems. However, when you are more than halfway across, the wind picks up and with so little freeboard, waves begin to slop over the side. You realize that unless you reduce the weight in the boat it will fill with water and sink. You need to act quickly and decide to throw one of the boxes overboard.

- Which one do you choose to jettison and why?

- The box sinks rapidly beneath the waves, water stops coming in, and you row on as quickly as you can. But soon the waves get higher and you can see that you'll have to ditch another box. Which one of the remaining six do you throw overboard and why this one?

- Then you realize you'll have to ditch another box to stay afloat. Which one of the remaining five do you throw overboard and why this one?

- Then you realize you'll have to ditch another box to stay afloat. Which one of the remaining four do you throw overboard and why this one?

- Then you realize you'll have to ditch another box to stay afloat. Which one of the remaining three do you throw overboard and why this one?

- Then you realize you'll have to ditch another box to stay afloat. Which one of the remaining two do you throw overboard and why this one?

- You finally reach shore with just one box, which you carefully stow in the hut. But the next morning you're amazed to see that one of the boxes has washed up on the beach. As you rush toward it you hope it's the one that contains...?

- Why this one?

WHAT DID HE TELL YOU?

In this exercise what's important to your man is just as significant as how thoughtful he is about his choices. We're not only interested here in which box your man regarded as the most important—whether, for example, he considered literature, jokes, or survival to be salient—but also how reasoned he was about his choice of mind food. These decisions could have many variables. Which books held vital information for his survival? Which books would he tire of first? Which material did he feel he just couldn't part with? The more factors he comes up with, the slower the decision-making process might be.

So how long did he spend thinking about which box to throw out? Did he still choose the box he threw out last as the one he hoped had washed ashore or did he change his mind? This could show that he values the opportunity to review his decisions in case there's something he may not have considered.

Was he open in sharing his thought processes with you by talking out loud as he examined his options, or was he closed, just giving minimal answers? (If he wasn't particularly forthcoming, you could always ask him why he made the decisions he did. And you can share with him the reasons for the decisions you made.)

212.

THE GREAT OUTDOORS

THIS EXERCISE WILL TELL YOU HOW HAPPY YOUR MAN IS, AND WHETHER HE'S AMBITIOUS OR COMPLACENT. YOU MAY NEED PEN AND PAPER TO NOTE DOWN HIS ANSWERS.

ASK HIM THIS: "What do you figure you'd like to do in different environments? I'm going to read you a series of scenarios, and I want you to answer the questions that follow."

- You are on a lake. What are you doing?

- You're in a jungle. What are you doing?

- You're in the Arctic. What are you doing?

- You're on a prairie. What are you doing?

- You're on a beach. What are you doing?

- You're in the wetlands. What are you doing?

- You're in a forest. What are you doing?

- You're by a river. What are you doing?

- You're on a farm. What are you doing?

What Did He Tell You?

We've found that men answer the questions in one of three different ways. They generally relate to the different environments either contentedly, exploitatively, or actively.* What they're doing won't necessarily be the same in each place, but you'll probably be able to spot a trend.

CONTENTED: The contented man feels at one with nature. He is happy in his habitat, respects the things around him, and doesn't need to change things. He'll use passive words such as *sit, lie,* and *look*. He'll be sipping gin in a jungle clearing, walking over farmland, or sunbathing on the beach. He'll be easy to live with, but may not be such a great provider.

EXPLOITATIVE: The exploitative man is more driven, seeking his relevance in external projects that may change his environment, rather than being able to find peace internally. He'll use words such as *build, make,* and *change*. Chances are he'll be setting up an ice hotel in the Arctic, damning the river, or building a new barn on the farm. He'll be a good provider, but you may not see too much of him unless you work side by side.

ACTIVE: The active man finds satisfaction in doing things within the environment. He doesn't want to exploit it, but he's not going to be sitting down for too long either. He'll use words such as *play, explore, walk,* or *run*. He'll be fishing in the river, mountain biking across the prairie, or kayaking through the wetlands. He'll be a good provider as long as he's prepared to turn his energy into work.

So what sort of impact does he have in these different environments? What implications can you draw from this regarding how he approaches everyday life and your relationship? Did his answers ring true with what you know of him? If they did, you're obviously with the man you want to be with. If his answers were at odds with what you know, get him to elaborate. It may be that he feels frustrated with what motivates him and where he's going.

Because most men will have initially visualized a setting, you can take this further by going back to each environment and asking him to describe it in more detail. For example, was the beach small and private, or expansive with big surf and lots of people? What about the forest? Was it light and open, or dark and gloomy? By asking for these extra details you'll discover where he feels most comfortable, and whether he likes to be around people, or whether he appreciates nature in solitude. In other words, you'll find out which environments make him feel good and which make him feel bad. Are they the same for you? Do you like panoramic views with big skies, or quiet leafy glades and sparkling streams? Would you both like to build a home in the same environment, and how would it relate to its surroundings?

* Some men find certain environments unpleasant or threatening, and they'll usually tell you this right off. They might say, "I hate the jungle! I wouldn't want to do anything in there!" In which case you should simply pass on to the next environment and make a note not to take him on a vacation to Borneo.

213.

KEEP IT CLEAN

ASK HIM THIS: "Can I take you anywhere? Imagine that I'm taking you to meet my parents for the first time. I'm going to read you a series of statements, and I want you to complete them as quickly as possible, but you have to keep your answers clean."

- You're a pain in the...
- Why, you dumb...
- Why don't you just shut the...
- I've got you by the...
- I don't give a flying...
- Now you're really in the...
- He thinks the sun shines out of...

- What the...
- Son of a...
- Stick it up your...
- You're full of...
- Kiss my...
- Take it up the...
- You mother...

WHAT DID HE TELL YOU?

This exercise will tell you whether he can modify his speech and adapt to different social situations. How hard did he have to work on finding clean alternatives? Was it seamless or were there long silences as he attempted to find "acceptable" phrases? Did he even realize that there was a crude option? How comfortable was he with this exercise?

214.

MARGARET LOVES MICHAEL

THE TWO SCENARIOS IN THIS EXERCISE MAY SEEM
STRAIGHTFORWARD TO YOU, BUT MOST MEN FIND THEM
EXTREMELY DIFFICULT TO UNDERSTAND. HOWEVER, TO
GET THE MOST ACCURATE RESULTS, MAKE SURE YOU ONLY
READ THE SCENARIOS OUT ONCE EVEN IF HE ASKS YOU TO
REREAD THEM—AND HE ALMOST CERTAINLY WILL.

ASK HIM THIS: "How's your memory for detail? I'm going to read
you two scenarios just once and I want you to answer one question at
the end of each one."

Here's the first one:

> Margaret goes to a party and meets her dream man, Michael.
> But Michael is married to Rachel and Margaret is engaged
> to John. Unbeknown to Margaret, John works in the same
> building as Michael and Rachel has seen John there. She really
> fancies him and fantasizes a life with him. Michael believes that
> marriage is forever and Margaret doesn't want to break John's
> heart. John is also attracted to Rachel but doesn't want to tell
> Margaret that.
>
> • What could happen?

Here's the second scenario:

> Tom meets Debbie at a party. He finds her very attractive and wants to ask her out. But Debbie is married to David and Tom is engaged to Kate. Tom doesn't know that Debbie works on the same floor as Kate and that David has seen Kate there. David really fancies Kate and wonders what it would be like to be with her. Debbie believes that marriage is sacred and Tom doesn't want to break Kate's heart. Kate is also attracted to David but doesn't want to tell Tom that.

- What could happen?

What Did He Tell You?

So how did he do? Was he able to keep up with the stories and tell you who could get together with who? Most women find these two stories very easy to grasp while their men call for several rereadings in order to comprehend them. To men, both story lines read like one-sided telephone conversations, in which prior knowledge of the people being discussed is essential for understanding the likely outcomes. Actually, all the information is available but they seem to freeze when they perceive that too much detail has been supplied.*

The fact that the scenarios are about relationship dilemmas may also flick his "off switch" pretty early on. Because the first sentence of the first scenario centers on a woman's desires, men tend to lose the plot fairly quickly. However, if your man is still vital and on the lookout, he'll generally find the second scenario easier to follow because the action starts with a man on the hunt for a woman. This is also something the still "active" male can relate to, and he is more likely to understand the dynamic and suggest an outcome.

This brings up an issue that bugs a lot of women. Why do men, who are in apparently settled relationships, still find the need to look at other women? This is an issue we've heard often from couples we've talked to during the writing of this book. It can cause much stress within a relationship, which is a shame because it's stress that is often due to a misunderstanding of male and female priorities.

Generally speaking, a woman's physical appearance is more important to a man than a man's physical appearance is to a woman. (See #711 footnote for an important exception to this.) In this respect it seems that men and women are wired differently—something the makeup industry is well aware of. It's the reason men reportedly spend a much shorter amount of time on matchmaking websites than women. They just flick through looking at each woman's picture and go for the one that has physical appeal, while women take time to read what the man has written and base their decision to make contact mainly on that. Women start from the inside and work out. Men look on the outside first, and then work in.

So when a man checks out another woman he's simply responding to a stimulus he's wired to receive. It's much the same with women checking out each other's clothes—something they do automatically because it affects their social interactions.

* Men's brains are structured differently from women's, a fact that gives some credence to those clichés about men not listening, and women not being able to read maps. However, nothing is absolute and an increasing number of men and women are what is referred to as "bridge brains," a term coined by social philosopher, Michael Gurian. Their brains have developed in such a way that they are capable of thinking and acting in a more cross-gender fashion. Bridge-brain men, for example, have greater verbal ability than other men and are more nurturing and emotional. Because these are traits that many women seem to want in a man, more women will select bridge-brain men to mate with, and so the number of these men in the population will rise. Gurian estimates that around twenty-five percent of men are now bridge-brains.

LEVEL 3

A Personal History

There is a theory that in order to understand the present or to predict the future, you must first look back to the past. All the secrets are there. Never is this more relevant or true than when we're looking at individuals. The past is like a gold mine for understanding a person's character and behavior. In fact, it's almost impossible to really "know" someone unless you do look back.

In *A Personal History,* we explore your man's childhood and family background to give you information that will help you understand him better. What was he like as a boy? Did he have many friends? How did his parents treat him? What was his early view of the world—was it a good place or a bad place?

Level Three covers the most influential time of a person's life, and needs to be explored thoroughly. Because there is such a rich vein of information in these exercises, the process may be a lengthy one and you'll need to allow plenty of time for them. Don't try to do too much at one sitting, and remember, some men find this section particularly difficult, especially if their childhoods were not positive. Tread lightly and be prepared to shelve questions for a later time when you feel he might be more open to them.

But most men love *A Personal History* because you're asking them questions that only they have the answers to, and often they'll be telling someone for the first time in their lives. Consequently, they become absorbed. The more questions they answer about their early years, the more immersed they become in it. Usually we're only asked one or two questions about our childhood at a time. But the extent of these exercises allows him to stay with his boyhood long enough for it to become a reality again. When this happens, memories and feelings become vivid and lead him to a deeper understanding of the influences that have shaped him. Remember, simply by asking these questions you'll be showing a level of interest and care that most men will welcome.

Many of these exercises are also reversible, and you will probably want your man to take you through the same sets of questions. Together, you might discover all sorts of things about yourselves that you either didn't previously know, or didn't think were relevant to how you are today. As a way of initiating intimate disclosure, *A Personal History* should prove invaluable for both of you.

301.

HOME SWEET HOME

HOME SWEET HOME HAS THE POTENTIAL TO BE AN
ABSOLUTE MINE OF INFORMATION, SO DON'T BE PUT OFF
BY ITS LENGTH. AFTER ALL, HIS CHILDHOOD REPRESENTS A
HUGE PART OF HIS LIFE. ASK HIM TO EXPAND ON ANY OF
THE STATEMENTS IF YOU WANT MORE DETAILS.

ASK HIM THIS: "What do you remember about your home life as
a kid? I'm going to read you a series of statements relating to your
childhood, and I want you to complete them as quickly as possible."

- You'd describe your childhood as...

- You'd describe your parents' relationship as...

- Your mom and dad's style of parenting would best be
  described as...

- In your house, signs of affection were...

- When you were a child, being naked was regarded as...

- If your parents heard you swearing, they...

- If your parents punished you, they usually did so by...

- As a child, you mostly got into trouble for...

- Mealtimes at your house mostly consisted of...

- When it came to table manners, your parents...

- Weekends at your house mostly consisted of...

- In your childhood, religion was...

- At vacation time, your family would usually...

- As a child, one vacation that stood out was...

- Family trips in the car were...

- In your childhood, Thanksgiving could best be described as...

- In your childhood, Christmas could best be described as...

- In your childhood, Halloween could best be described as...

- In your childhood, birthdays were...

- The pets you had in your childhood included...

- Your favorite was...

- In your childhood, you'd describe your health as...

- Physically, you would have been described as...

- If one type of music dominated your household back then, it would have been...

- Your favorite television/radio show back then was...

- The television/radio show you most wanted to watch/listen to but weren't allowed to was...

- Where did you come in the family? Were you the eldest, a middle child, the youngest, or an only child?

- Thinking back, you'd describe your status in the family as...

- With regard to feelings of security and warmth, you'd describe your home life as...

- Thinking back to your Mom and Dad, you had more interests in common with your...

- These interests included...

- Your parents' opinion of you back then was that you were...

- When describing you to other people, your parents used to say...

- What you most loved about your Dad back then was...

- What you most loved about your Mom back then was...

- What you most hated about your Dad back then was...

- What you most hated about your Mom back then was...

- Looking back, you probably most take after your...

- What you most love about your Dad as an adult is...

- What you most love about your Mom as an adult is…

- What you most dislike about your Dad as an adult is…

- What you most dislike about your Mom as an adult is…

- Apart from your parents, the adults you most saw in your home were…

- Apart from your parents, the adults you most thought of as role models were…

- Thinking back to your very first day at school, you'd describe it as…

- Your favorite teacher in your childhood was…

- Your best friends back then were…

- You'd describe your relationship with your siblings as…

- The family from television or movies that you would most identify with would be…

- The family from television or movies that you wish you'd been a member of was…

- If your family had a coat of arms, the motto underneath would read…

- If you could change just one thing in your childhood, it would be…

- If you could bring up your children the same way that your parents brought you up, it would make you feel…

What Did He Tell You?

Did he tell you things about his childhood that you didn't know? Did he surprise himself with facts that he thought he'd forgotten? Did he look back on his early years with sadness, regret, or pleasure?

A lot is written about nature versus nurture, and there's no denying that we are born with a set of genes inherited from our family, and that we also arrived with our own personality and characteristics.

But our family life also has a huge bearing on how we turn out. It affects our behavior in all sorts of areas. It's where we form our attitudes, our moral code, our goal setting, our self-confidence, and whether we view the world as a good or a bad place. And, of course, it colors us emotionally, which in turn affects the way we form relationships.

All in all, this exercise should provide you with new insights into the psyche of your man, and thus help you to understand him better. (See also the interpretation of the next scenario, *When You Were Just a Little Boy*.)

It would also be very helpful for him if *you* could complete this exercise. What factors did you have in common? What disparities were there? Do they matter to you both? And do you think your family backgrounds have had any bearing on why you're with him now?

302.

WHEN YOU WERE JUST A LITTLE BOY

THIS IS ANOTHER SCENARIO IN WHICH YOU MAY NEED TO TREAD LIGHTLY. IT MIGHT BE THAT HE LOVES TALKING ABOUT HIS CHILDHOOD, BUT IF HE DOESN'T, EASE UP, OR EVEN SHELVE IT FOR ANOTHER TIME.

ASK HIM THIS: "What do you remember about your childhood? I'm going to read you a series of statements and I want you to complete them as quickly as possible."

You have been hired by a director who is doing research for his new movie. It will be set in the same era and location in which you grew up, and he interviews you to get a better feel for the role of the young boy who is the star of the film. These are the director's questions to you:

- As a little boy, you were at your happiest when…

- When you were a little boy, you were really scared of…

- When you were a little boy, you hated…

- When you were a little boy, you loved eating…

- When you were a little boy, you hated eating…

- When you were a little boy, you loved going to...

- When you were a little boy, you really looked forward to...

- The thing that most made you cry when you were a boy was...

- What you most loved about Christmas was...

- What you most hated about Christmas was...

- What you most loved about your birthday was...

- What you most hated about your birthday was...

- When you were a little boy, the thing that most embarrassed you was...

- When you were a little boy, the thing that most made you laugh was...

- When you were a little boy, you were loved by...

- When you were a little boy, you were admired by...

- When you were a little boy, you were really good at...

- The thing that got you most into trouble was...

- The best thing about being a little boy was...

- The worst thing about being a little boy was...

(Now go back and ask him whether his answers would be the same now that he's an adult. For instance, do his loves and hates about Christmas still apply?)

What Did He Tell You?

How much of his boyhood is still present in his likes and dislikes now? Does he think his boyhood has shaped the way he is today? How much has he changed? How good was his memory? Were there things about his boyhood that he just didn't have an answer for?

His childhood experiences will have had a major impact on him one way or another.* People whose childhoods were unpleasant tend to react in one of two ways. Either they bounce out of it and become determined to give their own children the quality of life they deserve, or they become slightly bitter and treat the world as if it owes them a favor. If a person's childhood has largely been happy, they will reflect this in their attitudes to other people. They will generally feel good about themselves and know that they are lovable and valued.

While there are no hard-and-fast rules about the effects of parenting on children, there are general indicators that should help you to see patterns or tendencies. Parenting styles are often neatly bunched into three categories: authoritarian, permissive, and authoritative. But within the first two there are many variations, and the outcomes in adulthood can be profound.

Obviously, hostile or punitive parenting can make a child abusive and distrustful, which in turn can lead to self-punishment and guilt. Rejecting or shaming parents will probably create a child who is hostile, self-centered, and socially ill at ease.

But the wrong kind of upbringing doesn't have to be through physical or mental abuse. Neglectful parenting will tend to make a child very reserved, have commitment problems, and have a feeling of never belonging. Inconsistent parenting makes the child feel angry, stubborn, and misunderstood. Parents dominated by their children will probably lead to the child becoming lazy, selfish, and arrogant. Ambivalent parenting encourages identity crises.

Warm and well-intentioned parenting can also have its pitfalls. If, for instance, parents are overprotective it could lead to the child feeling insecure, submissive, and dependent. Indulgent parenting can lead to feelings of narcissism and issues with authority. Adoring, uncritical parenting can make the child manipulative and temperamental, bordering on the histrionic. Equally, parents who are emotionally seductive—in other words, use their child as a source of love— can encourage eating disorders/addictions, depression, and self-deprecation.

Note, though, that the field of brain science has discovered a phenomenon they call "resilient genes," genes that counter some of the unfavorable conditions that an individual may experience. Scientists assert that these genes explain why siblings can go through almost exactly the same childhood environment, and turn out at opposite ends of the spectrum.

However, the one constancy that seems to prevail in arguments relating to parenting is that a child's behavior, whether it be good or bad, is largely learned. The degree to which this behavior is presented may be dictated by inherited character genes, but overall, a child will mimic what he or she sees and hears, and react one way or another to situations that he or she encounters. We hope that *When You Were Just a Little Boy* and the previous exercise, *Home Sweet Home,* will help you to gain a clearer picture of each other's backgrounds and consequent attitudes.

* Try this scenario out on yourself. What insights did it provide? Are you able to share them with your man?

303.

PLAYTIME

FOR SOME PEOPLE, TALKING ABOUT THEIR CHILDHOOD
IS QUITE DISTRESSING. THE LAST THING YOU WANT TO
DO HERE IS MAKE YOUR MAN UNCOMFORTABLE. IF HE'S
EVEN SLIGHTLY RESISTANT, LEAVE IT AND COME BACK TO
IT ANOTHER TIME. BUT IF HE IS WILLING TO DO THIS
EXERCISE, YOU MAY STILL NEED TO PROMPT HIM ALONG
WITH YOUR OWN QUESTIONS.

ASK HIM THIS: "Could you ever work with children? I'm going to read you a scenario, and I want you to answer any questions by using your own childhood experiences."

You are applying for a job as a teacher's aide in an exclusive preschool. The owner of the facility, Mrs. Tremain, interviews you and explains that her line of questioning is to determine if you have the ability to truly relate to children.

First, she asks: "Did you grow up in the city, a small town, or the country?"

- She asks: "How much did you play outside?"

- She asks: "Did you need toys to play with, or could you make your own fun?"

- "Did you have a fort?"

- "Did you have a special place where you went for play?"

- "Did your parents encourage you to play?"

- Then Mrs. Tremain asks: "Were you able to play without adult supervision? For instance, did you go to the local park on your own for extended periods of time?"

- "Did you have many friends?"

- "How much did your parents play with you?"

- "What sort of games did you play with them?"

- "What sort of games did you play with other children?"

- "Who was your first fight with?"

- "Who did you most go to for help if you were hurt or in trouble or needed a conciliator?"

- Mrs. Tremain then asks: "Were you allowed to play anywhere at home, or were there rooms or areas that were off limits?"

- "Were there any set ground rules for your play?"

- "In a pickup game of baseball, were you one of the first to be chosen for a team?"

- "As a young boy, do you think you were popular?"

- "Were you a leader?"

- "Were you happy as a boy?"

- "Who were your superheroes when you were a boy and did you pretend to be them?"

- "When you have fantasies now, do they have similarities with those you had when you were a boy?"

- Finally, Mrs. Tremain asks: "How would you define 'play' in an adult world? And how do you play now?"

WHAT DID HE TELL YOU?

Can he see how his childhood may have influenced the way he is now? How relaxed is he when talking about play or his own childhood? If he is a parent now, how has it shaped his role in reaction to his own parents? In other words, if his parents were enthusiastic and playful, has this translated to the way he is with his kids now? Would you regard him as a playful person? Does he have a sense of fun?

And what about you? How did you play as a child? Maybe you could get him to run the exercise by you. Then you might discover any differences between your play styles and whether these differences reflect the way you are now.

This all begs the question: How important do you think play actually is? Psychologists and educators tell us that play is an essential part of human development. In childhood, it acts as a sort of dress rehearsal for adulthood. Play is where a child can safely explore and improve such skills as communication, knowing right from wrong, creativity, and self-image. It also allows the child to simply be him- or herself. The shame of adulthood is that either we tend to lose our ability to play, or we suppress it because we think that it's childish and irrelevant. Never could this be further from the truth.

A child's world is not governed by logic, so children can circumvent the conventions and assumptions that in adulthood have a way of stifling us as individuals. For instance, they might make up an "invisible friend" and gain great security from this pretend companion. An ignorance of the subtleties of language will also help them to keep their understanding of the world simple. Take the following conversation as an example. "Johnny, what have you got in your mouth?" "Candy." "Where did you get it?" "Off the floor." "That's disgusting!" "No, it's yummy." This ignorance of language at that point in the three-year-old's life enabled him to enjoy the taste of the candy, rather than worry about where it had come from.

We're not suggesting that as adults we should have imaginary friends and reduce language to its most obtuse form. But we can learn so much from children's play. If we could combine their fearless imagination and our rationality, just think how creative we could become. It would also allow us to take risks within our relationships, and open us up to more of our own potential. In fact, that's what this whole book is about—playing as a way of exploring each other within a lighthearted, nonpunitive climate that allows you to see new possibilities within your relationship.

304.

SCHOOL DAYS

APART FROM HOME, SCHOOL IS THE SINGLE BIGGEST
CHILDHOOD INFLUENCE IN ANYONE'S LIFE. WE SPEND
MORE TIME THERE THAN ANYWHERE ELSE. SO THIS EXERCISE
SHOULD GIVE YOU SOME INSIGHTS INTO YOUR MAN'S
FORMATIVE YEARS. GET HIM TO TRY THESE QUESTIONS ON
YOU TOO BEFORE YOU READ THE INTERPRETATION.

ASK HIM THIS: "What do you remember about your time at school?
I'm going to read you some questions and I want you to answer them,
giving as much detail as possible."

- Do you remember you first day at elementary school?
  What was it like?

- What were recess and lunchtime like?

- Did your mother prepare your lunch? If so, what was it?

- What did you like most about elementary school?

- Do you remember your elementary teachers? Who did
  you like the most?

- How were kids punished at your school?

- Were you ever punished? How?

- Did you have many friends at your school?

- Were you ever bullied in elementary school?

- How common was bullying in your school?

- Did you join in bullying others?

- Did you ever try to protect others being bullied?

- Did you ever try to confront the bullies?

- What about high school? Was there bullying there?

- Do you remember your first day at high school? What was that like?

- Think of some of the friends you had at school. Why were they your friends?

- Were you a bit of a loner, or did you hang out with a group of schoolmates?

- Do you still have contact with any high school friends?

- Have you ever been to any school reunions? If so, what was it like?

- Were you popular?

- Were you ever voted into a position of responsibility by your classmates?

- What about the teachers? Did they like you?

- What sort of student were you?

- Did you cut many classes?

- What was your favorite subject in high school?

- Did you have a favorite teacher?

- What after-school activities did you participate in?

- What was the best year you had in school? Why?

- Were your parents supportive of your achievements? Did they take an interest?

- What's the most embarrassing thing that ever happened to you at high school?

- What's the worst thing that ever happened to you at high school?

- What about the best thing?

- What do you think school did for you?

- What do you think school did *to* you?

WHAT DID HE TELL YOU?

Was school good for him? Were his experiences mostly positive or negative? What about you? How did your school days compare with his? How do you think it's affected both of you?

For many people school was just one long nightmare. Pressure from parents, teachers, and peers made it a miserable time, and it probably had all sorts of short-term and long-term effects. If parents regarded only academic achievement as a real measure of success, and you weren't particularly gifted in this narrow area, then a sense of failure could be a very real result. This could in turn manifest itself in a form of rage that would include truancy, bullying, and opposition to authority figures. At the very least, this sense of failure could impact future self-esteem, self-worth, social acceptability, and ability to achieve.

Thankfully, for most people, there is always something positive that they can remember from school, whether it be a kind teacher, a good friend, or even just one really good grade. There is also that strangest of animals—resilience. So how resilient were you both? The last two questions in this scenario could be particularly enlightening for each of you.

This may also be a good time to discuss what sort of school you'd like your children to go to. Based on your own school experiences, what are your priorities for your own children's education?

305.

MOMMIES AND DADDIES

DID HIS PARENTS HAVE A LOVING RELATIONSHIP, OR DID
THEY CONSTANTLY BICKER? HERE'S YOUR CHANCE TO FIND
OUT HOW ALL THIS MIGHT RELATE TO YOU. YOU SHOULD
GET HIM TO TRY THIS EXERCISE ON YOU TOO.

ASK HIM THIS: "What can you remember about your parents'
relationship? Think back to when you were growing up. Now,
I'm going to read you a series of statements regarding your
parents, and I want you to complete them as quickly as
possible."

- You'd describe your parents' relationship as…

- The way they normally displayed affection for each
  other was by…

- This was mostly initiated by…

- The kinds of gifts they'd give each other would be…

- The activities they enjoyed most together were…

128

- If you had to describe their style of communicating with each other, you'd say it was...

- When it came to domestic chores, they...

- When it came to intelligence, your father treated your mother as...

- Intelligence-wise, your mother treated your father as...

- In a crisis your parents were...

- The frequency of your parents' quarreling was...

- Some parents try to keep any fighting out of sight of their kids. For the most part your parents...

- If they did fight, the chances of it getting physical were...

- Your parents generally managed to resolve conflicts by...

- You'd describe the atmosphere around your parents as...

WHAT DID HE TELL YOU?

How much did he know about his parents? How does he think the way his parents related to each other has affected his own ability to have relationships? What about problem solving? How does his ability in this area differ from his parents? And what about signs of affection and communication? Is there a pattern here? And what did he learn about your parents? Was there much of a difference?

Given that parents are the first role models that anyone has regarding relationship dynamics, this exercise should give you a fairly solid idea as to where he's coming from or what he's reacted against. Just as children are affected by their mothers' and fathers' parenting style, so too are they influenced by their parents' relationship style. Whatever it is, they will have unconsciously taken note, and it will impact on their own relationships when they grow into adults.

Relationship styles, like parenting, can be a generational thing. Before the emergence of the feminist movement, for instance, many couples worked off the stereotypical blueprint of the husband being boss of the household, the breadwinner, and the dominant force. The wife was expected to be submissive or, to quote the now seldom used wedding vow, to honor and obey. But even within this model there was still room for mutual respect.

In more recent times, a combination of factors has irrevocably changed the blueprint, and most everyone either practices or is at least aware of what could be described as a more enlightened attitude to relationship dynamics. In some sectors of society, equality might still be a vision rather than a reality, but it's much closer than it was.

You might consider gender equality to be irrelevant when it comes to discussing relationship styles, but to us it's fundamental. So the question is, if you or your man's parents were part of the old school, have you followed suit, or have you both grown with the times? And whatever your parents' styles were, do you like each other's way of expressing your love and respect?

306.

MOTHER

WAS SHE A MISS HONEY OR A MISCREANT? THIS EXERCISE
MAY GIVE YOU THE LOW-DOWN ON HIS REAL FEELINGS FOR
HER, SO IT'S IMPORTANT TO CHERISH THIS INFORMATION
AND NOT ABUSE IT. ASK HIM TO EXPAND ON ANY OF HIS
ANSWERS IF YOU WANT MORE INFORMATION.

ASK HIM THIS: "What do you remember about your mother
when you were a kid? I'm going to read you a series of incomplete
statements relating to your childhood, and I want you to complete
them.

- If you had to describe your mother, you'd say she was...

- You'd describe your relationship with her when you
  were a boy as...

- If there was one word that would best sum up your
  mother, it would be...

- Back then, her hair was colored...

- When it came to clothing, she mostly wore...

- And makeup? She mostly...

- If you had to say whether your mother had a lot of friends or just a few, you'd say she had...

- These friends included...

- Did she have a paid job away from the house? If the answer was yes, this job was...

- Did she encourage and support you in the things *she* wanted you to do? If so, she did this by...

- Did she encourage and support you in the things *you* wanted to do? If so, she did this by...

- When she asked you to do things for her, it mostly took the form of...

- And this made you feel...

- If there was a time in your childhood when you stopped wanting to do things for her, it was...

- The times you got to be alone with her were...

- When you got to be alone with your mother, away from the other siblings, you felt...

- The special places your mother most took you to were...

- When it came to giving you hugs or kisses, she did this...

- One of your mother's favorite expressions was...

- She read you storybooks when...

- She told you made-up stories when...

- Your mother babied you when...

- When she spoke about her own childhood, she sounded...

- The clubs, societies, groups, and organizations that your mother belonged to included...

- Her interests were...

- Her passions were...

- Where religion was concerned, your mother was...

- Where politics was concerned, your mother was...

- As far as hands-on political involvement goes, she was...

- When it came to drinking, your mother was...

- When it came to gambling, your mother was...

- Your mother smiled when...

- This made you feel...

- Your mother laughed when...

- This made you want to...

- Your mother cried when...

- This made you...

- Your mother sometimes got angry when...

- To avoid her anger you would...

- She was usually angry with you when you...

- You and your mother would argue about...

- The worst thing you ever did to your mother was…

- You and your mother would have interesting discussions about…

- She was most proud of you when you…

- The thing you most regret about your mother is…

- What you'd most want for your mother now is…

What Did He Tell You?

How does he view his mother? How do his answers compare with what you know about her? Can he draw any parallels between his relationship with his mother and his relationship with you?*

We've all heard that cliché about men spending their whole life looking for a woman who's just like their mother. Or that when a man finds a woman, he spends all his time trying to have the sort of relationship with her that he didn't have with his mother. However, it's not just men who have hidden agendas, as you'll see later, and it's not as insidious or incestuous as it sounds.

If your man spoke with warmth and fondness about his mother then it's actually very good news for you, because it speaks volumes for his attitudes toward women in general. If his mother was loving, supportive, caring, and fun, then he'll tend to expect all women to be like that. There is, however, a negative aspect to a son's love for his mother. The mother's importance can reach godlike status and make it impossible for you to live up to her. On the other hand, if he doesn't have a strong bond with his mom it could be a plus, because you won't have to compete with her. The trick is to make sure that he's not looking on you as a substitute. It'll be up to you to decide whether, unwittingly, you're falling into this trap and enabling him to do this. You might also like to consider to what extent he might be a substitute father for you.

*
A major milestone in a child's life is when he or she gains independence from the mother. It's a particularly difficult thing for a boy to do. Boys, like girls, are biologically and psychologically attached to their mothers, but a boy needs to make much more of a break in order to prove his separate identity as an independent male. If a boy doesn't make this break in a positive way, it can cause problems with his romantic relationships. Similarly, if the mother is domineering and doesn't allow him to easily untangle himself from her apron strings, he may fear losing his independence in relationships with women and avoid commitment. Even when he has found a degree of autonomy, the way his partner criticizes him or asks him to do something may cause him to react negatively because he subconsciously feels he's still being treated like a child by his mother. By indirectly connecting him with her control again, he feels robbed of his hard-won independence and may resist perfectly reasonable requests. In the exercise we included a question about when he might have stopped wanting to be "mother's little helper." His answer here, along with many others in the exercise, could give you a clue as to whether he really has succeeded in breaking free from his mom.

Just as men can be influenced by their relationships with their mothers, research shows that women can be equally as affected by their relationship with their fathers. For instance, if a woman's father was distant or left the family, she may be overly needy in her relationships with men as a result of fearing their distance or eventual abandonment.

307.

FATHER

HOW MUCH IS YOUR MAN A CHIP OFF THE OLD BLOCK? AS IN *MOTHER*, THE INFORMATION YOU WILL RECEIVE IN THIS EXERCISE SHOULD BE RESPECTED AND CHERISHED. AGAIN, ASK HIM TO EXPAND ON ANY OF HIS ANSWERS IF YOU WANT MORE DETAILS.

ASK HIM THIS: "What do you remember about your father when you were a kid? I'm going to read you a series of incomplete statements relating to your childhood, and I want you to finish them as quickly as possible."

- If you had to describe your father, you'd say he was…

- You'd describe your relationship with him when you were a boy as…

- If there was one word that would best sum up your father, it would be…

- If you had to say whether your father had a lot of friends or just a few, you'd say he had…

- These friends included…

136

- Your father's job was as a...

- The thing he liked about his work was...

- What he hated about his work was...

- You went to his workplace when...

- When it came to his income, your father considered himself to be...

- Your father saw his role in the family as...

- He saw his role in the community as...

- When your father came home from work each day, you would...

- What he most wanted to do when he got home from work was...

- Did he encourage and support you in the things *he* wanted you to do? If so, he did this by...

- Did he encourage and support you in the things *you* wanted to do? If so, he did this by...

- Mostly, your father talked to you about...

- He read you storybooks when...

- He made up stories to tell you when...

- His favorite expression was...

- The way you used to hang out together was by...

- The times you got to be alone with him were…

- When you got to be alone with your father, away from the other siblings, you felt…

- Sometimes on the weekends you and your father would…

- The places your father most took you to were…

- When he spoke about his own childhood he sounded…

- The clubs, societies, groups, and organizations that your father belonged to included…

- His interests were…

- His passions were…

- Where religion was concerned, your father was…

- Where politics was concerned, your father was…

- As far as hands-on political involvement goes, he was…

- When it came to drinking, your father was…

- When it came to gambling, your father was…

- Your father smiled when…

- This made you feel…

- Your father laughed when…

- This made you want to…

- Your father cried when…

- This made you…

- Your father sometimes became angry when…

- To avoid his anger you would…

- He was usually angry with you when you…

- You and your father would argue about…

- He was most proud of you when you…

- The thing you most regret about your father is…

- What you'd most want for your father now is…

WHAT DID HE TELL YOU?

How much like his father is he? How much influence has his father had on him? Have these influences been good or bad? Has he tried to be like his dad, or has he moved in completely the opposite direction? What do you think of his dad? Have you learned anything new?

Parents have the awful responsibility of being the first adults their children will see. The child will either accept these visions or reject them. So if your man has responded to this exercise with a soft attitude and spoken in kind ways, then he obviously thinks that his father represents the type of man, husband, and father that he'd like to emulate.

If your man spoke in less than positive tones during this exercise, then he may have rejected his father's model and has gradually shaped his own image. But even if he's done this, it's still his dad's image that he's working from. This could explain a lot. For instance, if his dad was very authoritarian, your man may be reacting to this, and may have developed a much more laid-back or permissive approach to parenting.

On the other hand, despite his negative feelings about his upbringing, he may still have subconsciously adopted his father's approach purely because it's all he's known.

The father-son relationship is complicated. As the first male role model, the father reaches virtual hero status, and as a consequence it's only natural that the son will seek out approval and praise. But with the onset of adolescence, the son goes through a period of questioning and resistance as he seeks out his own male identity. The degree to which this conflict plays out is dependent upon the time and quality of time the father has spent with the son in early childhood.

Other factors can accentuate the conflict, particularly if the father's role was that of discipline enforcer. To compound matters, dads usually have more common interests with their sons, so they're thrown together with such pursuits as sports, cars, or the outdoors. Unfortunately, this can lead to a competitive/combative streak, which, along with the father's enforcing role, instills in the son a feeling that he is a disappointment to his father. This can have quite a lasting effect, and for some men it's only in their thirties and forties that they begin the process of acceptance and forgiveness. As a subsidiary question, it might be worth asking how he sees his father now.

Also, based on his own childhood experiences, how would he or does he parent his own children differently?

308.

BIG BOYS DON'T CRY

HOW IN TOUCH WITH HIS EMOTIONS IS HE? *BIG BOYS DON'T CRY* EXPLORES WHAT EFFECT HIS FAMILY CULTURE MAY HAVE HAD ON HIS ABILITY TO EXPRESS HIMSELF. BEFORE YOU READ THE INTERPRETATION, HAVE HIM TAKE YOU THROUGH THE SCENARIOS TOO.

ASK HIM THIS: "What was it like when you were a kid? I'm going to read you a series of scenarios relating to your childhood, and I want you to answer a question at the end of each one."

Think back to your childhood and then imagine yourself in each of these situations.

1. One of your friends takes your favorite pencil and breaks it. You retaliate by pushing him into the corner of a coffee table and he gashes his knee. Feeling guilty, you hide behind the couch, crying. In this situation, *your* parents would most likely have said to you either:

   A. "You can't just push your friend around like that. If he does something to make you mad, come and see us. In the meantime, we want you to say you're sorry to him."

B. "We don't care what he did. You know you shouldn't push him around. Now, go to your room."

C. "Stop that crying! You're not the one with the cut knee. Now, apologize to your friend."

D. "It's not nice to hurt your friend, is it?"

So, which of these options would *your* parents have said?

2. You have your heart set on going to Disneyland, and the whole family has been talking about it for weeks. But a couple of days before you're due to go, your parents receive news that your granny is sick, and so the trip is called off. You, however, are inconsolable. In this situation, *your* parents would most likely have said to you either:

A. "We know you're disappointed, and we're sorry. We wanted to go too."

B. "Don't be sad. We'll go another time."

C. "You're so damned selfish! Can't you see that your granny's sick?"

D. "Life is full of disappointments, son."

So, which of these options would *your* parents have said?

3. You walk into the living room to find that the family cat has killed George, your pet guinea pig, and is busily eating it. You run crying to your parents for comfort. In this situation, *your* parents would most likely have said to you either:

A. "You poor thing, having to see that. We know how much you loved George. Come and have a cuddle."

B. "Well, honey, you knew when you got George that there was always a chance of this happening."

C. "That'll teach you for letting it out of its cage, won't it?"

D. "Poor George! Poor you!"

Which of these options would *your* parents have said?

4. Your mother won't let you go to the movies with your friends because you haven't done your chores. When you turn to your dad for support, your dad sides with your mom. You become so enraged that you let fly with a torrent of obscenities aimed at both of them. In this situation, *your* parents would have said either:

A. "Look, we know you're mad, but don't take it out on us. You know the rules. Chores first, then the movies."

B. "That's no way to talk, young man. You should know better than that."

C. "Right, that's it! Not only are you not going to the movies today, but you're grounded for a month."

D. "Boy, what a mouth!"

Which of these options would *your* parents have said?

5. You're playing baseball at a Little League game. When you try to catch a foul, you miss the ball and it hits you smack on the nose. It's so painful that you burst into tears and run to your parents in the bleachers. Which of these options would *your* parents have said:

    A. "Ow! That must hurt. Let's put a bit of ice on it. Then you could go back on the field when it stops hurting."

    B. "Come on, son. Shake it off. Your team needs you."

    C. "God son, you're pathetic. It's just a bit of blood. Now get out there and play ball."

    D. "Wow! That's going to be a big bruise."

Which option would *your* parents have said?

WHAT DID HE TELL YOU?

Which of the answers did your man mostly attribute to his parents? His choices in this exercise could tell you a lot about how his family dealt with emotions, and what effect this has had on him as an adult.

If he thought that his parents would mostly have answered the A options, then he will have been brought up in a supportive and directed environment. His parents would have allowed him to own up to his emotions, and they would have been available to guide him into appropriate or safe ways of expressing himself. As a result, this will mean that he is better able to articulate his feelings and share them with people around him. It also means that, like his parents, he'll be able to offer empathy and support.

If he thought his parents would mostly have answered the B options, then by and large, his parents would have been dismissive of his emotions. Phrases like: "Don't cry," or "Buck up," or "Better luck next time" will have littered his childhood. The underlying message he would have learned from this response would be that he should hide his feelings, and that his parents would not be sympathetic to his needs. This, in turn, would gradually create a rift between him and them. If you want to get a more accurate handle on this, try asking him if he can remember a point in his life when he stopped confiding in his parents, and why. People brought up in this dismissive environment will tend to be emotionally repressed, and they will find it hard to connect on an intimate level with others.

The C options indicate a shaming/abusive parenting style. If your man mostly identified with these responses, then it's likely his parents not only tried to suppress his feelings but also punished him for expressing these feelings in the first place. As an adult, this would lead him to being intolerant of any negative displays of emotion, and he might even see these displays as nothing more than ploys to gain advantage. For instance, in reaction to someone breaking down in tears he might say: "Oh typical! When all else fails, turn on the waterworks."

The D responses point to a permissive or noninterventionist parenting style. Children brought up in this climate will feel that their parents may have acknowledged their emotions, but because there aren't many visible boundaries put in place and little guidance to help them deal with the best way to express these emotions, a sense of chaos will gradually take over. Because their displays of emotion will have been allowed to reach extremes, they'll subsequently find it difficult to control themselves, and will have limited ability at self-soothing. As adults they may be given to aggressive behavior and depression, and will have difficulty in problem solving.

Options B, C, and D in this exercise are indicative of dysfunctional family life. Children brought up in these backgrounds can be profoundly affected in later life. There is a widely held belief that children who endure an abusive early life—whether it be mental, emotional, or physical—take on one of four distinctly different personas, personas that they carry with them into adulthood.

First, there is the family hero or responsible/good child. This child becomes the third parent. They are high achievers and are usually popular in their peer group. But to maintain this image they adopt a very judgmental, rigid attitude that has no time for introspection. Their outward confidence masks a deep insecurity.

Second, there is the problem child or scapegoat. They are usually highly sensitive but lack the defensive mechanisms to counter the disharmony raging around them. This inherent honesty leads to problems at school, addictions, and self-loathing. But because their reactions are so extreme, they are usually the first in the family to seek help and move toward recovery.

Third, there is the caretaker. These children see their role as deflectors or pacifiers and they'll do anything to paper over the cracks. As adults they gravitate toward abusive relationships, adopting a rescuing attitude, and spend their life trying to please.

Fourth, there is the lost child. Their defensive mechanisms are simple. They disappear into a world of fantasy and daydreams. As adults, they have low self-esteem and are often commitment phobic. They become socially isolated and unhappy. Many writers and actors fall into this category—their art allowing them to express themselves from the relative safety of their characters.

These four roles, of course, are generalizations—no one fits perfectly into them. But overall, you should both be able to piece together a general trend, which will help explain your current modes of expression and why you choose them.

LEVEL 4

Go Forth, Young Man

Based on the information gathered from the last chapter, we now step into his adult world and examine his attitudes toward women, his perceptions of the roles within a relationship, his expectations of a relationship, and his core beliefs.

Level Four is the biggest chapter in the book, and this is no accident. Having looked at his graduation from his most formative years, we now explore the next influential phase of his life: his first forays into adult relationships. In this level we try to help you discover how past relationships have further added to his persona. He will have had successes, disasters, joy, and pain. Have these experiences enriched him, or made him gun-shy and entrenched? The scenarios in this chapter will hopefully answer these questions, and shine some light on how this might be impacting on your relationship with him.

We'll also explore how his past relationships have influenced his attitudes. Some of these attitudes will be set in stone, others he may still be formulating, which means, of course, that as in the past, he's still being shaped by his environment and experiences. The big difference though, is that now *you're* in his life, and by using this book, you will be making the kinds of connections that will be positive and rewarding for both of you.

401.

CHAOS IN MANHATTAN

THESE LITTLE SLICES OF LIFE WILL SHOW YOU HOW HE SEES THE WORLD'S HEROES AND VILLAINS. WE'D RECOMMEND YOU READ THROUGH THE INTERPRETATION FIRST.

ASK HIM THIS: "How are you at figuring out what's going to happen next? I'm going to read you a series of scenarios, and I want you to complete them as quickly as possible."

- The museum was only the second publicly commissioned building undertaken by the fledgling architect. Questioned by reporters about the work, the architect said that...

- Speaking on national television, the scientist proclaimed that while winning the Nobel Prize was a huge honor, it wouldn't significantly change...

- Chaos reigned in Manhattan today when location filming of a movie got out of hand. Unwitting bystanders, assuming a ten-foot exploding cucumber was for real, ran for their lives. But the film's director said that city ordinances had been complied with, and stated that filming would resume the next day. However, in a gesture of good will to the citizens of New York...

- A person believed to be about seventy-five years old paused in the middle of the road right in the path of an oncoming truck. Then at the last minute...

- The defendant, accused of murder, took the stand and in a show of defiance...

- When the surgeon who'd just operated on your child walked toward you with the thumbs-up sign, you were so relieved and grateful that you just wanted to rush up and give...

- You apprehend a mugger trying to make off with an old lady's handbag. The lady is so grateful that she gives you a substantial reward. The next day a reporter from a local TV station visits you. But instead of asking about your heroic deeds...

- You're the first to the scene of a drunk-driving accident. The driver is unconscious and a fire has started in the engine of the car. You...

- While you're on vacation, you get a terrible toothache. So you go to the nearest available dentist, whose behavior is so comforting and professional that you decide to show your gratitude by buying...

- You're trapped in an elevator with three other people. One of them panics and begins banging on the doors. You...

- You walk out of a party and find a friend lying on the ground in a drunken state. You...

- You're working for a department store as a security guard when you notice someone shoplifting, so you...

What Did He Tell You?

If your man is right now sitting back with a glow of satisfaction from having been wonderfully creative, let him wallow for a while. After all, yes, there is an element of creativity to this exercise, and the scenarios appear to have little or no connection to each other, but they would have taxed him intellectually. So if he still managed to come up with some inventive answers, despite the fact that he may have been wondering where it was all leading, then he's done well, on a cognitive level at least.

But how many of the people in the scenarios he had to interact with or speak for were actually women? All of the scenarios included professions or behaviors that could have been attributed to either men or women. So which ones did he attribute to women? It might say a lot about his gender perceptions and expectations.

Of course, there may be other explanations for his answers. For instance, if he thinks the old person on the road is a man, he could be associating frailty with men and therefore could see himself as vulnerable when he's old.

His past experience may also have dictated some of his answers. It may be, for example, that he's only ever dealt with male doctors, or the only people he knows who have drinking problems are male. Still, this won't account for all of his replies, and you may see an interesting pattern emerging.

402.

BREASTS ARE FOR...?

By placing him in this slightly detached situation, you're going to learn something about how he sees women, and what impact they've had on his life.

ASK HIM THIS: "What do you know about women? Imagine that while traveling through space you meet an alien who is making a study of the female of the human species. So far the only information he's gathered has been from television sitcoms he's intercepted via satellite. You can help him to understand women by answering the following questions."

• Why do women have breasts?

• What are the nipples for on these breasts?

• Why do men have nipples?

• Why do some women have breast enlargements?

• Why is cleavage so important?

• Why do some women like to show off their belly buttons?

• Why do women and men have hair under their arms?

The alien then asks:

- Why is women's skin softer than men's?

- Why do women have higher voices than men?

- Why are women afraid of mice?

- Why do women wear skirts?

- Why do they wear high-heeled shoes?

The alien then says:

- In these TV shows the women often turn up late. Why is that?

- Why do they wear makeup?

- Why does it take them so long to put this makeup on?

- Why do women have so many shoes?

- Why are women more emotionally expressive than men?

- Why do women always ask men what they're thinking?

The alien then asks:

- Why do women always ask about their weight?

- Why do men always try to avoid answering this question?

- What is cellulite?

- Why do women always go to the bathroom with other women?

The alien then says:

- Everyone seems to make a big deal about a woman's period. What is this "period"?

- Why should you never have an argument with a woman in the week before she has her "period"?

- Why do women value their relationship above their career?

- Why do women need to feel cared for?

- Why are women often attracted to "bad men"?

- How come women seem to be filling more and more executive positions in the corporate world?

- Why do women make such good caregivers of children?

- Why do women want to get married?

- Why do women stay in abusive relationships?

- Why do women like chocolate more than sex?

WHAT DID HE TELL YOU?

This is a fun exercise to uncover some of your man's preconceptions about women. Just how much does he really know, and are his observations positive or negative? Also, did he think that television's portrayal of women and men was real?

Sitcoms often highlight stereotypical concepts by grossly exaggerating human traits. This form of caricature can be very funny, and given the nature of television, it's actually a necessity. Time restraints mean that writers just don't have room to develop individual characters. So they present recognizable images and then cut to the chase. Reality is never a factor. Well, not for the writers and producers, anyway. But as viewers we are left in a situation where we are subtly being convinced that the sitcom is, indeed, the truth.

Yet we're highly developed life-forms, aren't we? Surely we can sort out fact from fiction. Well, media analysts would have us believe otherwise. Some of them assert that television is a form of what they call panopticism*—a way of being insidiously coerced into believing in carefully prescribed social ideals.

But to suggest that television stereotyping is an establishment conspiracy seems to forget a basic human trait—laziness. Television is very formulaic. If a show was successful in the 60s, why mess around with the ingredients? Update it a bit and churn it out. And if the shows happen to promote a safe, conservative view of life, well, that's a bonus.

Still, your man may, like you, recognise these sitcom stereotypes very easily. But does he have a contrasting view of the real world to negate them? How many women does he know, for instance, who fit in to none of these categories? And are you one of them?

* Panoptics is a concept in which a small number of people can, through surveillance, enforce laws and create discipline, and was named after the Panopticon, a circular-shaped prison block designed in the 1700s by Jeremy Bentham. The inclusion of this useless piece of information is an example of men taking any opportunity to demonstrate their superior knowledge—thereby perpetuating yet another stereotype!

403.

THE WOMEN'S MAGAZINE

AT LAST YOUR MAN GETS TO SHOW YOU JUST HOW MUCH
HE UNDERSTANDS WOMEN. YOU'LL NEED PEN AND PAPER
FOR THIS ONE. NUMBER A SHEET FROM 1 THROUGH 35
AND THEN NOTE DOWN HIS ANSWERS. AND DON'T SHOW
HIM WHETHER YOU AGREE WITH HIS ANSWERS OR NOT;
OTHERWISE HE WON'T WANT TO GO ON.

ASK HIM THIS: "How well do you know women's needs? You've applied for a position as a staff writer on a women's magazine, and you are interviewed by the editor to see just how well you know women. The editor reads out a series of statements and asks you to answer with either true or false. Here's the first statement."

1. It's important to a woman that her man can cook.

2. It's important to a woman that her man will clean the house.

3. It's important to a woman that her man takes care of house and car maintenance.

4. It's important to a woman that her man organizes the family finances.

5. It's important to a woman that her man regularly gives her signs of affection.

6. It's important for a woman to know that her man wants to marry her and stay married to her.

7. It's important to a woman that her husband wears a wedding ring.

8. It's important to a woman that her man buys her lingerie.

9. It's important to a woman that he will show public demonstrations of love and affection for her.

10. It's important for a woman to see her man working with skill and application.

11. It's important to a woman that a man has status.

12. It's important for a woman to be patiently listened to by her man.

13. It's important to her that her man is sexually experienced.

14. It's important to her that her man is able to take the lead sexually.

15. It's important to a woman that a man has body hair.

16. It's important to a woman that her man is good at massage.

17. It's important to a woman that her man is a good dancer.

18. It's important to a woman that her man is well educated.

19. It's important to a woman that her man is good at sports.

20. It's important to a woman that her man remembers their anniversary.

21. It's important to a woman that her man is good with his hands.

22. It's important to a woman that her man is a skilled driver.

23. It's important to a woman that her man has good fashion sense.

24. It's important to a woman that her man has strong political opinions.

25. It's important to a woman that her man is competent in the use of firearms.

26. It's important to a woman that her man is well groomed.

27. It's important to a woman that her man is physically well endowed.

28. It's important to a woman that her man doesn't need her.

29. It's important to a woman that her man knows when to shut her up.

30. It's important to a woman that her man can say no.

31. It's important to a woman that her man comes from a close family.

32. It's important to a woman to be her man's last love.

33. It's important to a woman that there are limits to how much her man will forgive her.

34. It's important to a woman that her man is right.

35. It's more important to a woman to feel significant in her man's life than it is for a man to feel significant in hers.

(Now go back and ask him to explain his choices.)

WHAT DID HE TELL YOU?

If you were the editor, would you give him the job? Does he have a good understanding of what women want, or are you asking yourself if he's actually on the same planet? What's important here is not whether you think he's right or wrong but trying to get a handle on just where he's coming from. So by having him explain his choices, you will get a better understanding of his attitudes toward women.

If you share most of the same perceptions as your man about what is important for a woman, it obviously means you have a good basis for building a relationship. If he's way off the mark, it may be why you haven't been connecting with each other. Or it may be that he knows what's important to you, but he doesn't think it's important for him to do anything about it. A third option may be that because the exercise talks about women in general he hasn't associated these global views with his relationship with you.

404.

BELIEVE IT OR NOT

EVERYONE LIKES TO THINK THAT SOME THINGS IN LIFE ARE
SET IN STONE. IT MAKES US FEEL SAFE. SO HOW DO MEN
REACT WHEN *BELIEVE IT OR NOT* SMASHES SOME OF THEIR
CORE BELIEFS?

ASK HIM THIS: "What do you think are some of the differences
between the sexes? I'm going to read you a series of statements about
men and women, and I want you to respond by saying either 'I agree'
or 'I disagree.'"

- Women feel more pain than men.

- The structure of a man's brain is different from a woman's.

- Men's brains have more brain cells than women's, but
  women are three percent more intelligent than men.

- Women are generally better than men at recognizing
  emotions from facial expression.

- Men are better than women at recognizing anger in facial
  expressions, especially in other men.

- Men perceive their work and accomplishments as the most important thing in their lives.

- For a woman the quality of her relationships defines her self-worth.

- Men feel like failures if they're not right.

- Women like men more when men admit they're wrong.

- Women have lower sex drives than men.

- Women have better peripheral vision than men.

- Men have more zipper injuries than women.

- Women beat around the bush; men are more direct.

- Men like to impress with big words.

- Women *attempt* suicide three times more than men.

- Men *commit* suicide three times more than women.

- Men dream of power and owning status symbols. Women dream of being of service to others.

- Men consider "things" to be more valuable than relationships.

- Men want to be seen as dominant, bold, and admired; women want to be seen as loving, attractive, and generous.

- When a man has problems, he looks inward and talks to himself. Women share their problems with others.

- Women have a better sense of smell than men.

- Men are better than women at math, chess, musical composition, and physics.

- The more testosterone a man has, the less he smiles.

- As men age, their testosterone levels drop and they smile more as they mellow.

- Men are attracted to blonds because blond hair is a sign of high estrogen levels that play an important part in nurturing behavior.

- The longer a man's ring finger is, relative to his index finger, the more testosterone he'll have.

- The more testosterone a man has, the better he'll be at spatial tasks, such as parallel parking.

- The larger a man's testicles, relative to his body size, the more promiscuous he'll be.

- Young men who feel good about their looks are more likely to engage in risky sexual behavior.

- The larger a woman's breasts, the more promiscuous she'll be.

- Women want love; men want sex.

- Men who don't drink alcohol prefer women with small breasts.

- Extroverted men prefer women with large breasts.

- Large-breasted women prefer small-nosed men.

- Large-nosed men prefer flat-chested women.

- Men want power, achievement, and sex, while women want relationships, stability, and love.

- Recent studies show that the number of extramarital affairs young women have equals those of men.

- Men are more easily overwhelmed by marital conflict than their wives.

- Women are constitutionally better able to handle stress than men.

What Did He Tell You?

Some of the statements in this exercise may be generalizations, and there will be exceptions, but based on research all of them are true.

How did he score? How does he react when he's told that they're true? What areas is he particularly interested in? What does he dispute and why? How attached to an idea is he? How many of the facts in this exercise did you find surprising?

Not all men are right, and not all men think they are either. But there are some "facts" that we cling to because we need to feel certain about something. So when it comes to learning that women are more intelligent than men, it's natural for your man to argue the point. But when he disputes sexual biology, behaviors, and tendencies, it would suggest that he's got a few hang-ups on this front.

Like many of the exercises in this book, *Believe It or Not* is designed to generate some interesting discussions. It's not about who's right or wrong but rather about your willingness and his to explore your differences and come to a better understanding.

405.

LADIES' DAY

HERE'S A FUN ONE THAT'LL TEST YOU BOTH. TRY TO STAY
IN ROLE WHILE YOU'RE DELIVERING THIS SCENARIO. YOU'LL
GET MUCH MORE INTERESTING ANSWERS IF YOU CAN.

ASK HIM THIS: "What do you know about sports? I'm going to read you a scenario, and I want you to complete the unfinished statements as quickly as possible."

It's ladies' day on a sports radio talk show, and you've been invited along as a guest expert. This is the day that women can call in and ask absolutely anything about sports, and know that they'll be treated with respect and dignity.

Chad Zerko, the DJ, gives you your first caller.

"We've got Marlene from Baltimore on line one. Marlene, what's your question?"

"I just wanted to know why hockey is so rough? These guys know how to skate, don't they? So how come they're always smashing into each other?"

You say…

"Next we have Adrienne from Chicago."

"Yes, I want to know why male athletes spit so much."

You say…

"And now we have Betty from Columbus."

"Hello? Am I on the air?"

"Yes, go ahead, Betty."

"Well, I want to know how come in basketball you don't get more points for a slam dunk."

You say…

"Right, next up, Suzy from Little Rock. Your question, Suzy, and could you turn down your radio a bit?"

"Oh, sorry. Yes, well I've been watching football for years and I still can't figure out what that huddle thing is. What do they talk about in there?"

You say…

"This is NZKYG and it's Ladies' Day. Right, next caller, Rita from Newark. Go ahead, Rita."

"Hi, Chad. I just wanted to talk about Nascar racing. Don't they find it really boring going round and round and round? Why don't they change the shape of the track?"

You say…

"Hey all you gals out there. call in now! It's Ladies' Day here on NZKYG. Okay, we've got Felicia from Reno on line one. Felicia, your question."

"Yes, my husband has just spent a fortune on a new set of golf clubs. What I don't understand is why he needs so many. Couldn't he just make do with two or three? Why does he need fourteen? His bag wouldn't be so heavy for a start."

You say…

"Moving right along, it's Jill from Salt Lake City. Go ahead, Jill."

"Hi. I just want to ask a question about male track sprinters. Wouldn't they be able to run faster if they lost a little weight? They seem to be a bit bulky."

You say…

"Now we have Debbie from Eugene. Your question, Debbie?"

"Yeah, hi, Chad. I just want to know why my husband has to watch *SportsCenter* every night? I mean, he's already seen all the games."

You say…

"Next up from the French Quarter we've got Julianne from New Orleans. Bonjour, Julianne."

"Hi. I want to know why boxers hang on to each other all the time. I mean, they're supposed to be boxing, right? Isn't that more like wrestling? So what *are* they doing?"

You say…

"Okay, last up this hour we've got Stella from Biloxi. Go ahead, Stella."

"Thanks. Well, you see golfers squatting down to get a better read on the lie of the green before they take a putt. What I want to know is why golfers don't lie right down on the green to get a really accurate read on a putt?"

You say...

What Did He Tell You?

How was his knowledge base? Did he manage to treat the questions with respect and dignity? For instance, did he thank the women for their questions, or did he treat the callers as if they were bimbos? Could he answer all the questions, and if so, how does it make you feel to have a font of sports knowledge in your midst?

Many men are walking encyclopedias when it comes to sports, especially the sports they're really into. Your guy's probably no exception. But how willing was he to actually impart his knowledge? His answers in this exercise could be brief and lightweight, especially if he thinks that you were only humoring him anyway. And maybe you were. But think about it. What if you had to complete a similar exercise that asked you to explain why women wear lip liner or find high heels exciting? Would you be that keen to let him in?

Keeping information to ourselves, particularly in specialized areas, is quite normal. Why do we do this? Is it just for the power that it yields? Referring back to this exercise, you might be tempted to answer no. After all, do you really care whether a golfer has three clubs in his bag or fourteen? Probably not. But if your man has treated the women in the exercise very lightly or patronizingly, you could wonder why this is. Perhaps in this case, knowledge of the sports world is not power to him, it's ownership.

When it comes to areas of personal interest such as hobbies or pastimes, we guard this information because it protects what we covetously refer to as our personal space. In relationships we need these spaces because they define who we are as individuals. They can take many forms. It could be a physical space such as a study, the kitchen, a part of the garden, or particularly with men, the garage, the car, or the toilet. Alternatively, the area we're trying to protect could be something less geographic such as friends, family, or information. These domains are our secure preserves that we can slip in and out of, safe in the knowledge that everything is still okay on the home front. Indeed, if we feel free enough to mark out our personal space and feel comfortable in it, that says a lot about the confidence and trust we have in the relationship.

As with everything in a relationship, however, there needs to be a balance. When a private space turns into an escape this can cause problems, because while the escapee may feel safe, the partner will be feeling the opposite. Sometimes, though, this feeling of insecurity can be misguided. We may feel threatened by our partner's privacy and misinterpret their need for space as them trying to get away from us. Rather than address our own insecurities, we try to muscle in on their territory, or usurp it altogether.

Here are a few questions to ponder. What are your personal spaces within your relationship? How much do you feel you need to protect them? Do you ever feel shut out of your partner's spaces? Do either of you feel the need to infiltrate each other's space? And lastly, how important are these spaces for both of you?

406.

IN A WORD

HERE'S A QUICK, FUN WAY TO FIND OUT WHAT SECTORS
OF SOCIETY YOUR MAN ADMIRES OR DETESTS. IF YOU WANT
HIM TO TRY YOU OUT ON THIS AS WELL, DON'T READ
THE INTERPRETATION UNTIL YOU'VE BOTH FINISHED THE
EXERCISE.

ASK HIM THIS: "Who do you like? I'm going to read you a list of statements, and I want you to complete them as quickly as possible."

• Californians are...	They're also...
• New Yorkers are...	They're also...
• Christians are...	They're also...
• The police are...	They're also...
• Terrorists are...	They're also...
• Teenagers are...	They're also...
• Women are...	They're also...
• Firefighters are...	They're also...

- Musicians are...   They're also...

- Artists are...   They're also...

- Lawyers are...   They're also...

- Southerners are...   They're also...

- Athletes are...   They're also...

- Politicians are...   They're also...

- Homosexuals are...   They're also...

- Lesbians are...   They're also...

- Republicans are...   They're also...

- Men are...   They're also...

- Mothers are...   They're also...

- Fathers are...   They're also...

- Children are...   They're also...

- Democrats are...   They're also...

- Actors are...   They're also...

- Marines are...   They're also...

- People with tattoos are...   They're also...

- You are...   You're also...

(Add your own categories to this list if you like.)

What Did He Tell You?

So, who are his heroes, what's his view of life, and what are his prejudices? This exercise is a classic word association exercise that should quickly tell you things about his background, his intolerances, and the people he most admires.

In this exercise he has to give two opinions about the subjects, and they may contradict each other. So how can you decide what your man really thinks? Here's a tip: If he has two opposite views, then they cancel each other out. It's only when he gives two positives or two negatives that you'll get the real deal on how he perceives each subject.

Mostly, he'll have gathered his opinions from experience. He may, for instance, have a fairly unflattering stance on lawyers because he's been involved in civil or criminal suits. However, this may not be the only reason. He may simply know a few lawyers whom he doesn't particularly like as people. Alternatively, he may never have been to court, and doesn't know any lawyers, but has gained his opinion either through taking on the views of his family or peers, or through some perceived negative image that he's picked up from the media.

As with all word association exercises, it's the subsidiary questions you ask that will give you the clearest idea as to his reasoning. So if he displays opinions about any of the people in the exercise that you find either interesting or alarming, ask him why he feels this way, or whether he actually knows any artists or marines or Southerners. Dig a little, and you may be surprised at what you discover.

407.

THE GLENDA BENDER

THIS IS A NOVEL WAY OF SEEING WHAT YOUR MAN THINKS OF HIMSELF. BUT TO MAXIMIZE THE RESULTS, KEEP YOUR DELIVERY ANIMATED, AND WHERE APPLICABLE, SEXY.

ASK HIM THIS: "Are you good at selling yourself? I'm going to read you a scenario, and I want you to complete the unfinished statements."

While chilling out in a hotel room the night before a job interview, and paging through the information you've been sent, you notice something odd about the business card of your prospective employer. On the back, in very elegant handwriting, is the name Glenda, plus a phone number.

Out of curiosity you decide to call her. (Ask him to hold his cell phone, or imitate holding a phone, to get him into the role.) You explain where you got her number and she says in a deep, seductive voice: "Are you normally so impulsive?"

You say…

She says: "Have you ever done anything like this before?"

You say…

She says: "Well, I have to admit that I'm finding this a little bit disturbing, but it's also rather...exciting. How do you feel?"

You say...

Then Glenda says: "God, you've got a lovely voice. Tell me what you look like."

You say...

She says: "What's your best physical feature?"

You say...

She says: "Tell me about your hands. I like men telling me about their hands and telling me what they can do with them."

You say...

She says: "Tell me, do you have a big nose?"

You say...

Then Glenda says: "If you could describe yourself in one word, what would that be?"

She says: "What sort of woman do you think I am?"

She says: "And how old do you think I am?"

She says: "What do you think I look like?"

Then Glenda says: "What do you think I'm wearing?"

172

Then she says: "So, what's your idea of a good time? I mean, if we were to meet sometime soon, what could you offer me?"

Then she says: "What do you most like about women?"

Then she says: "What kind of woman do you respect?"

Then she says: "Guess what I most hate about men?"

Then she says: "You know, there are three things I really love about men. I like hands, knees, and…"

Finally, Glenda says: "Actually, I think this is getting a bit silly. I think I'll go. But ring me tomorrow night."

Then she hangs up.

• After this conversation you feel…

The position you're applying for is as a financial controller at a casino. The interview the next day goes well, though it seems rather brief. At the end you're asked if you have any questions of your own. You express surprise that, given the nature of the job and the environment it's in, you weren't asked any questions that would probe your moral character.

The manager just smiles wryly and says: "We got all the personal information we needed from Glenda. She's been my PA for ten years now. She's pretty talented, wouldn't you say?

You say…

- Do you think you got the job? Would you want it if you did get it?

- Do you think you were treated fairly?

- And if not, why?

WHAT DID HE TELL YOU?

So how is he at self-promotion? Did you like the way he described himself, and did you agree with his take on his strengths and best features? How realistic was he being?

We've found that men loosen up in this exercise because it's fun and slightly naughty. You might question our tactics and think that all we're doing is encouraging lurid fantasy play. But if you think this, then you're forgetting two things: (1) Fantasy play in this context is a nonthreatening way of communicating things that otherwise might never be exposed, and (2) You may be the object of his fantasy, regardless of the fact that you're in a different guise, i.e., Glenda.

So in *Glenda Bender* your man may be letting you know what turns him on, what his desires are, how he'd like to talk with you, and how he'd like *you* to talk with him, whether it be tentative, gentle, forceful, or outrageous.

What was it like for you? Did it make you feel seductive or uncomfortable? Did you have fun? And did he?

If he did flirt with Glenda, how was he at it? Did he look at you while he was talking to Glenda? He may have deliberately avoided eye contact to more accurately simulate the role-play and/or to help him to immerse himself in the story. Does he flirt with other women in front of you? If he does, are you okay with that? Does he think you flirt with other men, and if so how does he feel about that?

408.

SENSIBLE SHOES

IN THIS SCENARIO LATENESS AND WHO CAUSED IT ARE
MINOR DETAILS. WHAT'S IMPORTANT IS HOW ARGUMENTS
ARISE, WHAT FUELS THEM, AND HOW AWARE YOUR MAN IS
OF THEIR DYNAMICS.

ASK HIM THIS: "Who do you blame when you're late? I'm going to read you a scenario, and I want you to answer some questions at the end."

John and Prue arrive at the train station just in time to see the train pulling out. John says, "Oh no, now we'll be late for the movie."

Prue says, "I suppose you're going to say it's my fault for spending time putting on my makeup. Well, you wouldn't want to go out with me looking like a tramp, would you?"

"I guess not," says John.

"No! And anyway I didn't take that long, did I?"

"Well…."

"No! So what are we going to do now?"

175

"Well, Prue, we could take a cab to Wood Station, catch the 7:06 from there to Ellis Station, and if we walked quickly enough from there we might just make it."

"You know I can't walk fast in these shoes."

"Well, why did you wear them?"

"Because I wasn't planning on walking fast, besides which you wouldn't want me to go out looking like some frump in sensible shoes, would you?"

"Well, maybe not," says John.

"No! It's not like I'm stuck up or anything. I mean if you'd told me there was even the vaguest chance that we'd have to walk I could have worn my flats, couldn't I?"

"Yes, except then you'd have looked like a frump, wouldn't you?"

"So you *do* think I look like a frump in my flats?"

"No, I don't. *You* said you'd look like a frump."

"When did I say that?"

"Just before you said you could have worn your walkers if I'd told you there was even the vaguest chance we'd have to walk."

"And did you tell me there was the vaguest chance we'd have to walk?"

"No."

"No. So it's your fault then!"

"What's my fault?"

"Us not being able to get to the movie!"

"No, that's a different issue."

"Look, John, getting to the movie is the most important issue right now, isn't it?"

"Yes, it is."

"Well, then why are you standing here arguing the point about different issues?"

"I'm not arguing, Prue, I'm just saying it's a different issue."

"There you go again! Do you know what the problem is here?"

"What?"

"You! You are the problem because instead of taking action you just keep bringing up irrelevant issues! So take a deep breath, John, and tell me how we're going to get to the movie now."

"There's only one way to get there now."

"And what's that?"

"The only way now would be to get a cab all the way in."

"Are you insane? That would cost a fortune!"

"Look, Prue, I'm simply answering your question. You wanted to know how we could get to the movie on time and I told you. The cost is not the issue."

"There you go again about issues! Do you know what I think?"

"No, Prue, what *do* you think?"

"I think you're a complete moron!"

- So, what's going to happen if this argument were to continue?

- Is either Prue or John in the wrong?

- Why do you think Prue is so angry?

- What set her off?

- Is John helping or hindering the situation?

- Could John have a hidden agenda? If so, what could it be?

- If you were John, how would you have pulled out of the argument, and at what stage?

WHAT DID HE TELL YOU?

How perceptive is he when it comes to arguments in a relationship? Did either of you identify with John or Prue in the way this argument developed? Did either of you see any similarities in your own communication styles?

Most couples have differences of opinion. It would be strange if they didn't. These differences are usually very small. But sometimes they have a way of escalating into full-blown warfare, and this is usually because, at the back of the minor spat, a much bigger problem is lurking. Arguments also have a way of getting out of hand because of other circumstances. For instance, either of them might have a headache, or be preoccupied by another problem, or a particular word early on in the conversation may have triggered a disturbing or irritating memory.

It's often not what is said, but how it's said, that can press our buttons and put us in a bad mood. We're all sensitive to different underlying messages that we feel are implied by the words used, and also by who uses them and how. For instance, in this scenario you may have noticed that toward the end, both John and Prue begin to use each other's names. They could do this in a positive, neutral, or negative way, but in this case it's likely to have been in a quite scathing parental fashion, which would have added to their stress levels.

By listening to your man's answers to the questions at the end of the argument, how aware do you think he is of the subtleties involved? Did he apportion blame? Did he understand how the argument between John and Prue started? Did he think Prue had a hidden agenda? How did he see John's role—was John being understanding or was he fueling the argument? And did he think *John* had a hidden agenda? If so, how quick was he to supply answers?* His speed of reply could indicate that he's well versed, or at least familiar, with this type of ploy.

The last question—how would he have pulled out of the argument, and at what stage—should give you a clue as to your man's ability to predict trouble brewing, and whether he has the self-awareness and skill to avoid the type of conflicts that are counterproductive or downright destructive.

---

* One guy who did this exercise said that John was deliberately trying to fan the flames in order to avoid the movie, which he clearly wasn't all that keen on seeing. "It was probably some chick flick," he added.

409.

TWO FROGS

How can *Two Frogs* tell you about his attitude toward relationships? Prepare to be surprised.

ASK HIM THIS: "What do you see when you look at animals? I'm going to ask you to give names to some animals, and I want you to answer as quickly as possible."

- There are two frogs on a lily pad.   Their names are…

- There are two horses in a field.   Their names are…

- There are two birds in a tree.   Their names are…

- There are two pigs in a pen.   Their names are…

- There are two fish in a bowl.   Their names are…

- There are two tigers in the jungle.   Their names are…

- There are two dolphins in the sea.   Their names are…

- There are two eagles in the sky.   Their names are…

- There are two penguins on the ice.   Their names are…

- There are two beetles on a leaf.   Their names are…

What Did He Tell You?

We've found that a man's answers to these questions are a fair guide to whether he wants to be in a relationship or not.* If he gives a male and a female name to each pair of animals, then he sees a world of couples and will feel most comfortable conforming to that. If on the other hand he gives a male name to each animal, it indicates he's more likely to be into spending time with buddies. (Although, some people have asked us whether it's a sign that he's gay!) If he gives female names to each animal, then it suggests that he doesn't feel a part of the female world. He may feel alienated from women and see them as dominant.

* There is some evidence to suggest that people attribute male or female qualities to certain animals. If this is the case with your man, then the results could well be inconclusive. It's interesting to note that when women answer these questions they often give pigs and frogs male names because they can't imagine how such ugly creatures could possibly be female.

410.

PATTY-CAKE

OFTEN THERE IS A DISCREPANCY BETWEEN WHAT A MAN
WANTS TO GIVE AND WHAT HE EXPECTS TO RECEIVE. THIS
DISCREPANCY CAN TELL YOU HOW HE PERCEIVES HIS ROLE
IN THE RELATIONSHIP.

ASK HIM THIS: "Do you like receiving gifts? I'm going to read you
a series of statements, and I want you to finish them as quickly as
possible.

- You'd like your girlfriend/wife to make you…

- You'd love it if she wrote you…

- You'd like her to buy you…

- You'd like her to treat you to a…

- You wish she would prepare you…

- You'd like her to give you…

- You'd like her to tell you…

- You'd really love her to show you…

- You'd like to make your girlfriend/wife a...

- You'd like to write her a...

- You'd like to buy her...

- You'd like to treat her to a...

- You'd like to prepare her...

- You'd like to give her...

- You'd like to tell her...

- You'd really love to show her...

What Did He Tell You?

Were there any differences between the scale of what he wanted to receive and what he wanted to give? Did he have low expectations but grand desires? Did he have high expectations but very ordinary gifts? Or were his gestures and his expectations roughly the same?

There are a number of possible combinations, but essentially there will either be an equality or a disparity, and they'll mean very different things. For instance, if he wanted to buy his girlfriend a castle in Europe and expected her to buy him something equally outlandish, then he probably attacks his relationship with enthusiasm and high expectations, although it could be suggested that such grand gestures smack somewhat of self-consciousness and a need to show the world how much he loves her.

If he expected little in the way of gifts and gave an equal amount back, it suggests that he sees himself in a balanced relationship, and that the roles of both man and woman are supportive, independent, and secure. He might think they have no need for grand gestures to prove their love for each other. But it could also indicate that he lacks imagination or a romantic side.

So what if there is a disparity? If he wanted to treat her to a world cruise but only wanted her to treat him to a pizza, then it says one of four things: he feels unworthy of affection; he's conditioned to believe that it's a man's role to be a provider, not a receiver; he doesn't want to feel obligated; or he feels guilty.

Conversely, if he expects his girlfriend to write him a novel or a vast collection of poems dedicated to her love for him, but he's only willing to write her a thank-you note for last night's sex, then he probably sees himself as the power broker of the relationship. Either that or he has a distorted view of his partner's needs.

Admittedly, there are people of either gender who find it hard to receive. But in general, the ability to both give and receive indicate a generosity of spirit and a feeling of self-worth. It's up to you to decide on your man's intent regarding his gifts, but the contents may well be dictated by what makes him feel most comfortable when expressing his love, or how romantically inclined he is.

So how romantic is your man? How much nurturing does he need? How does he see your role in the relationship? And what about your needs? Does he have a clear idea of what you'd like to give him and what you'd like to receive?

To finish off, here are two more things to consider. How often does he ask you to do things for him? And how often do you ask him to do things for you?

411.

BUT YOU PROMISED

BUT YOU PROMISED MAY HAVE YOUR MAN PUNCHING THE
AIR IN DELIGHT, BUT THAT'S LIKELY TO CHANGE AS THE
SCENARIO UNFOLDS. IN THE END, YOU MIGHT BOTH BE
PUT UNDER THE SPOTLIGHT, WHICH ALWAYS MAKES FOR
STIMULATING CONVERSATION.

ASK HIM THIS: "Does the following argument ring any bells for you?
I'm going to read you a conversation between Mark and Maria, and
then I'll ask you some questions at the end."

Maria says: "Mark, how come you're watching TV? You
promised to clean up the yard."

Mark says: "Yeah, I know. I'll do it after the game."

Maria says: "But you promised to do it after lunch."

Mark says: "Yes, but I didn't know the game was on. I'll do it
after."

Maria says: "By the time the game's finished, you won't have
time. We'll need to go to the Barretts' barbecue."

"Well, I'll do the yard tomorrow."

"Can't you do them both at the same time? You could do the yard and come in for the replays when you hear the cheering."

"Well, I might as well not watch the game at all."

"Oh, so you can do the yard after all?"

"No Maria, I need to concentrate on the game. I can do the yard anytime. The game's only on once. It's really important."

"Well, there'll be other games that you can watch."

"But not this one."

"No, but how important is it, Mark? You didn't even remember it was on. Can't you just record it?"

"Yes, I could but when am I going to watch it?"

"You could watch it after the barbecue."

"Come on, Maria. David, Paul—all the guys at the barbecue will be talking about it."

"So you're saying that it's more important to watch the game than clear the yard?"

"No, I'm just prioritizing. And anyway, what's so important about clearing the yard right now?"

"Have you forgotten that your parents are coming over tomorrow?"

"No, I haven't forgotten. Look, I'll do it in the morning."

"But the forecast is for rain in the morning."

"Well, they're not going to be outside then, are they? So it won't matter."

"But they'll see it when they come in."

"Look, Maria, if it's so important why don't you do it?"

"I would but I have to bake for the barbecue. Janice and David, Debbie and Paul—they're all bringing something."

"Okay, but why didn't you do that this morning while I was washing the car and doing the lawns?"

"I was talking to Lucy."

"Yes, I know. All morning."

"It was the anniversary of her mother's death, and I was talking her through it. It was important."

"And that was the only time you could have called her?"

"Yes, it was. She's going away tonight!"

"Okay, but this is the only chance I have to watch the game. I've already missed the buildup. I'll do the yard in the morning."

"Mark, you promised to do it last weekend."

"It was raining, remember?"

"Well, it's not raining now."

"I know it's not raining now, but I want to watch the game. What's the big deal anyway? Why do you worry about what my parents think?"

"It's just being respectful. If the place looks nice, they'll know we made an effort and that means we care."

"How would they know we'd made the effort just for them anyway? I could have done the yard two weeks ago."

"I don't care. I just want the place to look nice. Besides, you didn't do it two weeks ago."

"Well, I've said I would do it some other time."

"But you said you would do it after lunch!" says Maria, as she walks off.

- Who is being the most reasonable, Maria or Mark?

- What are Maria and Mark trying to do?

- Is either of them in the right?

- How could Maria have got what she wanted and avoided the argument?

WHAT DID HE TELL YOU?

How well did he understand the dynamics? Did he recognize the pattern? (Did he see it as a typical "he doesn't do his share" versus

188

"she nags me so much I don't feel motivated"?) Did he recognize it in your relationship? Did he see how it started? Who did he side with? What about you? Did you recognize Mark and Maria's argument as being similar to ones you've had? Who did you side with? Did you notice the pattern? How could the pattern have been broken? Could either Mark or Maria have pulled out of it? How? If you and your man are able to have a constructive discussion about this hypothetical situation, it may allow you to be more objective about one of your own arguments in the future.

For the record, the pattern started because Maria's opening statement accuses Mark of being inconsistent—"why are you watching TV?...you promised to clean up the yard." This immediately puts Mark on the defensive, and he attempts to show that he's being consistent while pointing out inconsistencies in her position. The argument continues in this vein until it circles back to its original starting point and Maria gives up. How could Maria have avoided the argument? Well, that depends on just where Maria is really coming from. Is she complaining because she's annoyed that Mark is relaxing while she is working? Is she annoyed because he's just refusing to do what she asks, which is putting her in a weak position? Or is she really worried about the yard not getting done in time for his parents' visit?

Most of the men who've done this exercise empathize with Mark's position not just because they too want to watch sports undisturbed (see #102) but rather because he has remained in control and maintained a consistent position throughout. They see him as a reasonable guy who doesn't lose his cool while managing to watch a game and fend off the demands of an "unreasonable" wife at the same time. Given the importance of sports and the perceived difficulty of arguing with women, coupled with the male's poor multitasking ability, Mark's feat of juggling is seen by some men as nothing short of saintly!

(This scenario continues on the next page.)

NOW ASK HIM THIS: "What if the argument didn't end there? Imagine that instead of walking off Maria had put her hands on her hips and said:

> "You've always got an excuse, haven't you? Just look at you, slumped there on the sofa with your fat gut hanging out. Why can't you be like Debbie's Paul? He keeps himself very fit and trim, and I know for a fact that when he says he'll do something he does it! So does David. He says he'll take Janice skiing in Brekenridge and he does! And what's more, he arranges for the kids to be looked after! How many times have you said you'll take me to that cabin by the lake, and you never have and I bet you never will! God, you're just a useless fat slob! Useless around the house, useless at keeping your word... and useless in bed with that gut of yours. Debbie and Janice think I should sleep in the spare room until you come to your senses and lose some weight!"

- Why has Maria reacted like this?

- Has your opinion of Mark changed? If so, why?

- How do you think Mark would react and why?

- Do your arguments get personal like this?

- How do you resolve them?

WHAT DID HE TELL YOU?

Did his answers show that he understands why people react the way they do? Was he right in his assessments? Did he reevaluate his opinion of Mark? If so, were his reasons valid? Did he think Maria went too far?

What did he think would be the consequences of her outburst? What do you think? Is all fair in love and war or should there be rules? Will they have more trouble resolving this now? Will Mark go to the barbecue? If they both want to resolve it, how do you think they should go about it?

Our take is this: Out of frustration Maria raises the stakes (now her complaints have turned to global criticism: "you've always...") and she's also showing contempt by bringing up old hurts and comparing Mark's behavior and physique unfavorably with that of his male neighbors. As if that's not enough, she also demonstrates complete disloyalty by letting it drop that she's been discussing his performance in bed with the very people he is about to socialize with at the barbecue. Worse still, they apparently feel sorry for her, and for all he knows may have discussed it with their husbands. How humiliating! He suddenly feels weak and will desperately attempt to regain the control he enjoyed in the argument up until her final outburst.

Mark is likely to see Maria's action as so disloyal that he feels hopeless and angry about the relationship and may be drawn into escalating the argument by mounting a counterattack on her personality, body, past behavior, the way she's perceived by his friends—anything he knows that will be hurtful. Or he may just withdraw into his cave and maintain a semblance of dignity and control while he fights the hurt in private. Whatever he does, the perceived breach of trust may take some time to heal.

412.

TIGHT JEANS

YOU PROBABLY ALREADY KNOW HOW FUNNY HE IS. BUT
DOES HE UNDERSTAND THE POWER OF HUMOR? WHERE DO
PRACTICAL JOKES FIT INTO THE MIX, AND WHY DO WOMEN
LIKE MEN WHO CAN MAKE THEM LAUGH? THIS EXERCISE
SHOULD GIVE YOU SOME CLUES.

ASK HIM THIS: "What do you think of practical jokes? I want you
to imagine you're the script editor for a sitcom called *Jim and Jan*.
It's about a couple who have issues with each other's priorities. For
example, Jan thinks Jim spends too much time drinking beer and
watching sports on TV, and Jim thinks Jan buys too many clothes and
takes too long to get ready when they go out. A script outline has been
submitted to you that involves the couple playing practical jokes on
each other. You have to consider how the jokes will pan out.

In the first scene Jan gets mad that Jim is drinking beer and
watching sports on TV while she cleans the house. She furtively
opens the refrigerator and gives each of his beer cans a vigorous
shaking. What happens and how does Jim react?

Jim gets Jan back by filling her hair dryer with baby powder
when she's running late. She aims the dryer at her wet combed
hair and turns it on. What happens and how does Jan react?

The next evening Jim is passed out on the sofa from drinking too much beer. Jan superglues his zipper so that he won't be able to get his jeans off. What happens and how does Jim react?

The next day there's an argument about how long Jan takes to get ready. Determined to show that Jim is wrong, she tries on everything well in advance and has it laid out ready to get into right after her bath. But Jim secretly swaps the jeans she's chosen with an identical pair she bought six months before when she was slimmer. What happens and how does Jan react?

A few days later Jim has to give an early morning marketing presentation to a group of five women who run a fashion magazine. While he's shaving, Jan inserts a nude picture of Jim into each of the five folders he'll give out during the presentation. What happens and how does Jim react?

Jim gets back at Jan by opening the gift-wrapped bootees she's bought for a teenage mother's baby shower and replaces them with a packet of condoms. What happens when the present is opened in front of everybody, and how does Jan react?

- Whose pranks do you think were funnier, Jan's or Jim's?

- Would you pull any of these practical jokes on someone you were in a relationship with?

- Is there a difference between playing practical jokes on women compared with playing them on men?

- At what point does a prank cease to be fun and cross over into ridicule and cruelty?

What Did He Tell You?

Did he find the situations funny and become involved enough to add his own amusing embellishments? If you enjoyed his ideas it's likely you share a common sense of fun, which is usually an indicator of compatibility. Studies have shown that couples who joke with each other, and are able to find the humor in serious situations, tend to have more harmonious relationships than those couples who don't.

If he thought that Jim's pranks were funnier than Jan's, he may be conforming to a common male expectation that women aren't as good at pulling pranks as men. This is based on the fact that men, far more than women, use pranks to test each other and establish a pecking order and are therefore more practiced at it. For this reason many men find pulling serious pranks on women an inappropriate assertion of power that runs counter to their role of protector. Of course, while we love to hear about practical jokes being played on people, most of us are aware of how damaging they can be in a relationship, especially when they result in public ridicule as Jim and Jan's last pranks do.

Practical jokes aside, males and females seem to have quite different expectations when it comes to humor. For example, women almost always say that they want a man who can make them laugh* when this is not one of the qualities that men say they look for in a woman. Does this mean there's something about a man's humor that tells a woman whether or not he's relationship material? First, a good sense of humor demonstrates an ability to think laterally as well as indicating a youthful outlook and social confidence—useful traits in a relationship. But more important, a man who delights in the lighter side of life won't be boring. His humor signals that he's probably going to be flexible, understanding, able to diffuse conflict, and easy to have around for the long haul.

Second, research shows that laughing reduces stress hormones, lowers blood pressure, and boosts the immune system. It can also trigger the release of endorphins, which produce a general sense of well-being. With all these benefits, is it any wonder women want humorous men who will make them laugh? But why then, wouldn't men want humorous women? Why is it that many men report feeling uncomfortable with women who make jokes? Could it be that men feel their role is not only to ensure physical protection in the form of a well-defended home, but also to provide bodily sustenance to the mother of his offspring by encouraging laughter so that she can benefit from its health-giving effects? If this is true, it could be argued that a male may interpret his partner's joke telling as a threat to his role as the family medicine man and therefore denigrate it.

Whatever the reasons, a good sense of humor is so sought after in relationships that it even has its own abbreviation (GSOH) in personal ads. And there can be no doubt that laughter is one of the most pleasant and efficient ways we have of signaling and maintaining interest in a potential mate. Responding positively to a man's humor is one of the quickest ways a woman has of letting him know that she's on the same wavelength—or at least wants to be. Not laughing is the easiest way of telling him to shove off—even if she does find him amusing. Conversely, it's one of the first things a guy will do to find out whether she's interested. Try a funny line or two and if there's no reaction, chances are it's time to move on.

We think a woman is blessed if she's with a man who can laugh at her jokes as much as she laughs at his. It's a clear indication that he has good self-esteem and will be understanding and sympathetic. And of course men will be blessed with lower blood pressure.

* The annual romance report conducted by Harlequin Publishing in 2006, which surveyed over two thousand men and women in North America, reported that seventy-three percent of women said "a sense of humor" was what attracted them to a man in the first place.

413.

KICKING TIRES

HERE'S ONE THAT WILL HAVE HIM CHANGING INTO REVERSE REAL FAST. HE'LL SWEAR BLIND HE WOULD NEVER MAKE THE COMPARISONS YOU'LL BE ASKING HIM TO. AND MAYBE HE WOULDN'T. BUT THAT'S NOT THE POINT OF *KICKING TIRES*. READ IT THROUGH FIRST TO FIND OUT WHY.

ASK HIM THIS: "What are five things you would check for when buying a good used car?"

1. The first thing you would check for would be…

2. The second thing you would check for would be…

3. The third thing you would check for would be…

4. The fourth thing you would check for would be…

5. The fifth thing you would check for would be…

NOW ASK HIM THIS: "Think back to your answers. Are the things you found important in choosing a car the same as the things you would consider when choosing a woman? For instance, if the number

196

of previous owners of the car was important, does this mean that the number of previous relationships a woman has been in would be a concern to you?"

THEN ASK HIM THIS: "Now think back again to your original answers. Would the things you found important in choosing a car be the same things that a woman would consider if looking at you as a potential partner?"

WHAT DID HE TELL YOU?

Are you now looking for rust on your chassis or general wear and tear on your bodywork or interior? What color is your upholstery and do you have a powerful engine? Is your trunk big enough? Are you a high-maintenance classic or something more exotic with a foreign pedigree? This exercise may put your tail in a spin, and have you thinking about all manner of other considerations such as mileage, previous owners, air bags, cruise control, cornering, and economy.

But before you become completely insulted by the idea that you're being compared to an automobile, remember this: given how women think that men value their cars ahead of their wives, the comparison could, in fact, be seen as a compliment. Besides, the whole point of this exercise is to get you both thinking about your priorities when it comes to a relationship. And what did he think a woman would find important in considering him as a potential partner? Was it looks, safety, or performance?

414.

DOROTHY

THIS ONE'S ALL ABOUT HIS IDEAL RELATIONSHIP. BUT YOU
MAY NEED TO TREAD CAREFULLY. READ THROUGH IT FIRST
AND YOU'LL SEE WHAT WE MEAN.

ASK HIM THIS: "What do you look for in a partner? I'm going to
read you a story and then ask you some questions."

When Brian walked in on that hot Thursday night it was late,
real late, and Dorothy was already asleep. The smooth contours
of her firm body stretched out on the covers, glowed warmly in
the orange light from the street. She hardly stirred, but he knew
she would have heard the dull throb of the Dodge pulling into
their drive and he knew she would be pleased. Brian flicked on
the bedroom fan and took a cool shower. When he returned,
he lay down beside her on the bed and let the fan cool his still
wet nakedness. His hand brushed lightly across the side of
her cheek and then began stroking the back of her neck. She
stretched and seemed to smile a little.

In all the time they'd lived together, he'd never been able
to fathom what was really going on in Dorothy's mind. Her
thoughts remained a mystery. But ever since Alice had stormed
out of the house in a stinking rage, lugging all her belongings

and her damned intellect with her, and Dorothy moved in, he'd never been happier. She was never cranky or moody, and she didn't ask him smart questions that made him feel inadequate. Not once had Dorothy been mad at him for being late, and she never made snide comments. She simply loved being with him. Wherever he was she was happy to be there too. She never complained and they never argued. It wasn't that she was clingy, Dorothy had her own interests that kept her happy and occupied. Brian loved Dorothy, and as far as he was concerned it was the perfect relationship.

- In your opinion the best thing about the relationship between Brian and Dorothy is...

- The worst thing about their relationship is...

- Would you like a relationship like this?

- Do you realize that Dorothy is a dog?

(At this point he may suffer a cognitive crisis, and you might have to read the story to him again. If he really got sucked in, be prepared for him to call you Alice and storm out of the house!)

WHAT DID HE TELL YOU?

Okay, we admit this is a bit of a mean one. Most guys dream of an uncomplicated relationship where they have no obligations and they can be as self-centered as they like. So it should come as no surprise that a significant number of them will give this relationship the thumbs up. If your man did, it doesn't mean that he'd be happier living with a dog than with you. But it may mean that he feels stressed in the relationship and dreams of shedding his responsibilities and leading a less complicated life. (But then who doesn't?) It may also mean that he wants things to be less complex and/or confrontational.

At least now that you have him actually thinking about relationships, albeit the difference between canine and human ones, it may be an opportune moment to get him to say what he thinks is the best thing about being with you, and the worst—that is, if you're not too mad at him for wanting to have a relationship with a dog!

There are those who say that the way a man treats his dog is a sure sign of the way he'll treat his woman—if he beats his dog then he'll beat his woman. We think this is far too simplistic. For example, consider the following behavior: He pats his dog affectionately on the head in public; he deworms and de-fleas it every two months; takes it to dog obedience classes; never lets it off the leash; and insists that it sleep at the foot of the bed. Okay, come to think of it, maybe it's not too simplistic.

415.

SOUP OF THE DAY

YOU'LL BOTH ENJOY LISTENING TO HIS TAKE ON THE WORLD, EVEN IF HE DOESN'T KNOW HE'S GIVING IT TO YOU. FEEL FREE TO ASK HIM ADDITIONAL QUESTIONS IF YOU WANT MORE INFORMATION. IT CAN BE FUN TO PUT THE BOOK BETWEEN YOU AND TAKE TURNS ANSWERING EACH QUESTION.

ASK HIM THIS: "What are you like in different situations? I'm going to read a series of scenarios and I want you to fill in the gaps as quickly as possible."

- You're sitting in a restaurant and you're covered in soup. Why?

- You're lying on a rug on the ground, close to a babbling brook. It's a beautiful day. Why are you here?

- You're standing on a bridge looking down to a river that's far below. Why are you doing this?

- You're watching a burning building from the shelter of a fence. Why are you there?

- You're walking along the road holding a bunch of flowers. Where are you going?

- You're lying naked on the ground and surrounded by lots of people who are looking down on you. Why?

- You're hanging upside down outdoors. Why?

- You're walking across a golf course with a snake around your neck. Why are you doing this?

- You're standing at a street corner, pressed up against a building. You're holding something. What is it?

- You're sitting in a car on the edge of a lake, and the car engine is still running. What are you doing?

- You're standing on the top of a tall building and a helicopter is descending toward you. Why?

- You're standing in front of a group of armed soldiers. Why?

- You're running down the street with a ladder over your shoulders. Why?

- You're standing naked with your legs apart, and you're looking back between them. Why?

What Did He Tell You?

Is your man proactive or reactive? Negative or positive? Hopeful or fearful?* For instance, where was he going with the bunch of flowers? Was he bringing them home to you, or was he going to a funeral, or visiting someone in the hospital? And what about standing on the bridge? Was he merely taking in the view? Or was he about to do a bungee jump, or something altogether more dramatic?

Generally, his actions are indicators of his self-esteem. The more proactive he is, the higher it will be, and the lower it is, the more he'll avoid action because he'll be scared of failure and feeling even worse about himself. You've probably heard people say, "He can only love you as much as he loves himself." It's quite true, and if he has high self-esteem he'll love you *because* he feels good about himself. But if his self-esteem is low, he'll love you *in order* to feel good about himself. That's something you need to watch out for.

Of course all the scenarios in this exercise can be interpreted in different ways, but your man's take on them should tell you much about his attitudes and his view of the world. It might also remind him of past experiences or fuel his imagination, which may well lead to interesting conversations.

* You do have to take into account what mood he's in. While he may have participated in this exercise, he still may have been brooding about something that affected his answers. If you try him on another day, you may get a completely different response. Look for an overall trend in his answers.

JUST HOLD ME

IF YOUR MAN DOESN'T KNOW THE DIFFERENCE BETWEEN
INTIMATE TOUCHING AND CUDDLING, THEN HE'LL PROBABLY
LAUGH HIS HEAD OFF AT THIS EXERCISE. AND THAT'S OKAY.
BUT DON'T LET THE CHANCE GO BY TO ENLIGHTEN HIM.

ASK HIM THIS: "Do you feel like you're misunderstood sometimes? I'm going to read you a conversation between two people, and I want you to answer some questions at the end."

She says: "Oh, I love it when you lie close to me like this and cup your hands around my head. It makes me feel really loved. Do you feel especially loving when you do that?"

He says: "I guess so."

"Tell me what you feel."

"Well, you know, I like doing it 'cause... well, I guess it's like I'm kinda cradling you and that makes me think of you as little and me as kinda big and strong."

"Does feeling big and strong make you love me more?"

"Well, I guess it makes me react in a protective way."

"When you're feeling protective, are you feeling more loving?"

"No...I think I love you all the time."

"But there must be times when you feel more loving toward me."

"Well, I guess there are."

"Is this one of them?"

"Yeah, I think it must be."

She says: "No, don't put your hand down there yet... I want to talk more."

He says: "I'm still listening."

"No, you stop listening when you start down there. Cradle my head again and talk to me. I love it when you talk to me."

"What do you want to talk about?"

"Just talk about how you feel. How you honestly feel."

"Well... I feel really turned on."

"And...?"

"And I want to make love to you."

"And...?"

"And then I want to go to sleep."

"How do you think that makes me feel?"

"I thought you liked going to sleep with me afterward."

"I'm not talking about that…and stop holding my head; it doesn't feel right anymore."

"So what are you talking about?"

"I'm talking about your selfishness."

"How am I being selfish?"

"You just want what you want! You don't care what I want!"

"Well, what *do* you want?"

"Right now? Nothing! I just want to go to sleep!"

Later she says: "Are you awake? I can't sleep."

He says: "Me neither."

"Will you hold me?" she says. "Just hold me."

Now I'm going to ask you a question.

- Did any of it sound familiar, and if so, could you explain?

What Did He Tell You?

Did he laugh at this conversation? Why? And what did you feel about it? Most men do laugh when they hear this exercise. But it's not the dilemma that they find funny. They're laughing at some kind of recognition. There's something oh-so-familiar about this scenario—the different attitudes to physical touch and cuddling—that really hits the spot for men. It's almost a relief to see it happening to someone else, as if it's telling him that he's not the only guy in the world who goes through this.

This, of course, doesn't make it one shred easier for *you* though, does it? But instead of taking offense at his levity, you could take this opportunity to put your case forward, especially if you and he do see things differently.* Tell him what you need and what you want. Tell him why it's important to you.

Nonsexual touching has benefits on a therapeutic level, in that it can release endorphins that act as a pain/stress reliever. This works for both the toucher and the recipient. But on a much deeper level, it has a strong emotional significance. Nonsexual touching, such as stroking, massage, or cuddling, tells the woman that her man loves all of her, not just her sex. If you feel this, let your man know.

* An extra thing to note in the conversation is the way the two people are actually talking in different languages. The man prefaces a lot of what he says by using the term "I think" even though the woman has asked him how he feels. Either that, or the man takes the physical, tactile sense of the word *feel*, rather than the emotional meaning. It might be interesting to ask yourself how often you and your man also misunderstand or misinterpret these terms.

417.

WHAT ARE YOU THINKING?

THIS IS THE MOMENT WHERE YOU GET TO ASK THE
QUESTION ALL MEN HATE BEING ASKED. IT COULD ALSO
BE THE MOMENT WHERE YOU GET THE ANSWER YOU'VE
ALWAYS BEEN WAITING FOR. ONCE YOU'VE ASKED HIM THE
QUESTIONS, HE'LL NEED TO ASK YOU THE SAME QUESTIONS,
AND THEN YOU'LL NEED TO RUN THEM BY HIM AGAIN.

ASK HIM THIS: "What do you think about? I'm going to ask you some questions, and then I want you to ask me the same questions. I'd like you to sit comfortably, take some slow, deep breaths, close your eyes, and lean back." (Give him a few seconds to settle.)

- What are you thinking?

- What are you feeling?

- How did you feel about being asked that?

- What do you think my next question will be?

- What are you thinking now?

- What were you thinking about before this exercise?

- I can either ask you right now what you're feeling or thinking. Which one would you rather I asked you?

- Why?

- What are you thinking?

- Why do you think I'm asking this?

- What are you feeling?

- Why do you think this is?

Now I want you to ask me the same questions. (Hand him the book and show him where to start.)

WHAT DID HE TELL YOU?

His responses are likely to have been defensive, stilted, and confused with little or no information being given. (This will seem like familiar territory, no doubt.) Yours, on the other hand, will probably have been instantaneous, positive, and flowing, with an abundance of observations and feelings. He's likely to be amazed that you can "come up with all that stuff," and he may say: "Well, I could have come up with that, but…" If he does say something like this, it's quite likely you'll be able to get him to answer in a similar way to you when you continue the exercise (see below).

NOW ASK HIM THIS: "Can you see how I answered the questions? Do you think you could answer them like that too? I'd like you to try. So, sit comfortably, take some slow, deep breaths, and close your eyes.

- What are you thinking?

- What are you feeling?

- What did you think about being asked that?

- What are you thinking now?

- How did you feel about being asked that?

- What were you thinking about just before?

- I can either ask you right now what you're feeling or thinking. Which one would you rather I asked you?

- Why?

- What are you thinking?

- Why do you think I'm asking this?

- What are you feeling?

- Why do you think this is?

WHAT DID HE TELL YOU?

Were his answers different the second time around? Were his responses more like yours? And how did he react this time?*

What Are You Thinking? highlights some fascinating differences in the way men and women communicate. While there are many individual and cultural differences in cross-gender communications, studies show that most men use talk to hold attention or maintain status, whereas women talk in order to make connections and form relationships. For this reason men are more compartmentalized and defensive in their communication style. Having to impress means having to be on guard in case they let something slip, and that stops the natural flow.

Women, on the other hand, need to keep the flow going in order to demonstrate an easy openness and honesty that is essential to the building of lasting relationships. As a consequence, their style is less truncated and measured. It bubbles along unhindered—including all their thoughts as they come tumbling in. The more ideas and observations they share, no matter what their importance, the more points of connection they provide for others to link up with.

So how does this apply to a relationship? Take this scenario: A woman gives her man a detailed, free-flowing account of her day and asks him how his day was. Instead of reciprocating in kind, he simply says "fine" because his day had no particular drama. Reading this curt response as meaning there's something on his mind, she asks him what he's thinking. He says: "Nothing." This leaves the woman feeling that he's avoiding intimacy, or worried that he's hiding something. In turn, he thinks she's being intrusive, and he goes on the defensive. A stalemate ensues. When this situation occurs often enough, the woman may well stop asking. He'll feel like she's finally begun to understand his needs, but she's left feeling resentful and lonely.

In part, the conflict in this scenario stems from the word *think*. Women translate it as meaning the openly attentive, observational style that they always use. Men, however, equate *thinking* with a concentrated process of problem solving and figure they're being asked for some deeply significant thought. Being more status directed and thinking that they'll disappoint if they come up with something trivial, they protect themselves by saying "nothing."

You have to remember that in general, guys see themselves in terms of their place in the world, while women, on the other hand, see themselves in terms of their relationships. You could say that men come at themselves from the outside in while women come from the inside out. Women start with the detail and the background and work outward to the important action at the end. Men, on the other hand, start from the important action and then travel inward looking for any explanatory detail if necessary. Both styles are valid modes of communication, but they often don't work well together. When an inside-outer talks with an outside-inner, chances are there'll be frustration and misunderstanding.

So if your man is not bubbling with enthusiasm to share his day at the office, you may have to start with a question that works from the outside and goes in. It will start with the main action and then seek detail. In order to be noninvasive, it will need to be hypothetical, yet intriguing and ask for a solution—something that men love to give. Try a question such as: "Tell me, what sort of guy would prefer to turn up on time at an office meeting with a great big lipstick mark on his collar rather than change his shirt and be late?" Now right away he's going to ask why you want to know, and you're going to know that he's hooked. He'll soon be chatting about who does what in the office and why, and it shouldn't be too difficult to work back to how he feels in that environment and what it was like for him at work today. What does your man think about this type of approach? Would he rather be left to zone out in front of the television for a while before you hit him up with questions such as this?

* Asking him to follow your lead when you ran the questions past him a second time may have helped him understand where you're coming from, but it's unlikely to change how he operates in the future. Nevertheless, you can always play "tag talking" by having him describe things around him in detail and making observations about them as fast as he can. You let him go for a minute, then come in with a related observation, run with another series of observations, and let him come in again when you pause. The idea is to see how long you can keep it going—and find heaps to talk about at the same time.

418.

A SUMMER'S DAY

A SUMMER'S DAY WILL TEST YOUR MAN'S IMAGINATION, BUT THIS IS SECONDARY TO WHAT YOU SHOULD BE LOOKING FOR. READ THE INTERPRETATION CAREFULLY BEFORE YOU BEGIN.

ASK HIM THIS: "Have you ever had a great occasion spoiled by unexpected events? I'm going to read you a story line, and I want you to fill in the gaps."

- You're wandering in the countryside with your lover. It's a beautiful day. In the distance you see what appears to be a…

- But as you get closer you realize it's a…

- With it is a…

- There's also a…   and a…

- But then you're horrified to see that…

- In order to avert a disaster you…

- Unfortunately, this has no affect because…

- But as luck would have it, your lover is an expert in…

- She manages to…

- Then she tells you to…

- You're amazed when she…

- But possibly the most memorable thing she does is…

- And just when you think she's done everything she can, she…

- Reports in local newspapers later referred to her actions as being…

- Thinking back to the events of that day and what your lover did, you feel…

WHAT DID HE TELL YOU?

Does he find it easy to let the lover be the hero of the day? And does he do this with grace and fondness, or is there an edge of ridicule or disbelief? If you saw yourself as the lover, and he painted you in heroic terms, were you comfortable with this?

What you should be looking for in this exercise are his expectations of a lover. This is not to say that if he places her in a heroic light he necessarily wants to be saved, but that he wants to feel he could rely on her to be with him in hard times, and that he respects her for all her qualities, some of which he may not even know about.

If, on the other hand, he paints the lover's deeds as ultimately failing, it may not be a reflection on the lover, but merely that he's firmly entrenched in the concept that men are the protectors. This can be a stance that's extremely hard to shift, not just because it's a strongly held male notion, but also because it's still widely supported by the majority of women and society at large.

419.

GREEN CARD

You've seen the movie *Green Card*? Well, now's your chance to be in it. More important, you'll get an idea of how much your man knows about you.

ASK HIM THIS: "What are you like at official interviews? Imagine that you're about to marry your fiancée in a foreign country and live there with her. But immigration authorities want to ensure that you are marrying for love and not merely trying to gain citizenship. The female immigration officer asks you a series of questions in order to ascertain the veracity of your relationship with a female national of this foreign country.

This officer says that you have the right to refuse to answer any question, but this may prejudice her findings.

I want you to answer as if the woman you want to marry is me.

So the interview begins.

- Where did you first meet this woman?

- What most attracted you to her?

- And what did she most like about you?

215

- Where was she born?

- What is her favorite color?

- What is her favorite perfume?

- What's her favorite lipstick color?

- And eye shadow?

- Describe her fingernails.

- And her birthday is...

- Does she have favorite flowers? What are they?

- Are there flowers she dislikes?

- Does she like tea or coffee? Cream or sugar?

The immigration officer asks:

- What's her father's name?

- And her mother's name?

- What neighbors does she talk about from her childhood?

- Tell me about her siblings.

- Did she have a nickname when she was younger?

- Who's her least favorite relative?

- What's her favorite food?

- What about food that she hates?

- What distinguishing marks does she have?

- What's her bra size?

- What about her favorite movie star?

Then the immigration officer asks:

- How can you tell when she's nervous?

- How can you tell when she's lying?

- What sort of things does she remember about her last partner?

- What does she most hate about herself?

- What does she most love about herself?

- What sort of things frighten her?

- What sort of things upset her?

- What does she most like about you?

- What does she most dislike about you?

- If you had to describe her as either conservative or liberal, you'd say she was...

- Who's her best friend now?

- Who was her best friend in high school?

The immigration officer continues with:

- What would be your fiancée's idea of a perfect day out with you?

- What about her perfect day out on her own?

- And what would be her idea of a perfect evening in with you?

- And if she was on her own, what would be a perfect evening in for her?

- What do you think she most wants from you?

- What are the qualities about her you most love?

- Is there anything you wouldn't do for her?

- Would you lie for her?

WHAT DID HE TELL YOU?

Where are the gaps in his knowledge of you? Do they matter? It's a common perception that the more he knows the more he cares. But this is not always the case. Unlike women, men are seldom keepers of personal details and relationship history. So what your man knows about you in this exercise in part relates to his own priorities. However, a sign of his consideration for you will be that he also retains facts that are important to you. Only you will know this, but if you want to delve more, feel free to come up with some of your own questions. It should be fascinating for both of you to see how close your respective priorities are. You might also like to get him to run the interview by you. How much do you know about him?

420.

THE AD MAN'S WIFE

THIS IS A LONG SCENARIO, BUT IT'S WORTH THE EFFORT, ESPECIALLY IF YOU WANT TO FIND OUT HOW SUSPICIOUS YOUR MAN IS.

ASK HIM THIS: "How observant are you? I'm going to read you a scenario, and I want you to complete the unfinished statements when they come up in the story."

Bill is an advertising copywriter. He's thirty-nine going on forty. He's married to Lisa, a thirty-five-year-old lawyer. They live in a reasonably plush area on the outskirts of a large city. They have no children.

Lisa has only recently returned to work after a lengthy illness, and Bill wonders whether she's gone back too early. But she assures him that she's fine. Bill, meanwhile, is snowed under at the moment with two major ad presentations that could be worth millions to his firm.

One afternoon Lisa calls to tell him that she's staying in town to have dinner with his sister, which Bill thinks is odd because the two women don't normally have that much to do with each other. When Lisa finally does get home, it's very late.

• What Bill might want to know is…

Bill's workload is keeping him so busy at the moment that when he gets home all he wants to do is kick back and blob out in front of the TV. Lisa usually wants to talk about their day, but lately she seems to have picked up on his need to be left alone.

Then over the next couple of weeks he begins to notice odd things about her behavior, such as her abruptly ending telephone conversations when he walks into the room.

• He wonders whether…

Bill is starting to really stress out because of his work, and he's becoming a little forgetful. He's so tired that he's almost losing his sense of reality. At home the phone goes dead whenever he answers it, and he keeps misplacing personal items, such as his wallet. He wants to talk to Lisa about it, but she seems as scattered as he is. And besides, often when he calls her at work for a chat, she's unavailable or out to lunch.

Then Bill hears from two of his colleagues that they saw Lisa having lunch with his best friend, Tom. As it's coming up for Bill's birthday he calls Tom, a doctor at a city medical center, with the intention of asking him over for a celebratory drink. But Tom is noncommittal.

• So Bill is left with the impression that…

The next day Lisa tells Bill she's going to be working late again, but when he calls that evening she's not at the office. According to the firm's receptionist, she'd left suddenly an hour ago.

It's now Wednesday and Lisa isn't feeling well and decides to take the day off. But when Bill tries to contact her at home, she's not there. That night he finds her credit card statement on the bureau. One of the items is a large amount paid out to a travel agent.

On Thursday night Bill answers the phone and it's Lisa's mother, Judy. She calls three times in total this night, saying that she keeps forgetting to ask Lisa something. And while Judy is perfectly pleasant, she seems uncomfortable and abrupt talking to him.

• Bill wonders whether…

It's Sunday, Bill's birthday. He's been working so hard that he hasn't wanted to do anything special. But then, this is actually pretty normal. Birthdays aren't a big deal for him. Lisa complains of feeling a bit poorly, but despite this she persuades him to go to a swanky restaurant in town. Once there, however, she seems distracted. Halfway through the meal Lisa gets a call on her cell phone and becomes anxious. She wants to go home. Bill asks her who was on the phone.

• He wants to know because…

They get home and she says she's got something to tell him, and could he go into the living room and get them both a stiff drink while she goes to the bathroom.

• At this point he thinks she's going to tell him…

Bill goes into the darkened room, turns on the lights, and the place erupts with screams of "SURPRISE!!!" Everyone is there: his whole family, Lisa's family, his friends, and some of his colleagues. As a fortieth birthday present, his boss has given him two weeks' paid vacation time, and Lisa has bought them a resort holiday in Mexico.

- Now Bill feels absolutely...

What Did He Tell You?

So how suspicious was he? How quick was he to think that Lisa was having an affair? What other explanations did he have for the events?

There are at least three plausible explanations for Lisa's behavior. She could have been having an affair, she may have had a recurrence of her illness but didn't tell him because she didn't want him to worry, or she could have been planning a surprise party.

If your man headed down the medical alley, he will be showing his attentive, caring, and protective side, which is definitely a plus for you.

If he suspected early on that Lisa was being unfaithful, this could reflect a variety of things. First, a truly suspicious mind will target an affair from the start and be closed to any other alternatives from then on, regardless of any contradictory information provided.

However, he may have been burned in the past and hence have antennae finely tuned to any unusual behavior. Suspicion would rear its ugly head whether he wanted it to or not. A wary attitude could also mean that he's attentive, and that he sees patrolling the boundaries as his way of staking his claim on you.

If he correctly guessed early on in the story that Lisa was planning a surprise party, it shows that he feels worthy of such attention. This is actually a healthy state of mind. Of course he may guess the surprise option because he's secretly harboring a desire to have this happen to him.

421.

I'M A BELIEVER

IF YOUR MAN HAD TO WRITE DOWN HIS BELIEF SYSTEM, WHAT WOULD HE INCLUDE? THIS EXERCISE THROWS HIM A LIST OF BELIEFS THAT SHOULD LET YOU KNOW WHERE HE STANDS. GET HIM TO TRY THESE ON YOU TOO. FEEL FREE TO ADD TO THE LIST.

ASK HIM THIS: "What do you feel really passionate about? I'm going to read you a series of questions, and I want you to respond by saying either yes or no. For the purposes of this exercise, the word *belief* is defined as 'accepting a concept or thing with genuine enthusiasm.'"

- Do you believe in the right to bear arms?

- Do you believe in the sanctity of marriage?

- Do you believe in life after death?

- Do you believe in the possibility of time travel?

- Do you believe in love?

- Do you believe in luck?

- Do you believe in God?

- Do you believe in war?

- Do you believe in ghosts?

- Do you believe in a committed relationship?

- Do you believe in the death penalty?

- Do you believe in the existence of evil?

- Do you believe in civil unions?

- Do you believe in feminism?

- Do you believe in the social security system?

- Do you believe in globalization?

- Do you believe in psychoanalysis?

- Do you believe in nuclear deterrence?

- Do you believe in capitalism?

- Do you believe in democracy?

- Do you believe in genetic modification?

- Do you believe in human cloning?

- Do you believe in artificial insemination for humans?

- Do you believe in mercy killing?

- Do you believe in the right of parents to hit their children?

- Do you believe in abortion?

- Do you believe that global warming is caused by human activity?

- Do you believe in Darwin's theory of evolution—that we came from apes?

- Do you believe in sex before marriage?

- Do you believe in karma?

- Do you believe in Christmas?

- Do you believe in astrology?

- Do you believe in animal rights?

- Do you believe that nice guys always come last?

- Do you believe in magic?

- Do you believe in your country?

- Do you believe there's such a thing as a parallel universe?

- Do you believe in your job?

- Do you believe in relationship counseling?

- Do you believe in censorship?

- Do you believe in you?

What Did He Tell You?

Before you can really consider his answers, you need to remind yourself of the definition we gave for belief. Belief was defined as "accepting a concept or thing with genuine enthusiasm." So, while he may accept that democracy is a fair system, unless he is passionate about it, it's not really a factor in his life, and that's what *I'm a Believer* is trying to discover about him.

So how much does he actually believe in? Did he answer quickly and with certainty, or was he more considered? And where do his beliefs come from—parents, teachers, peers, personal experience, or his own deliberations? Does he hold any beliefs that don't suit his lifestyle or his self-perception?. Does he believe in things that you don't? And do you think men are expected to hold strong beliefs as part of their masculine image?

Because we rely on our belief system to help guide us through life, it can be very threatening when someone we're involved with holds a contrary viewpoint or questions something we hold dear. Usually, the best course of action is not to confront your partner's viewpoint head-on but instead take time to find out where your differing beliefs spring from and how they help you live your lives. That way you'll avoid unecessary conflict and reach a deeper understanding.

While a strong belief system can provide security, which enables us to move forward with clarity, if it's based on poor reasoning or research, it can quickly lead us astray. Unless we keep our minds open and inquiring, and are prepared to change our beliefs in light of any compelling new evidence that challenges them, we're likely to be overly rigid in our behavior and not respect the feelings of others. As author Robertson Davies warned, "Be sure to choose what you believe and know why you believe it, because if you don't choose your beliefs, you may be certain that some belief, and probably not a very creditable one, will choose you."

LEVEL 5

Behind the Shop Front

Having gained insights into your man's interests, skills, and personal background, we now start putting this information into the context of his present persona, and discover what effect all this has had on his behavior and character.

Behind the Shop Front has scenarios designed to give you a much better appreciation of who he is. Up until now you've had a few glimpses into his self-esteem and self-concept. But now, armed with his answers from the previous levels, you can begin to make more sense of this information and to see his fears and hopes, and why he looks at life either positively or negatively. This, in turn, will show you how resilient he can be, and whether he can tap into his emotional side and be brave enough to show his true self.

Most of the exercises in this book have an accent on novelty and fun. We've done this for a reason. Laughter is a powerful tool. It ensures that we don't take ourselves too seriously and gives us a clearer path to objectivity. In this level we've tried to keep the exercises light and entertaining, but there is a bit of an edge to one or two of them. You need to bear this in mind, and remind yourself that no matter how flippant your man's answers may be, there may be a jolt of awareness behind them, and discussion could and should emerge.

501.

THE RIVER

EVER WONDERED WHAT YOUR MAN IS AFRAID OF AND
HOW HE MIGHT HANDLE ADVERSITY? THIS EXERCISE IS
BOUND TO GIVE YOU SOME INSIGHTS. HAVE A PEN AND
PAPER HANDY TO JOT DOWN HIS REPLIES SO YOU CAN
DISCUSS THEM LATER. IF YOU WANT TO DO IT TOO, DON'T
READ THE INTERPRETATION UNTIL AFTERWARD.

ASK HIM THIS: "Do you like water? I'm going to read you a scenario, and I want you to complete the unfinished statements as quickly as possible."

You are sitting in a rowboat on a slow-moving river. It is quiet except for the occasional sound of water lapping up against the side of the boat. The day is fine and you are at peace with the world.

• With you in the boat is…

• You also have three valuable items on board. The first item is…

• The second item is…

- And the last item is…

- The only thing missing from this wonderful scene is…

- But just when you are feeling so rested that you could almost fall asleep, the peace is shattered by…

- You are so disturbed by this intrusion that all you want to do is…

- But then you think about the tranquility you were so enjoying and you try to return to it. However…

- Finally, the situation is resolved when…

- Looking down at your feet, you notice that…

- Now that the incident is over, you are determined to never again…

- But you remind yourself that things could have been worse. You could have…

- While all this is going on, your boat has drifted downstream and is seconds away from going over a two-hundred-foot waterfall. It will certainly be dashed to pieces on the rocks below, and you know that this is the end of your life. Before you die, you have a moment to…

- Which all goes to prove…

What Did He Tell You?

The choices people make in this scenario can be interpreted in light of a symbolic meaning that is given to each action or object. It's hardly a scientific exercise, but that doesn't mean you won't gain useful insights and stimulate interesting discussion if you enter into the spirit of it.* Remember the interpretations you come up with are only relevant at this point in time and are dependent on the person's state of mind and current situation.

Who you have in the boat with you—person or animal—will have qualities that you think may enhance your peace of mind. You will be comfortable sharing your personal space with them. Those that choose an object or an abstract concept rather than a person or animal, will tend to be independent and self-sufficient.

The precious items are things that you see as important in enriching your life.

The thing that is missing is something that you long for but feel you don't deserve. It could be dangerous despite its attraction and may represent your weakness or vice.

What shatters your peace, and how, represents the type of action or effect you are most afraid of.

What you do is what your gut response would be—physical or mental, fight or flight.

What happens despite your attempt to maintain equilibrium tells you whether your expectation is more of the same or something worse and therefore whether your outlook tends to be positive or negative.

If the situation is resolved by your actions, it suggests that you will be proactive in adverse situations. If it resolves itself or is resolved by another's actions, it shows that you favor a reactive, wait-and-see approach.

If you notice injury, disfigurement, or distortion in your feet, it shows that you have an understanding of the way in which adversity produces negative psychological effects. This is a sign of a self-aware individual.

The degree and scope of what you determined never to do again shows how self-critical you are. The more sweeping your proposed future action, the harder you tend to be on yourself.

How much worse you imagine things could have been shows the degree to which you can see the positive side of things. The more you are able to count your blessings, the happier you'll be.

If before you die you take the opportunity to perform some final, fleeting act, it shows you have unfinished business. If not, it suggests you may be more reflective and fatalistic.

"What it all goes to prove" indicates how philosophical you are. A lighthearted observation indicates a laid-back approach to life while a serious comment suggests a person who is often worried about life. The more amusing the comment is, the more youthful and proactive you feel.

* Don't be put off if your man turns this exercise into a comedy routine. Enjoy the fun and remember, the subconscious doesn't have a conventional sense of humor. The symbolism may still be applicable whether he's taking it seriously or not.

502.

STICKS AND STONES

WHAT'S IN A NAME? IN *STICKS AND STONES*, WE HAVE YOUR
MAN CHOOSE BETWEEN TWO SEEMINGLY OFFENSIVE TERMS
TO FIND OUT HOW HE SEES HIMSELF.

ASK HIM THIS: "What would you rather be called? I'm going to read
you a series of difficult alternatives, and I want you to make a choice."

Would you rather be called:

- A chauvinist or a copycat?
  Why did you choose this one?

- A big head or a big mouth?
  Why did you choose this one?

- A big shot or a bookworm?
  Why?

- A bully or a bungler?
  Why?

- A grouch or a groveler?
  Why?

- A dropout or a demon?
Why?

- A flirt or a fanatic?
Why?

- A spendthrift or a spy?
Why?

- A has-been or a hypocrite?
Why?

- A lightweight or a loudmouth?
Why?

- A name-dropper or a nitpicker?
Why?

- A smart aleck or a snob?
Why?

- A toady or a tightwad?
Why?

- A fascist or a fibber?
Why?

- A pervert or a psychopath?
Why?

- A slimebag or a sleazeball?
Why?

- A cheat or a coward?
Why?

- A wimp or a weakling?

- A whiner or a weasel?

- A killjoy or a kiss ass?

WHAT DID HE TELL YOU?

How does he see himself, and how worried is he about what others think of him? Can he find a positive spin from what would appear to be a bunch of no-win options? How realistic was he being? These alternatives are all difficult because on the surface none of them are positive. So the exercise is delving into his self-perceptions and his fears. By asking him why he made his choices, you might also find out about his prejudices and whether they are based on past experience.

The options in this exercise are all words or descriptions that men can find challenging or insulting. But what about you? How would you fare? How secure do you feel? Ask your man to try these alternatives on you. Would you rather be called:

- Frigid or flaky?

- A bimbo or a bitch?

- Fat or false?

- A gossip or a groupie?

- Abandoned or abused?

- A nag or a hag?

- Easy or erratic?

- A moaner or a manipulator?

- A slut or a shrew?

- A gold digger or a guilt tripper?

- A prude or a pushover?

503.

THE MORNING AFTER

IN THIS SCENARIO WE'RE LOOKING AT ARGUMENT STYLES, AND WHILE THE CONTENT MAY NOT SEEM RELEVANT TO YOU, KEEP GOING WITH IT BECAUSE IT MAY HELP YOU BOTH TO UNDERSTAND WHY LITTLE SPATS CAN SOMETIMES ESCALATE.

ASK HIM THIS: "What do you do when you go to a party? I'm going to read you a conversation between two people, Dave and Julie. Then when I've finished, I'm going to ask you a few questions."

Dave says: "Would you like some coffee?"

Julie says: "No."

Dave says: "How are you feeling this morning?"

Julie says: "Fine."

He says: "You seem quiet."

She says: "Am I? I didn't notice."

"So what's wrong?"

"There's nothing wrong, Dave, okay?"

"Hmm. Is that 'nothing's wrong,' or is it more like it's nothing you're going to tell me about?"

"Just drop it, Dave."

"Well, I could. But I have a feeling that it's not going to simply disappear. So why not spit it out, whatever's bugging you."

"I don't want to talk about it."

"So there is something wrong!"

"I said leave it, alright?"

"Leave what? You're being impossible."

"Why are you suddenly taking an interest in me now, Dave?"

"What do you mean?"

"What about last night at Gerry's party? You weren't so interested in me then."

"God, Julie, are you still going on about that? I thought we talked all that through."

"Maybe *you* did."

"Look, I don't see what the big deal is. We go to Gerry's. We have a few drinks. We mingle. And then I meet those two actors..."

"Two actresses."

"Okay, two actresses, and you..."

"And I get lumbered with Gerry's father."

"He's a nice old guy. Okay, he does talk a lot, but he's entertaining. In his own way."

"Yes, Dave, but that's not the point. You left me. I hardly saw you again all night."

"Julie, what did you want me to do? Hold your hand? Stick to you like glue?"

"Of course not. But you could have been a little more attentive."

"I don't get it. If you'd just wanted us to spend time together, we could have stayed home."

"But you wanted to go to Gerry's."

"I thought you did too."

"I did, Dave, but I didn't expect you to spend most of the night flirting with those two showgirls."

"They're actresses, Julie."

"You know what I mean."

"I don't. And for your information, I wasn't flirting. I'm considering using them in the film."

"But you were absolutely engrossed with them. And laughing and joking and…"

"It's my job, Julie. Besides, what's wrong with meeting people and having a laugh? They're very interesting women."

"So what are you saying? That I'm less interesting?"

"Of course not. But I was talent scouting."

"Right, for the film you've been talking about for ten years."

"That's not fair."

"I just wanted you to know how I feel. How you make me feel sometimes. I'm sorry I've upset you, but sometimes you just need to know the truth. Sometimes you just need to be a little more thoughtful. Okay?"

"Sure."

"Are you sure you're sure, Dave?"

"Yep."

"And you're okay?"

"I'm fine."

"Do you want some coffee?"

"No."

"Quite sure?"

"Yes. Quite sure."

- What just happened here, and why?

- Was Julie justified in her stance, or did you identify with Dave?

- Did you find it unusual for a woman to be sulking?

- Or did it seem more normal when Dave shut down at the end?

- How could this situation have been better handled by both Julie and Dave?

What Did He Tell You?

How in touch is he with the triggers that cause his own sulking? What about yours? Does he shut down in arguments with you? Does he know how to snap someone out of a sulk?

People tend to sulk as a result of feeling angry, embarrassed, or hurt. It's a simple way of shutting out the pain. Sulking is supposedly a childish behavior, but many of us continue to fall back into this mode in adulthood because it's something we've grown up with and it feels like we're punishing the other person. The problem is it can be self-perpetuating. The white rage, the deep mortification, and the consternation that we feel hold us in this horrible meltdown where we cook in the juices that got us there in the first place.

So it's incredibly valuable if either or both of you have an understanding of how sulking starts and how you can help to pull someone out of it again. Rule number one about these kinds of moods is that a person in a funk usually doesn't want to be there and is just looking for a way of saving face.

If your man has this understanding, he may have mentioned methods such as distraction, humor, or time. Sometimes we get lucky and a phone rings or a visitor calls, and that's all it takes for us to come out of it. But we've also had times when, left unattended, the blackness just seems to go on forever. So do either of you feel responsible for snapping the other out of a bad mood? Can your man get you out of a funk? Can you get *him* out? What methods work best for each of you?

504.

DEAR JOHN

HAS HE EVER HAD A DEAR JOHN LETTER? HAS HE EVER HELD OUT HOPE FOR SOMEONE DESPITE EVERYTHING POINTING TO THE CONTRARY?

ASK HIM THIS: "When does no mean no? I'm going to read you a series of excerpts from brush-off emails written by women. I want you to tell me which lines offer you even a glimmer of hope and why."

1. "I love you but if I stay with you, I know I'll hurt you."
   Would this line offer you any hope, and why?

2. "Being with you makes me sad."
   Would this offer you any hope? Why?

3. "But it's not you…it's me."
   Would this offer you any hope?

4. "I just need a little bit of space at the moment."
   Would this offer you any hope?

5. "I'm sorry. I'm just not ready for a relationship."
   Would this offer you any hope, and why?

6. "You're too good for me."
   What about this line? Would it offer you any hope?

7. "I love you too much, and that scares me."
   How would you react to this line? Would it give you hope, and why?

8. "We've had a great time, but I think we came from different places and we're heading in different directions." Would this offer you any hope?

WHAT DID HE TELL YOU?

His take on these brush-off lines should reveal plenty about his understanding of relationship dynamics and his past relationship experiences. For example, based on his history with women, he may actually see lines such as these as a plea for help or even a kind of low-level blackmail. Alternatively, he may see them for what they probably are—a need to take on the responsibility for ending the relationship so that the writer maintains control and lessens the likelihood of a come-back from the rejected partner. Also, by not blaming the other party and causing pain, the writer can feel better about initiating the split.

What we're also asking here is whether your man has ever been so gripped by a relationship that he's found it difficult to let go, despite all the signs that says he should. A brush-off email is a brush-off email, and nothing will change the fact that the writer in question wants out. When a sentence begins with "I love you but…" reality would suggest that everything before the "but" is irrelevant and should be ignored. But this is a lesson that can take a long time to learn. So, how realistic has he been in the past? When it matters, can he accept loss and move on? And what about you? Have you ever been delivered these brush-off lines? How did they affect you? (See also #609.)

505.

GIVE HIM ENOUGH ROPE

IN THIS ONE IT'S NOT WHAT HE DOES BUT HOW HE SEES
HIMSELF THAT'S IMPORTANT.

ASK HIM THIS: "Can you be a knight in shining armor? I'm going to read you a story line, and I want you to fill in the gaps as quickly as possible."

- A man sees a woman who is trapped on a roof by rising flood waters. He decides he must save her and ties one end of a length of rope to a power pole and then...

- After which he...

- But this fails, so he...

- Then he manages to...

- Finally, he is able to...

- The man is aged...

- How old are you?

What Did He Tell You?

Did he make the man younger or older than himself? In action stories such as this, your man will tend to perceive the age of the hero as younger than himself if he feels that he's past the height of his powers, and older if he feels that he's still not reached his full potential. If he asked someone else to help him, it could show either that he felt inadequate, or that he knew his limitations and was actually being quite resourceful.

Here are some other fun questions you might like to ask each other in order to get an idea of your differing self-perceptions.

- Someone has decided to make a movie of your life thus far. Which actor would you like to portray you and why?

- If you were the director of this movie, what pointers would you give to the person playing you?

- Which actor do you think your friends or relatives would pick to portray you?

506.

THE E-TRAIN ESCORT AGENCY

THIS IS A REACTION EXERCISE IN WHICH YOUR MAN IS PUT IN A SITUATION WHERE HE CAN GRAB THE MORAL HIGH GROUND. TRY TO KEEP YOUR DELIVERY AS AUTHENTIC AS POSSIBLE, AND MAINTAIN EYE CONTACT.

ASK HIM THIS: "What do you do when you spend the night away from home? I'm going to read you a scenario, and then I'll ask you some questions about it."

You're staying overnight on business in New York when you catch sight of an old fishing buddy you haven't seen in years. He's just leaving the hotel lobby but grabs an escort service card out of his wallet and scrawls his number on the back. You agree to call him next week. You take a meal on your own in the hotel dining room and turn in after watching Letterman. It's several days later and you're back home when your partner confronts you.

She says, "I'm very upset and I want you to answer some questions. I don't want you to say anything by way of explanation until I've finished. Just yes or no. Is that okay?"

You say…

"Was the purpose of your trip to New York purely business?"

"Did you go out with a woman while you were there?"

"Did you go out with a woman from an escort agency?"

"Did you have a meal with a woman?"

"Did you call a woman?"

"Did you sleep with a woman?"

"Did you have sex with a woman on a train?"

"I found this card in your suit pocket; it's from the E-Train Escort Agency, and on the back someone has written a phone number and it's not in your handwriting. Now don't say anything! Just answer me truthfully. Did you contact that agency?"

"Well, I rang the number on the back of the card and I got a lady named Sally. I told her who I was and asked her if she made a habit of sleeping with married men! She said it was none of my business and put the phone down! So did you or did you not speak with Sally at any time?"

"Well, can you explain what this card with this number on the back was doing in your suit pocket?"

WHAT DID HE TELL YOU?

This is your man telling you the truth! Okay, so you both know it's not for real, but how he handled it should give you some idea as to his reactions when he's being completely honest. Was he beaming with delight at you getting it so wrong, or was he concerned that you were barking up the wrong tree and wouldn't let him explain? If he was relishing being innocent, then it may be that he's not often in that position and was making the most of it. Whereas if he was wanting to stop you, it's more likely that he hasn't stepped out of line in the past.

If you're accused of something you didn't do it implies that you're not trusted. So it's natural to be indignant and upset if you're innocent. You want to clear the matter up as quickly as possible, both to ease your discomfort and protect the other person from looking stupid. However, if you've been dishonest in the past and been found out, then you're more likely to want your accuser to go on and on to demonstrate just how wrong they are, and by inference, just how innocent *you* are.

How did you feel putting him through the third degree? Is it the way you would normally handle this sort of situation? Did he empathize with your line of questioning? Would he put you through the third degree if the roles were reversed?

507.

CLASSIFIED INFORMATION

HERE YOU WILL SEE A LITTLE DEEPER INTO HOW YOUR MAN
VIEWS THE WORLD AND WHERE HE FITS INTO IT. GET HIM
TO TRY THIS EXERCISE ON YOU TOO.

ASK HIM THIS: "Who do you mostly mix with? I want you to imagine that you're applying for a position in a company that processes classified government information. To ensure that security is not compromised, the company needs to know that you will not be tempted to reveal secrets to your close friends. For this reason, they need to ascertain whether the type of relationship you have with your friends may entice you to impress them with confidential information. I'm the interviewer, and I want you to be as honest as you can about your friends."

- First, who are your three best male friends?

- What are these men's jobs?

- Now I want you to rank them according to what you see as their status.

- Last, where do you see yourself compared with them in terms of status?

What Did He Tell You?

Does he actually have male friends, or are they just acquaintances? Unlike women, many men are quite isolated and don't have the equivalent number of same-sex friends. How does he define a friend? How does he perceive himself in relation to his friends? What sort of people does he like to be friends with? Is there a mix of high and low achievers? Where do you think you would fit in his status ranking?

The wider the range of friends he has, the better. If he surrounds himself with underlings, then he may have an identity problem. If his friends are all higher on the status ladder than he is, then he may feel inferior, or he may not think they're real friends.

This may be a good time to discuss what he reveals to his friends. Does he feel he competes with them in sharing information? Is he aware of trying to impress them and does he think they have more of a need to impress him? What does he enjoy talking with them about? Does he talk about his relationship? How supportive are his male friends? Do they give encouragement and advice without minimizing his problems? How much good-natured teasing does he engage in with his friends? What does he think ragging achieves and does he ever feel it goes too far?

As a subsidiary question, you might like to ask him how he sees status. Does he simply look at it financially, or does he see status in terms of community kudos? Perhaps he sees status in an entirely personal way. For instance, one of his friends may be in an occupation that doesn't pay all that well but is in a field that he's always had the deepest respect and admiration for.

If you had to answer the first question in this exercise, who would your three best friends be? And how would you measure them? Would status come into it? What do you reveal to them? How different would your answers be from his?

508.

I LOVE THE WAY YOU TOUCH ME

WE ALL NEED A BOOST NOW AND AGAIN. IN THIS
EXERCISE YOU GET TO ELEVATE YOUR MAN TO DIZZY
HEIGHTS, AND HOPEFULLY YOU WILL ACTUALLY BE QUITE
SINCERE. BUT HOW DOES HE REACT? READ ON TO
THE INTERPRETATION FOR A BETTER UNDERSTANDING
OF HIS ANSWERS AND TO CHECK THE FINAL QUESTIONS.

ASK HIM THIS: "What sort of things do you like people to say about
you? I'm going to read pairs of statements, and I want you to say
which one you'd most like to hear."

A. You're wonderful.
or
B. You make me feel wonderful.

A. My friends all think you're great.
or
B. I love being with you.

A. People in the community really respect you.
or
B. You make me so proud of you.

A. You're a great lover.
or
B. I love the way you touch me.

A. You've got such a great body.
or
B. Our bodies seem to fit so well together.

A. You have such extraordinary insights.
or
B. I've never met anyone who understands me so well.

A. The reason people like you is because you're so honest.
or
B. You're the most honest person I've ever met.

A. Your clients really value your work.
or
B. I love watching you work.

A. Everyone commented on how clever and funny your speech
   was at your friend's wedding.
or
B. The poem you wrote to me on my birthday made me cry. It
   was so beautiful.

A. Your employees would walk over broken glass for you.
or
B. I'd do anything for you.

A. Everybody loves you.
or
B. I love you.

What Did He Tell You?

Is he more interested in having his ego stroked, or hearing specific things about his relationship?

The "A" sentences are all general compliments and signify what the outside world might think of him. The "B" sentences are more personal and specific things said by a partner. So is he more interested in what others think of him, or you?

We all want to be loved. To be popular. To be looked on with warmth and kindness. But we need to balance this by having enough self-confidence to know that essentially we're okay. We don't actually need to hear that the world loves us. But we do need to hear it from our loved ones. It's what enables us to continue in a relationship with trust and certainty.

However, any analysis of the human condition, by its very nature, is not scientific. There are many variables. If your man, for instance, opted for mostly "A" compliments, it could indicate that he feels a degree of insecurity about himself. But the reasons for this may have nothing to do with how he sees your relationship. At the moment he may feel very safe with you, but needs bolstering in other areas of his life.

Likewise, if your man opts for mostly "B" compliments, it should indicate his interest in the relationship. But it might also mean that he either doesn't feel all that safe at the moment, or he might simply be showing you the sorts of compliments he'd like to hear from *you*.

It could be that most men will choose the "A" option because they want to feel significant in the wider world. Women opt for "Bs" because the relationship is more important to them. This implies that if you want to butter him up, go for "A." If you want him to butter you up, he needs to understand that you'll want "B" options.

Some commentators suggest that women are born with a built-in significance and purpose based around their ability to bear and nurture children. Because men don't have this, they feel a strong need to seek relevance through their work. Women often say that men bury themselves in work as a means of escaping the family and that this places an unreasonable strain on the relationship. Some men certainly use their careers as an escape, but it seems to us that the majority use their work to prove their potency and relevance in the world.* It is one of the most powerful callings in our lives and the reason one of the first questions men ask each other is "what do you do?"

* If you want to check out just how much your man thinks about his significance in the world, try asking him these questions. You might be surprised to find that he actually has serious answers.

"You receive a call from the producer of the *Daily Show* who tells you that John Stewart would like to interview you. Why do you think he wants you on his show?"

"U2's Bono invites you for lunch. Why do you think he wants to meet you?"

"You're invited to the White House for an informal discussion with the president. What would the president want to discuss with you?"

"Film director Steven Spielberg calls to ask your opinion on something. What would he want to know?"

509.

WORST-CASE SCENARIOS

DOES YOUR MAN SEE LIFE AS A CUP HALF FULL OR HALF EMPTY? AND MORE IMPORTANTLY, DOES HE HAVE THE KIND OF RESILIENCE TO HANDLE THE BLEAKER MOMENTS? IF YOU WANT TO SHARE THIS EXERCISE, SPLIT IT IN TWO AND TAKE TURNS ANSWERING THEM.

ASK HIM THIS: "How do you deal with change? I'm going to read you a series of statements, and I want you to complete them as quickly as possible."

- If you were fired, it would be bad because...

- But it could have its benefits because...

- Winning the lottery would be good because...

- But it could be bad because...

- The breakup of a relationship would be bad because...

- But it could have a positive side because...

253

- Purchasing an expensive item on impulse could be bad because...

- But on the positive side it could...

- Hurting someone in a road accident would be terrible because...

- But it could have a positive side because...

- A death in the family would be bad because...

- But on the positive side it could...

- Having your house broken into would be bad because...

- But on the upside it could...

- Being diagnosed with a life-threatening disease would be terrible because...

- But on the plus side it could...

- Meeting the love of your life would be incredible because...

- But it could have a bad side because...

- Going to jail would be horrific because...

- But it could have a positive side in that...

• Being promoted in your job would be great because...

• But on the downside it could...

WHAT DID HE TELL YOU?

How flexible is he? Was he able to come up with negative and positive viewpoints to each situation? How easily was he able to do this? The more resilient a person can be, the more he or she will be able to show empathy, understanding, and tolerance to others. It will also mean being able to handle a crisis or a windfall without losing his sense of reality.

We often think that to be fully developed as adults, we have to be what is termed "well-balanced." But what does that mean? In part, it is the ability to be centered. Obviously, we can all be knocked off stride by what life throws at us. What *Worst-Case Scenarios* reveals is your man's ability to not only see both sides of a situation, but also whether, in the long run, he can regain his center. So it might show you that in life, no matter whether he's confronted by tragedy or good fortune, he won't go over the top but remain calm and even.

Some people, of course, have low expectations, and will have difficulty seeing any positives in bad situations. But rather than label themselves pessimistic, they'd prefer to call themselves realists. It's a mind-set you need to be aware of when looking at your man's answers. If he can't find positives when things go wrong in his life, he may also not recognize them when things go right. This means that he may find compliments uncomfortable to deal with, regardless of whether they come from you or anyone else. You may want to dig deeper to find out why this is so.

510.

BE HAPPY

THIS IS A QUICK EXERCISE FOR YOU BOTH TO GAIN AN INSIGHT INTO YOUR RESPECTIVE OUTLOOKS ON LIFE. YOU COULD GO THROUGH *BE HAPPY* BY ANSWERING THE STATEMENTS ALTERNATELY, OR YOU COULD SIMPLY GO THROUGH IT ONE AT A TIME.

ASK HIM THIS: "How do you see your life? I'm going to read some statements, and I want you to complete them for me."

- When you think of your early life, you thank your lucky stars that...

- Looking back at school, you count your blessings that...

- When you think about your present relationship or the last one you were in, you're really pleased that...

- One thing that you'll always be proud of is...

- In your work you're thankful that...

- When you think about your year so far, you're grateful that...

- When you think of yesterday, it really pleases you that...

- When you think about your friends, you're glad that...

- When you think about your family, you're thankful that...

- When you think about your body, you're grateful that...

- When you think about your future, you're pleased that...

WHAT DID HE TELL YOU?

Were you both grateful or did you have difficulty thinking of things to be happy about? Were either of you even downright negative?* What were the things you were grateful for? Were they positive things such as a wonderful upbringing or negative things such as being glad that you haven't been fired from your jobs yet, or that you're still alive? Your answers should give you a good idea of your current states of mind—whether you're feeling negative or positive and whether you generally have an optimistic or pessimistic outlook on life.

* Recent research has shown that answering questions such as this in a positive way can have a beneficial effect. The more people write down things that they're grateful for, the more they feel satisfied with their lives and the more their energy levels will lift. When positive feelings result in smiling, it can produce other effects. On a social level the person smiling is perceived to be more pleasant, attractive, and sincere and is therefore given more positive feedback. From a physiological standpoint, there is some evidence to suggest that smiling stretches our facial muscles in a way that stimulates the nervous system to produce cerebral morphine, a hormone that results in a pleasant, calming feeling. So if you're in a funk, try smiling anyway and it might just pull you out of it.

511.

WHO DOES HE THINK HE IS?

How we see ourselves may be affected by what others call us, but in the end it's up to us to either agree with the outside world or disagree. In this exercise you'll gain some insights as to how your man really thinks of himself. Note: keep your delivery reasonably fast.

Ask Him This: "How do people normally describe you? I'm going to read a series of words or phrases, and I want you to tell me whether you'd feel comfortable if someone used them with regard to you."

Would you feel comfortable if someone called you:

- A jock
- A doofus
- Frugal
- A groupie
- An airhead
- An animal

- A nerd
- Eccentric
- Easygoing
- Playful
- Arrogant
- Flighty

258

- Flaky
- A swinger
- Cunning
- Intense
- Naive
- A very good driver
- A bully
- Hard
- Multitalented
- Very generous
- Very creative
- Innovative
- A man of great vision
- Sexy
- A dedicated father
- Well endowed
- Altruistic
- Very special
- A great lover

- A geek
- Boring
- Pigheaded
- A womanizer
- An independent thinker
- Pedantic
- Self-centered
- A great conversationalist
- Very attractive to women
- A great leader
- Excellent communicator
- Highly entertaining
- A real comedian
- Anal
- A great cook
- A nonconformist
- Gentle souled
- Extremely popular
- a genius

What Did He Tell You?

Are you lucky to be with this guy, or what? How comfortable was he with exaggerated praise or downright condemnation? Did he find it easier to see his faults or his virtues? Just how honest and self-aware is he? This is an exercise in self-appraisal, desire, honesty, and wishful thinking.*

Some people find it easier to list their weaknesses than their strengths, but don't be fooled into thinking this necessarily means that they're weak or lacking in confidence. They might just be realistic. Similarly, someone who accepts the praise without a flicker of self-consciousness may not necessarily be full of his own self-importance. He may just feel confident or optimistic or valued.

Culture can also play a significant role in the way a person answers these questions. Some societies actively promote the blowing of one's own trumpet, while others insist on modesty and reward those who get others to blow their trumpets for them.

* Remember that some of his reactions may be based on his own definitions of particular words. For instance, he may feel deeply insulted by being called a flake, because it may have been something his father always called him. Ask him to elaborate if he felt strongly about any of the descriptions.

512.

WHAT'S UP, DAWG?

Is he more interested in the wood or the trees? Get him to try this one out on you too.

ASK HIM THIS: "How are you at coming up with explanations? I'm going to read you a set of scenarios, and I want you to answer the question that follows each one."

- Three people are in a field. Two of them are women, and one of these women is holding a child.
  What's happening?

- A man is sitting on a park bench. In front of him is a four-year-old boy using a stick to draw a picture in the dirt. Behind the man is a policeman.
  What's happening?

- Two men are looking down a storm culvert. One of them has a flashlight, the other one is holding a cup.
  What's happening?

- A man is staring at a letter he's just received. Next to him on the floor sits a cat by the fire.
  What's happening?

- A small girl is looking up to a man. She's holding something behind her back.
  What's happening?

- A policeman is looking up into a tall tree. Next to him is a woman sitting on the ground reading a piece of paper.
  What's happening?

- Two men are standing outside a bar after a night of drinking. One of them has his eyes closed while the other man pulls out a notebook and begins to write in it.
  What's happening?

- A couple is making out in the back row of a movie theater. Then immediately in front of them someone turns around and says something to the woman. At this point she gets up and leaves on her own.
  What's happening?

- It's nighttime and it's pouring rain. On a porch stands a woman holding a suitcase. In the lit room above, a couple is arguing.
  What's happening?

WHAT DID HE TELL YOU?

Is he more interested in explaining the logistics of the action, or the emotional dynamics occurring between the characters? If he attributes any emotional content to the scenes, then he's likely to be more understanding and supportive in his relationships. Does he empathize with anyone in these situations? If he does, this may be the result of significant moments from his past. It's also a good sign if he resolves the scenes positively. How different were *your* answers?

513.

THE LAST STRAW

THE LAST STRAW DEALS WITH YOUR MAN'S VALUE
SYSTEM AND EXPECTATIONS. WE'VE USED TWO FICTITIOUS
CHARACTERS IN THIS EXERCISE TO AVOID ANY PERCEIVED
FEELING OF THREAT, BUT YOU SHOULD STILL GET A FAIR
IDEA AS TO HIS THINKING IN GENERAL.

ASK HIM THIS: "Where do you draw the line in a relationship? I'm going to read you a series of statements, and I want you to complete them as quickly as possible."

- John thought Laura was the love of his life until...

- John thought Laura was the love of his life until she told him...

- John thought Laura was the love of his life until she did something he just couldn't forgive her for, which was to...

- He thought she was the love of his life until he saw her...

- He thought she was the love of his life until he found her...

- He thought she was the love of his life until her mother told him...

- He thought she was the love of his life until her best friend told him…

- He thought she was the love of his life until her ex-boyfriend told him…

WHAT DID HE TELL YOU?

How a man answers these questions* will tell you what he fears within a relationship. If most of his responses, for example, are concerned with Laura's faithfulness, then this could indicate either that this is a real concern for him or baggage from past betrayals.

Entering into a relationship is one of the most momentous things we do, even if we've had good experiences. If we haven't, then these fears are magnified, and trust becomes a real issue. A man's fears, apart from infidelity, could include dishonesty, betrayal, hidden character flaws, health issues, mental weakness, an undisclosed criminal record, or even mortality. Have you ever talked about these things with him?

The general opinion is that men's greatest fear is commitment, which could explain a reply such as: "John thought Laura was the love of his life until he met Sue." But in the context of this exercise, we think such answers shouldn't be taken too seriously. Indeed, we think that most replies are more useful as discussion starters rather than as definitive indicators. Now may be a good time to ask how past relationships have contributed to his fears, what he has learned from those experiences, and how he would do things differently now.

* Let him ask you these questions as well to stimulate a more interesting conversation. For example, Laura thought John was the love of her life until…

514.

AGONY AND ECSTASY

THIS IS A SCENARIO ABOUT EMOTIONAL AWARENESS AND
MAY TAKE SOME TIME. SO DON'T FEEL YOU NEED TO GO
THROUGH THE WHOLE THING IN ONE SITTING. YOU MAY
ALSO NEED TO ASK YOUR OWN QUESTIONS TO GAIN MORE
INSIGHT. BUT TREAD GENTLY.

ASK HIM THIS: "What are you like at characterization? I want you
to imagine that you're attending a writers' workshop and you've been
taught that in order to make your characters authentic, you should
base the dramatic moments in their lives on incidents and feelings that
you've experienced. I'm going to read you a series of statements, and I
want you to complete them, giving as much detail as possible."

- The most scared you've ever been was when...

- The most homesick you've ever felt was...

- The most angry you've ever been was...

- The most extreme pain you've ever felt was...

- The happiest you've ever been was...

- The most nauseous you've ever felt was...

- The saddest you've ever felt was…

- The most exhausted you've ever felt was…

- The most love you've ever experienced was…

- The most lost you've ever been was…

- The most rejected you've ever felt was…

- The most abandoned you've ever felt was…

- The most endangered you've ever felt was…

- The most frustrated you've ever felt was…

- The most nervous you've ever felt was…

- The most embarrassed you've ever felt was…

- The weakest you've ever felt was…

- The most guilty you've ever felt was…

- The most paralyzed you've ever felt was…

- The most unloved you've ever felt was…

- The most proud you've ever felt was…

- The worst pain in your head you've ever had was…

- The most unhinged you've ever felt was…

- The most hungry you've ever felt was…

- The most euphoric you've ever felt was…

What Did He Tell You?

How capable is he of exposing his feelings or recognizing them?* In this exercise you're asking feeling questions, which could be difficult for him to answer depending on how he chooses to interpret them. If he manages to keep himself detached, it won't be such a big deal. But if he really immerses himself in the subject, it will bring up emotions and memories that he may not feel comfortable with. Just remember, if you're unable to identify your emotions and talk about them with each other, it will make being in an intimate relationship difficult, and unsatisfying.

So, how did he react? Was he relieved to tell you some of these things, or was he embarrassed? We've thrown in a lot of physical questions as well as emotional ones, which will give him an easy out if he chooses to take it. Note, though, how he interprets some of the more ambiguous words such as *lost, paralyzed,* or *weak*. Does he follow the safe route and see them as physical sensations, or is he brave enough to interpret them emotionally?

You could do this exercise yourself, but be aware that some couples will compete with each other or feel the need to reciprocate feelings. For example, if the man said that the saddest he ever felt was when his dog died, his partner may feel obliged to come up with an equivalent situation so as not to feel left out. Or she may try to belittle his response by talking about something far more dramatic than a pet dying. Speak from your heart, and hopefully he will do the same.

If this exercise has helped him open up more, think what other feeling questions you can ask him that will help him share his emotions more fully and establish a closer connection.

* Emotional memories that are suddenly discovered always take time to come to terms with. So don't rush him. You may find he'll want to talk about something this exercise has brought up weeks later when he's processed it.

515.

THE CRYING GAME

In this exercise you'll be able to see whether he was brought up either with the "big boys don't cry" mantra or the "be a man and let it out" theory.

Ask Him This: "What do you think about men crying? I'm going to read you a series of story lines in which men cry, and I want you to tell me if you think it's okay for them to do so by replying either 'okay' or 'not okay.'"

- When the putt finally dropped and sealed victory for him in the U.S. Open, Michael was so overcome with emotion that he hid his face behind his hat.

- During a televised address in response to an act of terrorism that killed hundreds of Americans, the president broke down and cried.

- While being interviewed by a television reporter, a man who had just witnessed his house and all his possessions being destroyed by a twister broke down and couldn't continue the interview.

- Having tried to get his car started for over half an hour, Barry finally began to cry out of frustration.

- The celebrated religious leader had to fight back the tears as he publicly admitted to embezzling hundreds of thousands of dollars to service his gambling problem.

- Bernard was yelling at his wife for disclosing their financial situation to the neighbors. But when she also let slip that she'd told them about his impotency, he began sobbing with rage.

- When Malcolm saw his new baby for the very first time, he welled up with tears.

- When questioned by reporters today, Thompson tearfully admitted that he had taken a dive in his title bout last night in Atlantic City.

- When Gabrielle told Brandon that she was leaving him for another man, Brandon couldn't restrain himself and wept.

- When Suzanne told Dave that she was leaving him for another man, Dave was so stunned that he said nothing, and it wasn't until she left the apartment that he broke down and sobbed.

- Alex went to the movies with his girlfriend. While watching a particularly heartrending scene, Alex wept silently.

- The second movement of the symphony moved him so much that Steven felt tears rolling down his cheeks.

- When Gary saw his son decked out in his first baseball uniform, tears filled his eyes.

- William hadn't seen her in five months, and when he spied her walking down the concourse toward him, he had to fight back the tears.

- When Russell saw the beautiful deer that he'd just shot, he burst into tears.

Finally, not a story, but some questions.

- When's the last time you cried?

- Under what circumstances can you remember trying to fight back tears?

- How does it make you feel when someone very close to you cries?

- Do you feel the need to stop them crying by distracting them, or making them laugh?

(Now, go back and give him *your* take on each of the scenarios.)

WHAT DID HE TELL YOU?

What's his attitude to crying? Is he the stiff-upper-lip type, or is he able to let his emotions out? How did you view the scenarios? Was there much difference between your reactions and his? Was he at all surprised by your attitudes?

When people cry it's usually provoked by grief, rage, relief, pride, joy, empathy, or shame. Obviously, men feel all these emotions, but why do so many of them not cry? Part of it is biological. Males don't have the same capacity to cry as females who have larger tear glands and sixty percent more of the hormone prolactin that controls tear gland production. Also, men's brains are wired differently from women's, and are programmed to delay emotional reactions until any perceived threat has disappeared. Hence, the phenomenon of men remaining stoic in stressful situations but then finding it perfectly acceptable to cry in private later when the danger has passed. In fact, the male brain can become overstimulated by emotion, and the call to repress feelings often comes from older males who understand how indulging certain feelings can actually increase male stress rather than reduce it.

Another factor is conditioning. If a man's early male role models managed to keep a lid on their emotions, and if they were also contemptuous of boys or men crying, then the chances are high that he will follow suit. In these circumstances, any emotional outpouring on his part would probably be very confusing for him, and he may well feel a sense of shame for being "weak."

Opinion is divided on whether or not crying enables men to reduce tension and so avoid aggression. In fact, in Japan and China where boys are shamed for crying, much lower rates of male violence are recorded than in the United States where men are encouraged to express their emotions and cry more.

One thing is for sure—women's changing expectations of male emotionality have placed men in a difficult position. They now want their males to be more intimate and sensitive, but at the same time they have to be tough when it's required. They don't want weaker men, but men who can go from truculent to tender, from football to flamenco, in thirty seconds or less. Their ideal man is industrial strength and designer label all at the same time, which is a very tall order. Let's just remember, when disaster strikes, a man's ability to suppress his feelings and stay in control has high survival value, and deep down it's something that women rely on.

THE TREE, THE CAT, AND THE BICYCLE

HOW WOULD YOUR MAN RECOGNIZE HIS IDEAL WOMAN?
YOU'LL BE SURPRISED JUST HOW MUCH INFORMATION THIS
SCENARIO REVEALS. AND BECAUSE IT'S EASILY REVERSED,
YOU CAN TRY IT TOO. REPLACE THE WORD *SHE* WITH *HE*,
AND THEN COMPARE NOTES.

ASK HIM THIS: "Have you ever had a big wish come true? I'm going to read you a scenario and then ask some questions."

You find an old lamp in an attic. Just for fun you rub it and much to your surprise a genie pops out and says he'll grant you one wish. You wish for the most wonderful woman in the world. The genie says he'll grant your wish but to be sure that you're capable of recognizing such a woman, he will disguise her as three different things in three different locations, and you will have to pick her out. She will be disguised as a bicycle in a cycle shop, a tree in a garden, and a cat in an animal shelter.

• Let's start with the cycle shop. What sort of bicycle would she be disguised as? What characteristics would she have that would enable you to recognize her? How would you go about finding out?

272

- And in the garden, what sort of tree would she be? What sort of qualities would the tree have?

- And in the animal shelter, how would you recognize her from the other cats? How would you interact with the cat and how would she behave?

WHAT DID HE TELL YOU?

When we are asked to make parallels between someone we know and an object or animal, we discover new ways of describing that person. These new descriptions can lead to valuable insights, and make for interesting and often hilarious discussion. We can also find ourselves exploring and relating to the person in a new way. For example, did he just look at the tree or climb into its branches and smell its blossoms? Did he stroke the cat or ride the bicycle? In the end his descriptions could be very close to what he wants in a mate.

Was he more interested in describing the physical attributes of the bicycle or did he spend more time on its qualities? We've found that most men go for looks initially, whereas women usually opt for characteristics first off. So was the bicycle a sleek new racing model or a sturdy mountain bike with big tires? Was his chief concern how stylish it was or how useful? In other words, is his bicycle/woman a beautiful status symbol to be proudly displayed or something to be enjoyed for the excitement it provides and the places it can take him, or both? Was it secondhand or new? Did he test-ride it and where did he take it? All these things can be relevant, and while you may be a little unsure about interpreting some of the answers, most of the comparisons will be fairly obvious. For example, whether it had a comfortable seat and full suspension as opposed to being light and fast on corners with thirty-six gears and disc brakes may well suggest a liking for a homely woman as opposed to someone more exciting and responsive. And focusing on accessories such as lights, water bottle, wing mirrors, pump, or a trip meter might indicate a rather rigid requirement for certain characteristics.

Was the tree a graceful weeping willow or a sturdy oak? Whether it stood alone in the garden or with other trees could tell you if he perceives his ideal woman as being surrounded by friends or as his alone. If it was big enough to climb into or small and fruit bearing, it may suggest whether he wants a woman who'll inspire him or one who's a good provider. Whether his tree/woman is evergreen or deciduous may point to his desire for someone who is constant as opposed to changeable. Was his tree large and protective, providing shelter from fierce winter winds and shade from the summer heat? Did it have sweet perfumed flowers or lots of nesting areas for birds? Did it need pruning or transplanting, and was its bark rough and interestingly textured or pale and smooth? These are all attributes that are open to interpretation and discussion.

And what about the cat? Does he recognize her because she runs over and rubs against his legs, or did he need to entice her out of a corner and stroke her until she purred? Is she playful or asleep? Does he know her because she has the most beautiful soft fur or because she looks deep into his eyes and licks her lips? Does she roll playfully on her back or stretch and saunter off with a casual flick of her tail? In the end it'll be up to you to decide.

517.

THE MOTHERS' LEAGUE

IMAGINE, WHEN YOU TAKE YOUR MAN HOME TO MEET YOUR MOTHER, THERE ARE EIGHT MORE MOTHERS WAITING THERE, EACH WITH A DIFFERENT QUESTION TO TEST HIS SUITABILITY. SOME OF THEM ARE FLIPPANT AND OTHERS ARE DOWNRIGHT SNEAKY.

ASK HIM THIS: "What are you like with mothers? I'm going to read you a scenario and then I'll ask you some questions."

I want you to imagine that the girl you've been dating for a while wants to take you home to meet her mother. You agree, but when you get there you and your girlfriend are surprised to discover there are eight other mothers in the living room, all waiting to meet you.

However, you're relieved to see that they're a jolly lot who are all laughing. They explain that Wendy has just tried out one of her wicked questions on them. She'd told them that a female zoo keeper in Berlin had been fired for having sex with one of the animals and asked them to guess which animal they thought it might be. Julie said "A Panda," and then Wendy said "Okay, what's your second choice?" They all break out into peels of laughter and you can see it's going to be a fun session.

Your girlfriend's mother explains that these women are all members of her quilting group and when she asked them last week what she should be asking you, they all offered to come along with their own questions. "I've limited them to just one question each," she says, "and I'm going to kick off."

1. This is what your girlfriend's mother wants to know: "I want you to name five household chores and then rank them in order from the one you like the most to the one you like the least. And tell me why."

You say...

2. The next mother asks: "What's the worst thing that's ever happened to you?"

3. The next mother wants to know: "Why do women get so mad at men for leaving the toilet seat up, and why don't men get mad at women for leaving it down?"

4. The next mother's question is this: "What's one thing you could do to improve your relationship right now?"

5. The next question is: "If you could be suddenly transported to anywhere in the world, where would you go and what would you be doing there?"

6. Another mother wants to know: "What's the most embarrassing thing that's ever happened to you?"

7. The next mother says: "I want you to do a little hand reading for me. I want you to open your palm and choose one of the longer lines on it. Now I want you to imagine that your life starts at one end of the line, and ends at the other. If you look closely at the line you'll notice that there are little marks on it and little

lines running off it. These represent significant moments in your life. Starting at the beginning of your line, I want you to tell me what a few of these significant points are."

8. The next question is: "What's been the happiest time of your life to date?"

9. Finally, it's time for Wendy's question. "Well," she says, "my question is rather personal, but it's divided into two halves and once you've answered the first question it's entirely up to you whether you choose to hear the second question. If you don't want to hear the second question, I'm sure we'll all understand, won't we, girls?" she says with a twinkle in her eye. They all nod and lean forward expectantly. "So my question is this," says Wendy. "Have you ever measured the length of your erect penis with a ruler?"

"Now," says Wendy, "Do you want to hear the second question?" (If he doesn't want to hear it, the questions stop at this point.)

"The second question that we all want answered is this," says Wendy. "How long...are you prepared to put up with very silly questions like this?"

WHAT DID HE TELL YOU?

Question 1. So how was he on the domestic front? His girlfriend's mother obviously thinks that it's important for a man to help around the house, so she uses this sneaky way of finding out if the guy has ever done much housework. If he can come up with five chores, he at least has some understanding of what needs doing around the place.

Then, if he can rank those jobs and give reasons for his choice, you can be fairly certain that he's actually had some practice. If he has a particularly good overview, he'll have included a few of the dangerous jobs that can easily result in injury—jobs that women expect men to do, such as climbing up ladders to clear gutters or change light bulbs.

Question 2. This mother wants to know what he considers to be the worst thing in his life. It tells her about his sensitivities. Was it a romantic breakup or a nasty accident? Does it have to do with his family or his job? Whatever the answer, it will provide valuable clues to understanding what's tough for him.

Question 3. The problem of the toilet seat is probably as old as Mr. Crapper himself. But what this mother is looking for is whether he is able to empathize with the opposite sex's point of view. How much thought has he given to this problem, and is he able to see both sides clearly enough to make a case for each one and even come to a considered compromise? If you want to see how well he can think himself into understanding a physical situation, ask him if he'd consider sitting on the toilet the other way around, facing the wall. See how long it takes him to realize the problem.

Question 4. This question is aimed at finding out what his overview of the relationship is. Does he regard it as something both parties have to work on, or does he expect it to chug along without ever having to change the oil or the tires?

Question 5. This mother wants to find out if he's contented and ready to settle down or if he's still looking for his direction in life. The important thing, if he does want to go off somewhere amazing to do something equally wonderful, is whether he takes you along too.

Question 6. What embarrasses us is a real clue to the areas we feel most sensitive about. The more a man is embarrassed by minor things, the more sensitive he will tend to be. If he's not particularly embarrassed by anything at all, then he may be insensitive to you.

Question 7. By asking him to tell her what he sees as significant periods of his life, this mother is inviting him to show whether he has an overview of his own life's course and how much understanding he has of the forces that structure it. If he has this understanding, he should also be able to play a significant role in guiding the course of your relationship with him.

It seems likely that this mother will also have taken the opportunity to look at the relative length of his fingers. Intuitively, she knows that a man with a ring finger longer than his index finger is likely to have high fertility and be more competitive than a man with a ring finger of the same length or shorter than his index finger. In fact, research backs this up. Scientists have discovered that men with longer ring fingers have higher levels of the male sex hormone, testosterone. Conversely, women with ring fingers shorter than their index fingers, tend to have high fertility levels.

Question 8. Here again, if he can look back on his life and identify what it was that made him happy, then he can return to it again. This mother knows that a happy man is a loving man.

Question 9. In essence, what Wendy wants to know is whether he can take a joke. Men who can laugh at themselves and still be warm and positive are definitely keepers.

L E V E L 6

The Bottom Line

In Level Six you will finally be able to see the character beneath the man. Not his personality, or foibles, or outer appearance, but his character. In other words, you will be able to identify the difference between what he says and what he does.

Personality is the style of someone's expressiveness. Words such as extroverted, vivacious, serene, funny, and quirky are all descriptive examples of personality. But they shouldn't be confused with character. Someone doesn't have to be extroverted or serene to be a good person. In fact, many decent people often display the opposite traits. They can be short-tempered or high-strung or simply dull. But when it matters, they can still be relied upon to do the right thing and to act from their conscience.

We're not born with great character. We have to work at it, and it can be damned hard and very painful, especially if we've listened to our inner voice—our conscience—and ultimately acted on what we've heard. In this level you'll see how much your man has learned from his own past. It includes exercises to reveal his sense of loyalty, consideration, commitment, kindness, understanding, and emotional expression. Try not to be judgmental about his responses. The great thing about character building is that it never stops.

601.

DOES HE STILL LOVE YOU?

You can gauge what really matters to someone by listening to the questions they ask. This exercise gives him the opportunity to do just that. You can add your own questions in order to learn more.

Ask Him This: "Are you an inquisitive person? I'm going to read you a series of unfinished statements and I want you to complete them as quickly as possible."

- Your ex-girlfriend surprises you by telling you that she's pregnant. The first thing you'd ask her is…

- Your wife has been at an office party and arrives home very late. The first thing you'd ask her is…

- Your wife tells you that she's had a coffee with an ex-lover. The first thing you'd ask her is…

- A friend tells you that he's met a girl you'd really like. The first thing you'd want to know about her is…

- Your lawyer calls and tells you that you have a half brother who wants to meet you. The first thing you'd want to know about him is…

- Your wife's been arrested for shoplifting. When you meet her at the police station, the first thing you'd ask her is…

- Your political party has announced its latest candidate in the upcoming presidential race. The first thing you'd want to know about him or her is…

- A new boss has been appointed at your workplace. The first thing you'd want to know about her is…

- You've been asked to hire a Santa Claus for the department store where you work. For each applicant, the first thing you would ask is…

- Your realtor suggests you look at a house in a suburb you're unfamiliar with. The first thing you'd want to know about the area is…

What Did He Tell You?

Does he have a suspicious mind? Is his first instinct to think that he's being betrayed or hoodwinked? Or does he have an open, optimistic outlook on his world?

If he mostly responded in a negative way to these situations, it probably suggests that his world hasn't always treated him kindly. This may sound too simplistic and he may scoff at this reasoning. He might say that these situations weren't actually happening to him, or that he'd simply worked off secondhand evidence he'd picked up from friends or the media. But even this would still beg the question: "Why did he apply a negative spin to the situations?" It's worth asking him.

Conversely, if he mostly responded positively, we think it infers that, on the whole, life has been good to him. He is open to change, to new experiences, and to growing as a person. This stance, of course, has its own pitfalls. People who are too open are often described as naive. They always see the best in everything or everyone, and occasionally they get it horribly wrong.

The ideal is to be a mix of caution and cavalier, to have a nose for sniffing out trouble, and a heart to appreciate it when things go right.

602.

THE WRONG FLOWERS

These scenarios are testing dilemmas and should be fascinating for both of you. But note, you should be looking at how much of the big picture he can see and not whether his solutions are necessarily right or wrong.

ASK HIM THIS: "How good are you at thinking on your feet? I'm going to read you four stories and at the end of each one I want you to complete the unfinished sentences, and try to give as much detail as possible."

1. It's rush hour as you drive to work but you've allowed extra time because you have an important meeting this morning. You notice a woman on the side of the road. Her car has a flat tire. So you pull over to ask if she needs help. She's grateful because she has to pick up her child who's been staying overnight with a friend. But just then your office rings your car phone to tell you that the meeting is now earlier. You figure you've still got time to change the tire. When you get back to the woman's car, though, she's tried to loosen one of the wheel nuts and has hurt her wrist. She insists that she'll be okay to drive. At this point you would... And then you'd...

2. You're driving late at night on a remote road. It's raining and visibility is poor. Then from nowhere a young deer bounds on to the road straight in front of you. The impact slews your car sideways and you only just manage to regain control. The deer is lying in the middle of the road. Both your headlights are smashed and you're still about five miles from the nearest town on a straight highway. You have no cell phone. At this point you would... And then you'd...

3. You've ordered flowers for your wife with a naughty message that reads... (Ask him to tell you what the message says.)

   The flowers are to be delivered, but you've left work early so decide to pick them up yourself and give them to her personally. It's very busy at the florist's and the assistant is stressed out and a little offhand with you. By the time you get home, however, your mood has brightened, particularly when your wife is so pleased with the flowers. In fact, you end up making love, so it's not until much later that you notice she hasn't opened the envelope with your card. You say: "Honey, you haven't read my note." She asks you to read it out, and it's only then that you realize you've got the wrong flowers. You find a bereavement card for a woman with the same name as your wife. At this point you would... And then you'd...

4. At an office party you are introducing everyone to Joan, a new staff member you've hired. She's bright, hardworking, and honest. Things are going well until one of the board members turns up with his wife. Joan freezes and then escapes to her office. When you follow her and ask her what's wrong, she confides in you that she once slept with the board member many years ago and he was not a very nice guy. But you convince her to return to the party, saying that she shouldn't let her past get in the way. However, Joan

finds that the easiest way to deal with the situation is to hit the bottle. She gets pretty loaded and, armed with Dutch courage, decides to confront the board member. Before you can intercept her, she announces to everyone that the board member is a total asshole. At this point you would... And then you'd... And then...

What Did He Tell You?

In reality this exercise is all about consideration. Each of the four scenarios asks your man to exhibit a degree of thought and consideration for the people (or animals) involved. What you should be looking for is his ability to see past his own interests and think about others. Below are a list of some of the things he might have suggested.

1. This should be relatively straightforward. Given that he has stopped to help the woman with a flat tire, you should assume that he's now committed to a series of actions. First, he needs to know whether she'd like him to follow her to pick up her child in case she's underestimated the injury to her wrist. He could also offer to let her use his phone to call ahead and say that she's on her way. And last, he could call his work and tell them that he might be late.

2. The first thing he might do is to get his car to the side of the road and put on his hazard lights. Then he should make sure the deer is dead and not in pain. He might try to drag it off the road so that it won't be a danger to any other drivers. Next he would try to clear away any broken headlight glass from the road, again in consideration of other drivers. Having done all this, he's then left with the problem of trying to get help. Some more adventurous souls might

suggest putting on the hazard lights, turning the car around, and then reversing to the nearest town using the backup lights for extra help. This would seem a little foolhardy. However, it might depend on how much traffic is around at the time. The safest option would be to leave his hazard lights on and sit it out until another car comes along. He may also suggest taking the deer to provide food for some needy soul.

3. The worst thing he could do here is to keep the flower switch to himself, destroy the card, and do nothing more about it. But this is hardly necessary because he really has nothing to hide. However, he might decide that by telling his wife, it will spoil the magic of the night. His silence would be understandable because it's hard to imagine that she wouldn't find the mix-up appalling, especially when he tells her what he wrote in his card. But he should contact the florist at once and let them know of the mix-up so they can intercept the flowers going to the bereaved woman if they haven't already been delivered. If they have, he could offer to deliver the right card himself. He could also talk to the owner of the florist shop to make sure that the assistant doesn't get into trouble.

4. His first consideration should be to rescue Joan. Otherwise her job could be over before it's really started. Part of his motive here, of course, is selfish because he wants her to be on the payroll. He might whisk her away on some pretext, put her in a cab, and say to everyone that she'd been on flu medication or whatever and it had reacted with the alcohol. He would then need to pacify the board member and his wife by apologizing on Joan's behalf. And because the party is a team-building exercise, he needs to talk to people individually and try to elevate the atmosphere again. His last consideration, though, should be to himself.

In this situation, he really does have something to lose—his job and his reputation. After all, he's the guy who hired her in the first place. So he needs to cover himself in some way. He shouldn't wash his hands of Joan, but does he need to separate himself from her behavior by lying on her behalf?

In the 1960s and 1970s a new philosophical movement was developed called "objectivism," which spread into virtually every corner of society, including music, art, language, bureaucracy, and politics. One upshot of it was that virtues such as consideration and thoughtfulness were downgraded in favor of a more ruthless model. Objectivists claimed that each individual needed to be solely responsible for his or her behavior and welfare, or to paraphrase a biblical quote: "Do unto yourself." It also contends that if we are affected by the actions of others, then it is up to us to deal with it, not them.

Yet in each of the scenarios in this exercise, we're asking your man to return to a concept in which we are responsible for both ourselves and the people we come into contact with. Therefore, in an indirect way, we're not only challenging him to show consideration to others, but also asking both of you whether you think such thoughtfulness is really necessary or right. Do you think we should still live in an age where we try to help others? For instance, in scenario 4, would you have cared whether your man let Joan sink into professional oblivion? And in scenario 1, should he have gone out of his way to help the woman with the flat tire? In an objectivist world he could have said, "It's her problem, not mine." What do you think?

603.

SUPER BOWL

A RELATIONSHIP REQUIRES A LOT OF COMPROMISE AND AN ABILITY BY BOTH PARTNERS TO SEE THE OTHER'S POINT OF VIEW. THAT'S HARD ENOUGH, BUT WHEN A THIRD PARTY STICKS THEIR NOSE IN, WELL...

ASK HIM THIS: "Do you like attending big sporting events? You've been given a ticket to the Super Bowl by a friend at the last minute, but there's no one to look after the kids because your wife has arranged to see a sick friend on the same day. It's caused quite a conflict, made worse when she tells you about a conversation she's just had long-distance with her mother. I'm going to read what your wife says to you. Feel free to make comments as I go along."

"I've just been talking to Mom, and I can't believe her. I'm stunned. She said I was being selfish about you having to stay with the kids instead of going to the Super Bowl."

"She said you'd only get this opportunity once in a lifetime. But I'd promised Jenny. I planned this two weeks ago."

"Mom kept saying how important the game is, as if I didn't know. But Jenny's dying of cancer. How important is that?"

"So Mom says why don't I put it off for a day. She's so impractical. I've got to work the next day."

"Well, you know what she comes back with? Why don't I take compassionate leave?"

"But I can't get compassionate leave for a sick friend and I've got important meetings on Monday and Tuesday."

"But she wouldn't let up. She kept going on about how disappointed you'd be. But Jenny needs me. She's my oldest friend. I'd never forgive myself if she died before I saw her."

"But Mom just doesn't listen. She says why not go the day before the game? Well, Jenny's got other people there that day. She wanted me to herself on Sunday."

"And anyway, it's not like you'll miss the game. You can still watch it on TV. She said it wasn't the same. But I said that you could always create your own atmosphere, invite the guys over, that sort of thing, like you always do."

"And she said: 'Exactly. Like he always does. He'll never get another chance to actually be there.'"

"But Jenny needs me. Well, you know what Mom said? That I was putting friends before family. Then she accused me of not understanding your needs, and that after all the sacrifices you've made, I was being selfish as usual. That's when I hung up on her. I just can't believe her. What do you think?"
You say…

• How did hearing this conversation make you feel?

• What do you think about the mother's point of view?

What Did He Tell You?

So how loyal is he? How understanding? And unlike her Mom, is he actually listening to the wife? This is an exercise designed to test his ability to empathize with you and understand you, despite the fact that he'll be losing out. It may also prompt an interesting discussion about mothers-in-law.

His loyalty will be revealed either by his final comment or by what he says and how he says it during the exercise.* Is he soothing, sympathetic, and supportive of you? Does he take the opportunity to side with your mom in order to get his way? Or did he think the wife in the scenario had an ulterior motive for not wanting him to go to the Super Bowl—for instance, did he think that this whole story was more of a control issue? It's an interesting conflict and could demonstrate to both of you just how compromising and creative you can be.

Have you had similar situations in which your loyalty has been tested by mutual friends or family? How often have you gone to a mutual friend to help resolve an impasse? Men are often reluctant to share marital problems with their friends as it can be seen as a sign of failure. Under what circumstances would he seek advice from a male friend, and who would that friend be? What about a female friend? Would that make any difference? Would he go to a relative?

---

* One way of telling who he agrees with in this discussion is to be aware of when he says "Uh huh." Research shows that men use "uh huh" when they agree with someone, while women tend to say it in order to encourage a person to continue, even though they may not agree with what's being said. This can lead to misunderstandings in male-female discourse. Because the man thinks the woman has been agreeing with him all along, he's surprised when she's then critical of what he's been saying, and he feels betrayed. Women, on the other hand, feel that men aren't interested because unless the men agree with them, they say nothing.

604.

SPEECH NIGHT

WOMEN ARE OFTEN SURPRISED AT HOW MEN DEAL
WITH TRAUMATIC SITUATIONS. THIS EXERCISE MIGHT
SHED SOME LIGHT ON WHY MEN HANDLE TRAUMA THE
WAY THEY DO.

ASK HIM THIS: "How do you handle difficult situations? I'm going to read you a scenario and at different points I'll stop and either ask you questions about it or ask you to complete a statement."

Roger's wife, Tania, is out of town visiting her parents, so he must attend his 12-year-old daughter's speech night on his own. His daughter, Abby, has made the finals of a regional speech contest and she is very excited.

Roger is driving to the school (Abby is already there) when his father-in-law calls on his cell phone and tells him that Tania has been involved in a car crash, and that she died at the scene only an hour before.

- If you were Roger, would you still go to the speech night?

Roger decides he will go to the school. On his way he calls his parents and his brother and gives them the bad news.

As a result of the calls, he is late. The contest is about to start, but he can't simply hide away at the back of the auditorium. Abby has reserved a seat for him near the front so when he sits down, he can't fail to notice her sitting with the other contestants on the stage. She sees him and waves.

- What would Roger be thinking at this moment?

Finally, it's Abby's turn to give her speech. The topic for the night is: "The Most Special Thing I've Ever Done." As she begins her speech, it slowly dawns on Roger that she is going to describe how she played the flute at her parents' wedding.

She says, "Mom and Dad had lived together for ten years before they finally decided to get married, which was great for me. I mean, how many children get to be at their own parents' wedding? Even better, I got to play a part in it."

Up until now Roger's been okay, but as she begins giving details of the day, he starts to crumble. It's made worse by the fact that not only is her delivery excellent, but also that she continually looks to him for approval.

Even when she's sitting back on stage with the other contestants, she keeps her eyes on him and gives him a puzzled look. There's a break in proceedings while all the marks are being tallied, so she steps off the stage and comes down to Roger. The first thing she asks is: "What's wrong?"

- Roger says…

Then the big moment arrives and the results of the contest are announced. Not surprisingly, given her performance, Abby wins. It's only then that Roger remembers that he's promised to take her and her three best friends to dinner at a swanky restaurant that night if she were to win. Her friends are already racing up to celebrate and hit the town.

• At this point Roger…

WHAT DID HE TELL YOU?

Don't be surprised if your man would go right through the entire evening without telling his daughter the terrible news. This is possibly what many men would do.

Men's and women's brains are structured differently. The male brain takes a different route in absorbing data. The emotional response often comes much later. That's why your man could probably do what Roger did in *Speech Night*. He'll just be trying to keep things on an even keel. Why? Genetically and historically, men have been wired to stay calmer in stressful situations because their roles were to be protectors.

This cool response to trauma doesn't mean that men don't still "feel" it. But they would put such considerations on hold until any perceived danger was averted. Many men would do what Roger did, probably in an effort to delay breaking the news to the daughter until he could both digest the information for himself and control the setting, i.e., at home and away from other people.

He may also reason that his daughter should not be denied this moment of triumph and joy when the next months are going to be full of sadness and misery for her.

605.

LIFE, DEATH, AND RECYCLING

FOR SOME MEN, THIS EXERCISE MAY BE LIKE REVISITING
THEIR WORST NIGHTMARE. BUT IT'S LOTS OF FUN, AND IT
WILL ALSO SHOW HOW MUCH HE KNOWS ABOUT LIFE AND
DEATH AND RECYCLING. YOU COULD MAKE UP YOUR OWN
SCENARIOS TO FIND OUT WHAT HE KNOWS ABOUT OTHER
TOPICS THAT INTEREST YOU.

ASK HIM THIS: "How good are you at tricky questions? I'm going
to read you a scenario, and I want you to complete the unfinished
statements as quickly as possible."

It's Sunday morning and you've just woken up. Your five-year-
old daughter, Lucy, comes into the bedroom and sits next to
you. She wants to talk more about her pet mouse that died the
day before.

She asks: "Daddy, why do things have to die?"
    You say…

She asks: "Why?"
    You say…

She asks: "Why?"
    You say…

She asks: "Why?"
    You say…

(Keep going for as long as he can cope. Then try him with the following question.)

"Now I want you to try another scenario with Lucy. This time see how long you can keep going."

You've come down into the kitchen and notice that Lucy has put a banana skin into the nonorganic recycling bin. You ask her to take it out and put it in the compost bin. As she's doing this, she looks up and asks: "Daddy, why do we have to recycle things?"

        You say…

She asks: "Why?"
    You say…

She asks: "Why?"
    You say…

(Continue this for as long as you can.)

WHAT DID HE TELL YOU?

How did he hold up? How did he talk to Lucy? Did he talk down to her, or talk over her head, or was he dismissive? What was his patience level? What did he actually know about life and death, and recycling? More important, did he put a negative or a positive spin on his answers? He could legitimately be quite cynical about these topics, but if he's considerate and able to empathize, he'll have taken account of the child's age and tried not to be pessimistic.

No matter how clever someone is, there's always going to be another "why" at the end of it. Some men find this challenges their knowledge and reasoning ability and continue to provide answers when most of us would have given up. Others see the problem and look for a distracting technique that will get them out of looking stupid.

In this situation the child simply wants attention and is usually not interested in the correct answer. Women often understand this dynamic better than men and use the situation as a way of engaging with the child rather than trying to be right. So did he make it fun and play, or did he answer as if he'd been put on the spot and required to come up with a definitive answer? Did he come up with terms such as "maybe" or "could be" that show he's not rigid in his thinking and open to other possibilities. Did he engage by throwing the question back and encouraging the child to think for herself?

Did he enjoy the challenge of the second situation? This exercise is also a wonderful opportunity for him to show what he knows and how well he's able to think logically. It might also reveal whether he knows how to end this form of one-track questioning. For instance, did he try to turn the questioning around on Lucy so that she ended up being the target? Or did he try that other old trick of simply talking and talking until Lucy (and you) got tired of it?

606.

A FRIEND IN NEED

GIVING ADVICE CAN BE VERY TRICKY, AND STAYING
OBJECTIVE IS THE KEY. *A FRIEND IN NEED* MAY GIVE YOU
SOME CLUES AS TO YOUR MAN'S OPINIONS AND EXPERIENCE,
AND WHETHER DESPITE THIS, HE CAN STILL IMPART USEFUL
SUGGESTIONS AND KEEP HIS OWN AGENDA OUT OF THE
EQUATION.

ASK HIM THIS: "Do your friends often come to you for advice? I'm
going to read you a series of situations, and I want you to tell me three
things you would need to know about each of them before giving
advice."

- Your best friend is considering moving to a better
  neighborhood and a bigger house and wants your advice.
  What three things would you need to know before you
  advise him?

- Your best friend works for an advertising agency and is
  considering going out on his own. He wants your advice.
  What three things would you need to know before you
  advise him?

- A friend is considering leaving her apartment and moving in with her boyfriend and his parents, and she wants your advice. What three things would you need to know before you advise her?

- Your best female friend is considering leaving her partner because she suspects that he's just not that into her. She asks you for your advice. What three things would you need to know before you advise her?

- Your best friend is being hit on by a very attractive woman at his work. He's very tempted to have an affair and wants to know what you think. What three things would you need to know before you advise him?

- Your best friend comes to you for advice. He tells you his wife is having an affair, but she says it's just a fling and that she needs to get it out of her system. Before you would advise him, what three things would you need to know?

What Did He Tell You?

Did he rush in with his own advice before considering what he needed to know in order to give that advice? Was he sympathetic or judgmental? Did he try to work through the problems logically, or did he have a knee-jerk reaction to them? Was he thinking about the best interests of his friends, or was he projecting his own interests colored by his past?

Objectivity can be elusive. When it comes to giving advice on houses or careers, we're usually able to remain neutral and thus helpful, because we've nothing to lose or gain. But when it comes to more personal situations such as separation or infidelity, our own agendas have a way of muscling in whether we know it or not. For instance, if two of our best friends are considering breaking up, there is a temptation for us to talk them out of it purely based on the fact that it's going to affect our world. We may enjoy socializing with them on a regular basis and have even taken annual vacations together. Not only would their splitting up affect this social life but it could also undermine our own sense of relationship security.

Similarly, when giving advice on an affair, we can be tempted to put ourselves into the same situation. So we give advice based on how we would feel, forgetting that our friend may have completely different needs. That's why being able to ask the three or so questions before giving advice is so helpful in this exercise. It's an artificial way of removing oneself from the situation, and for laying the target of advice squarely on the friend, and not on our own agendas.

607.

ON THE ROCKS

THERE'S A THEORY THAT MEN PUT MORE STOCK IN THEIR CAREERS THAN IN THEIR RELATIONSHIPS. BUT DOES THIS MEAN THAT THEY DON'T HAVE A CLUE ABOUT RELATIONSHIPS AT ALL? *ON THE ROCKS* SHOULD GIVE YOU A FEW ANSWERS.

ASK HIM THIS: "How are you at predicting what people will say? I'm going to give you a scenario, and I want you to help me by completing the unfinished lines as quickly as possible."

Ruth and Gavin's marriage seems to be breaking down. For instance, when he comes home from work one day, she says...

Then Gavin says...

Ruth tries to...

But Gavin ...

So she reacts by...

The problem for Gavin is that Ruth ...

Ruth, on the other hand, feels that...

Her friends tell her...

Gavin's friends tell him...

Ruth is always saying to Gavin that...

And he is always saying to her that ...

You'd have to say that the fault lies with...

This is because ...

The situation for Gavin and Ruth could be resolved...

WHAT DID HE TELL YOU?

Does he have a handle on the dynamics within a relationship?* More importantly, how are his opinions shaped by his own experiences? And can you see any parallels within your own relationship with him? Last, how does he see conflict within a marriage? Does he see strife as normal, and what type of help has he used in the past to handle a relationship crisis?

* On The Rocks will give your man an opportunity to be flippant and therefore sabotage a serious conversation. But don't assume that this indicates he's not even vaguely interested in the subject. While we stress that there are no right or wrong responses in these scenarios, he may not look on it like this. He may still feel defensive. So if he does, don't sweat it. Enjoy his humor and leave it for another time.

608.

THE FLIP SIDE

THE FLIP SIDE IS AN EXERCISE DESIGNED TO SEE HOW YOUR MAN THINKS THROUGH PARTICULAR SITUATIONS, AND IT TESTS HIS ABILITY TO SEE THE BIG PICTURE. THIS IS A CLASSIC CONVERSATION STARTER BECAUSE IT WILL BRING UP ETHICAL AND MORAL ISSUES.

ASK HIM THIS: "Have you ever lost an important phone number? I'm going to read you a scenario, and I want you to complete the unfinished statements as quickly as possible."

While at a party you meet a very beautiful woman whom you are immediately attracted to. The attraction is mutual and you talk together at some length. But she has to leave to attend another engagement, so she writes her phone number on the back of your business card.

Later on that evening, you meet a man called Andrew who you think could use your business expertise, and so you swap cards. It's only the next day that you realize you've given him the card with the woman's number on the back. So you call Andrew and explain your problem. You tell him that the woman is gorgeous, and that you want to meet her again.

Andrew is very cooperative and finds your card. After reading out the number on the back there is a pause, and then he asks you:

"There were several gorgeous women there last night. I wonder if I met her? Tell me what she looked like and I'll see if I can remember her."
 You say...

He asks: "What was she wearing?"
 You say...

He says: "God, she sounds wonderful. What did you talk about?"
 You say...

He asks: "So, you think you're in with a chance, do you?"
 You say...

He says: "Well, I thought you and I were going to do some business together, but it seems like you're going to be a bit distracted. Maybe I will be too. You see, the number I've just given you belongs to my girlfriend." Then he hangs up.

• What do you do?

• If you were Andrew, what would you do?

What Did He Tell You?

Does he defer to the other man, or does he treat it as if it's one of those "all's fair in love and war" situations? To help you get as clear a picture of your man's motives as possible, you may need him to elaborate on his course of action. For instance, does he consider the boyfriend's feelings? Does he question the morals of the woman? Would he contact the woman to warn her?

Other questions to consider are, how close to your looks was his description of the woman? And what about the conversation topic? Do you have conversations with your man on this topic?

If you were the woman, what would you want the man you'd met at the party to do? And what would you say if your boyfriend confronted you about this other man?

609.

STALEMATE

WE ALL ADMIRE HONESTY, BUT IT CAN BE HARD TO TAKE.
HOW MUCH ROOM IS THERE FOR A LITTLE TENDERNESS?

ASK HIM THIS: "Can you speak your mind? I'm going to read you a story line, and I want you to complete the unfinished statements as quickly as you can."

Imagine you've been going out with a woman and you have had grave doubts about her. The sex is great but you're finding her too high maintenance. After talking about her with your best friend, Daniel, you decide that the fairest thing to do is break up with her. But when you next meet her, she rushes straight in with a needy question.

She says: "I've missed you so much! Have you missed me?"
    You say…

(As soon as he dumps her the exercise is completed. If he avoids the truth, carry on.)

She says: "What do you most like about me?"
    You say …

She says: "If you could think of one word to describe me, what would that be?"
You say …

She says: "If we could go on vacation together, and money was no object, where would you want to go?"
You say …

She says: "Do you think I'm beautiful?"
You say …

She says: "In what way am I beautiful?"
You say …

She says: "When we first met, you said that I made you hot with desire. Did you mean it?"
You say …

She says: "How do you feel now?"
You say …

She says: "I just love you. You're so wonderful to be with."
You say …

She says: "You still love me. I know you do. What do you love most about me?"
You say …

She says: "So it's not true what Daniel said—that you want to break up with me?"
You say …

She says: "So why would he say that to me?"
You say …

What Did He Tell You?

Whether he's evasive or truthful is not the point in this exercise. Breaking up with someone is an extremely stressful situation for both parties. Therefore, what you should be looking for is how tactful he can be, how gentle, and how much he's able to leave the woman intact.

But this doesn't necessarily mean he should delay telling her of his decision. It could be argued that ultimately the best way to break up with someone is to do it fast and clean, because no matter how much you try to sugarcoat the moment, the person being dumped is still going to suffer the pain of rejection. But again, even this method can be handled gently.

What about you?* Did you imagine yourself as the woman? How did you feel about the way he responded?

* This scenario brings up some other issues. For instance, what's your definition of "high maintenance"? Do you think that it's only a term used by men who take their partners for granted and thus feel constantly like they have to prove their love? Or do you think some people really are so insecure that their need for affirmation can be stifling? What are your expectations within a relationship? How often do you need overt gestures of love? Do you think this is reasonable?

You might also like to ask your man to define "dumping." Does this mean no future contact, or "let's just be friends"? In your experience, which one of these works better? Has he ever been dumped? And if so, how was it done? Was it similar to the way he dealt with the woman in the scenario? What has he learned from being dumped or dumping someone himself? How would he behave differently in the future?

610.

THAT FOUR-LETTER WORD

We've found that results from this exercise vary wildly, depending on what stage your relationship is in, but *That Four-Letter Word* is always lots of fun. On the other hand, the discussion afterward can be uncomfortable, so go easy on him.

Ask Him This: "What are you like at repetition? This is possibly the easiest exercise in the book."

I want you to say "I love you" fifty times, starting now.

What Did He Tell You?

Was he comfortable with the word *love*? How was his delivery? Was it monotone or expressive? Did he enter into the spirit of the exercise? Did he look straight at you when he said it? What were his eyes telling you?

If he was very deliberately saying the phrase the exact number of times, and even counting down with his fingers, then he may be more literal. But be careful not to jump to conclusions. He may be treating the countdown as a way to build intensity. Therefore, you should note his last "I love you." It may say more than you think.

What about the pace of his delivery? Was it fast, slow, or measured? Where did he place the emphasis? Did he say *I* love you, I *love* you, or I love *you*? Don't read too much into this, however, because in all likelihood he's simply copied the way you said it.

Just a note—some guys may actually resist participating in this exercise because it's making or exposing a commitment. He may feel that you'll take his "I love you" seriously. If he asks whether you'll take the phrase personally, it shows he doesn't treat emotional expressions lightly, and he should be respected for this. On the other hand, do you feel that having him say it fifty times is trivializing the whole thing?

Remember, for many guys saying "I love you" is an admission of dependence. It's comparable to saying he needs you and that's quite possibly not the independent impression he wants to leave.

One school of thought also holds that men put more store in action than words. If you want to know whether a man cares about you, you need to determine whether what he gives you is what he loves. For example, if he loves his car, does he let you drive it? If he treasures his family, does he truly include you in this family circle? Apart from gifts, he may feel more comfortable expressing his feelings by doing things for you, hugging you, or simply spending time with you.

Could it be that the main reason some men find it difficult to say "I love you" is because they're not sure whether their idea of love is the same as a woman's? Or do they know exactly what the woman is asking, but don't want to be cornered into an admission that they might regret? And while you're at it, why not ask your man whether he thinks it's more important for the woman to be in love with the man or the man to be in love with the woman.

611.

THE ROMANCE WRITER

BECAUSE THIS EXERCISE IS SET IN A ROMANCE WRITERS' CONFERENCE, IT MAY PROMPT YOUR MAN TO LOOK AT LOVE IN PURELY STORYBOOK TERMS. BUT ONCE *THE ROMANCE WRITER* GETS INTO FULL SWING, IT SHOULD REVEAL WHAT OPINIONS HE ACTUALLY HAS ABOUT GENUINE LOVE AND THE DYNAMICS WITHIN A RELATIONSHIP.

ASK HIM THIS: "Have you ever participated in a public question-and-answer session? I'm going to read you a scenario, and I want you to answer any questions when they come up during the story."

You are one of the country's leading experts on the psychology of love, and you have been invited to a romance writers' symposium as the guest of honor. Your main task during the symposium is to take part in a question-and-answer session.

The first question you have to field is from an attractive woman near the front of the auditorium who stands up and asks: "Could you explain what true love is?"

Then another writer asks: "How do you know you're really in love? What are the symptoms?"

A young woman asks: "If I were to write about a male character, how would his idea of true love differ from a woman's?"

From the back of the auditorium comes a question from a man: "What do you think motivates us to try to find love?"

One of the more well-known writers then stands up and says to you: "You've been quoted in the past as saying that romantic fiction offers the public false hope of finding a lasting relationship. Could you explain your comments?"

Another famous writer then asks you: "What would you say to people who think that love is just a distraction from the ultimate goal of trying to accept and live with our own strengths and weaknesses?"

Then a younger man asks: "Could you explain why some women find the bad boy image so attractive?"

Next comes a question from a quietly spoken middle-aged woman, who asks: "How does a healthy sex life really help a relationship to develop positively?"

The same woman then asks: "How *would* you define a healthy sex life?"

Another middle-aged woman then asks: "Critics of romantic fiction argue that we mostly highlight the first flush of love. If we had to write sequels to our books, what would these lovers need to feed their relationships with in order to truly live 'happily ever after'?"

A rather cynical man then stands up and asks: "We all know that you represent science. So I guess you would dismiss the whole concept of 'soul mates.' Or would you?"

Finally, the emcee intervenes and puts forward a question: "I'm sure everyone here today would like to know about some personal experiences of your own regarding romance. Could you tell us about your first love, and your last?"

What Did He Tell You?

How much does he know about love? How does he feel about love? How well can he express his feelings? Have you ever heard him talk about love like this before? Have you ever asked him?

If he is less than articulate, this shouldn't necessarily count against him. After all, how often is a man ever asked to explain true love or the concept of soul mates? Remember, the whole point of this exercise is to gain insight, not to show him up as a tongue-tied idiot. So you might learn more if you repeat the questions he had difficulty with.

Many of the scenarios in this book work best when you can get your man to answer off the top of his head, but on this occasion time for him to think through the issues may prove more valuable for both of you.

If he has been able to express himself reasonably well, he's either thought a lot about the topics, or he's very fast on his feet. Either way, it should help you to know where you stand with him. Is he a romantic, or is he a realist? If he's a romantic, does this sit comfortably with you? And if he is a realist, how much room is there for the romance that you might want?

THE MEDICINE MAN

THE MEDICINE MAN SHOULD GIVE YOU SOME VALUABLE
INSIGHTS INTO HOW HE APPROACHES DIFFICULT
PREDICAMENTS AND WHY HE'D WANT TO SAVE YOU.

ASK HIM THIS: "Do you like quests? I'm going to put you in a scenario about climbing a mountain. You're going to come across a series of challenges, and I'm going to ask you to tell me how you'd overcome them. There are no right answers."

The woman you love more than anyone else in the world has contracted a disease that is almost always fatal, and she has only a short time left to live. A doctor tells you that he knows of a medicine man who has a secret formulation that can cure this particular ailment. The only problem is that the medicine man lives at the top of a mountain and can only be reached by climbing a narrow trail that is well guarded.

You decide to try to reach him, even though you are not allowed to take any weapons or any other equipment with you. You may take no food or drink, and you can only wear ordinary clothes and shoes. You have no magical powers.

The first obstacle you come to as you walk up the steep, rocky trail is a six-foot-high picket fence. There is no gate in it.

- What do you do?

Next you come to a smooth sheet of ice that slopes across the trail at a forty-five-degree angle. It is three yards wide and twenty yards from one end to the other. If you slip off it, you will fall over a five-hundred-foot cliff to your right and be dashed to pieces below. On your left is an equally high cliff, making it impossible to climb above the ice.

- What do you do?

A little further along the trail, you come to a narrow archway guarded by a huge chained dog. The archway is set into a sheer cliff that rises above it to the left, and another sheer cliff drops away to the right. It is impossible to proceed without going through the archway and past the dog.

- What do you do?

Next you come to a sentry box. There is a soldier sitting inside with a gun. He warns you that he will shoot you if you attempt to pass him.

- What do you do?

You go further up the trail, but it suddenly ends at a rock wall. However, standing beneath a fir tree is a beautiful woman who tells you that if you give her pleasure she will show you the secret staircase.

- What do you do?

The beautiful woman shows you the secret staircase, and you're halfway up it when you find your way blocked by a very large and venomous snake who glares at you and shows its fangs.

- What do you do?

You climb the rest of the stairs and find the medicine man sitting at the top. He tells you he will give you the medicine you need to cure your beloved if you first tell him five things about her that make her worth saving.

- What do you tell him?

The medicine man shows you a metal container that holds the secret remedy. He explains that it must be kept in the container and carried carefully back down the mountain. If it is dropped or rolled in any way, it will be ruined.

You thank him and go to take the container but find that it's so heavy you can scarcely pick it up, let alone carry it. What's more, the medicine man tells you he can't help you with it.

- What do you do?

WHAT DID HE TELL YOU?

We think it's safe to assume that deep down almost all men are on a quest to prove their worth and relevance. Even today, the experience of the heroic quest seems to be central to the male journey as evidenced by the burgeoning popularity of quest-type video games. As males we're aware, perhaps unconsciously, that women choose those of us who aspire to protect them by using our physical prowess, our financial power, our mental agility, or some special form of magic.

So it should come as no surprise that most men will do their best to get to the medicine man and back down with the secret remedy, especially if you are his beloved. There aren't many who opt to forgo the hazards of the journey in favor of returning to spend the last remaining days with their loved one. That may be a very lovely thing to do, but it's not a very male thing to do. If he gives up on a challenge, he simply won't feel good about himself.

Just how he tackled each challenge should give you an idea of how he approaches problems in real life. Was he optimistic or pessimistic? Did he approach each challenge as though he would undoubtedly find a way through, and portray a confidence in the viability of his ideas, or did he express doubts that his solutions would really work? Were his answers slow and considered or quick and light? Did he show a flexible approach by being prepared to retrace his steps if need be? How tireless was he in pursuing solutions, and were they realistic? Did he rely on his physical strength or his intellect? Was he overbearing or diplomatic? Did he make friends whose help he could call on later, or did he burn bridges?

What interpretation did he put on the word *pleasure*? Did he give her pleasure by reciting poetry, singing her a song, or having sex with her? To what extent did he consider his beloved's feelings in this regard?

Finally, and perhaps most significantly, how difficult was it for him to tell the medicine man five things about his beloved?* Did he tackle this task with more or less enthusiasm than the other challenges? Why do you think that was? Did he describe his beloved's worth in terms of her contribution to her family and society, or did he focus on her worth to him? How did his observations make you feel?

* We've been told by a friend that her neighbor tried *The Medicine Man* on her husband, but changed the number of things that made her worth saving from five to fifty! Last she heard he was up to thirty-nine and struggling, but her neighbor has a new spring in her step.

LEVEL 7

The Big Picture

Finally, in *The Big Picture* we step out into the wide, wide world and take you and your man's character for a joyride. In the process we put the spotlight on his integrity, his discernment, and his core values. We'll also be challenging both of you with some ethical dilemmas.

If you've systematically approached this book by working through all the levels, you should now have a much clearer idea of where your man has come from and what he stands for. Along the way, you'll probably have discovered much about yourself as well. In *The Big Picture,* we've provided some situations that will challenge both of you. In a sense, this level is less about revealing your man's character and more about how both of you can work through problems together. The situations in the following scenarios may be hypothetical, but they encompass broad subjects that you just might have to encounter in your lives. Maybe you already have.

Keep in mind while you're doing these scenarios that you should avoid being judgmental. There are no right or wrong answers. These are simply opportunities to learn more about each other and to enrich your lives with conversation, insight, and honesty.

701.

THE NUDE, THE DUDE, AND THE SHREWD

THIS STORY SHOULD GIVE YOU AN IDEA OF A MAN'S SENSE OF RIGHT AND WRONG. WHAT HE THINKS IS OKAY AND NOT OKAY IN THE WORLD OF WHEELING AND DEALING MAY ULTIMATELY REFLECT ON HOW HE DEALS WITH YOU.

ASK HIM THIS: "Have you ever found a real bargain? I'm going to read you a story about a young man and a porcelain vase and ask you some questions along the way."

A young man is browsing in an antique store when he comes across a small porcelain vase decorated with a hand-painted nude figurine. He thinks it will make a great gift for his girlfriend's birthday, as she collects this type of porcelain, but he knows it's likely to be out of his price range.

Still, he takes it up to the old man behind the counter and says, "There's no price on this, how much is it?"

"What?" says the old man adjusting his hearing aid. "You'll have to speak up. I'm a little hard of hearing."

"How much is this?" repeats the young man, raising his voice.

"Hmm, I'll have to ask my son," says the old man. He goes to the stairwell and calls down:

"Nathan! How much is that little blue porcelain vase with the nude on it?"

"Four hundred and seventy-five dollars!" Nathan calls back.

"What?" says the old man.

"Four hundred and seventy-five dollars!" repeats Nathan.

"It's one hundred and seventy-five dollars," the old man says.

"One hundred and seventy-five dollars," the young man says in amazement, having clearly heard what Nathan had called out.

"That's what Nathan said," says the old man.

The young man can hardly believe his luck. It's really more than he can afford, but at this price it's clearly a bargain, so he buys it.

I'm going to tell you a bit more of the story in a moment, but I just want to stop here and ask whether you think the young man was right to have bought the vase at that price.

So now the story continues. The young man is so excited with his bargain that he takes it into another antique store nearby to see if he can actually make money by selling it at a profit.

"How much will you give me for this vase?" he asks the owner.

"Let's see now, a pretty little piece, I mean the vase not the nude, but I wouldn't be able to sell it for more than a hundred dollars," he tells the young man. "So I'll give you fifty for it."

"Oh, come off it!" says the young man. "This was on sale up the road for four-hundred and seventy-five dollars, so it's clearly worth at least two hundred and twenty-five dollars."

"Oh really!" says the owner. "And at what store were they asking that price? It wouldn't by any chance be the store on the corner run by the old man and his son Nathan, would it?"

"Why yes, as a matter of fact it was," says the young man, beginning to feel uncomfortable.

"And I bet it didn't have a price on it, did it? And you took it up to the counter and asked the old man how much it was, and he adjusted his hearing aid and asked you to repeat yourself, and then he called out to Nathan who said the price was four-hundred and seventy-five. And the old man asked him to repeat it a few times, and then he told you a much lower price, and you were completely sucked in because you thought he couldn't hear. Am I right?"

The young man nods and looks at the floor.

"Well," says the owner, "if it's any consolation to you, there've been plenty of smarter and older people than you sucked in by their little ploy, and I dare say you won't be the last."

- Have you changed your opinion about whether the young man should have bought the vase at the "bargain" price?

- Do you think it's okay for the old man and his son to use this sales technique?

- What do you think the guy in the story should do with the vase now? Should he still give it to his girlfriend? Should he own up to what happened?

WHAT DID HE TELL YOU?

Does your man have a sense of right and wrong, and more important, can he justify his opinion? Is his moral position based on whether or not he will be found out, or is it based on not wanting to feel guilty later?

Or could it be that it's based on what he believes is right regardless of the consequences or his feelings? Did he evaluate the consequences of his action? For example, did he express concern that the old man was making a terrible mistake from which he and his son may suffer financially? Did he consider that the father and son could fall out over the father's mistake?

Did he question the fact that the man in the scenario had gone in to buy a gift for his girlfriend, but having gotten a bargain, was now switching his motivation toward making some money for himself? After all, if his sole concern had been to buy his girlfriend a gift, wouldn't he have just bought the vase and given it to her, rather than looking to make a profit for himself? And did he wonder what the guy would do with the vase? Would he still give it to her, knowing that it wasn't worth what he thought, and that the gift itself could feel sullied by his own dishonesty?

Here's some information to ponder. In 1958 psychologist Lawrence Kohlberg formulated his six stages of moral development. It was based in part on the theories of Jean Piaget and Erik Erickson. His theory contends that we all go through moral reasoning in six distinct stages, and that this process can take a lifetime. These stages are:

1. Obedience—actions considered either right or wrong depending on consequences. In other words, an action is only wrong if punishment follows.

2. Self-interest—an action is perceived as right if it will be of personal benefit.

3. Conformity—actions are dictated by how they will be seen by others. For instance, children might see an action as being "right" because it's what their parents would expect them to do.

4. Law and order—actions are dictated by social conventions and laws.

5. Human rights—actions are dictated by a sense of justice, even if it means breaking existing laws.

6. Universal human ethics—an action based on the perception that this action is intrinsically right, not because it is an expectation or law or convention.

Apparently, while stage six does exist technically, people very seldom if ever reach this elevated state. Kohlberg suggests that there may even be a seventh stage that links religion with moral reasoning.

So where do you think you fit on Kohlberg's ladder? Are you both at the same stage? And where does the concept of "conscience" fit in?

702.

THE WRITER AND YOUR WIFE

THIS SCENARIO REVOLVES AROUND JEALOUSY WITHIN A GROUP DYNAMIC. STAY IN TUNE WITH YOUR OWN REACTIONS BECAUSE IT MIGHT TOUCH AS MANY NERVES FOR YOU AS IT DOES FOR HIM.

ASK HIM THIS: "Have you ever been on vacation with people you don't know that well? I'm going to read you a scenario, and I want you to answer a couple of questions when I've finished."

You've met Charlie and his wife Jude at the golf club a few times and found them to be a very pleasant couple. So you're delighted when they invite you and your wife to accompany them on a five-day cruise on their sailing boat.

Charlie is a writer and takes quite a shine to your wife. They end up having long conversations about books and writing, a subject that doesn't interest you at all. Jude is very nice, but you don't have anything in common with her.

Jude is obviously put out by her husband's conversations with your wife and becomes grumpy. Later you hear them arguing in their cabin and overhear enough to learn that Charlie has had quite a few affairs since he and Jude have been married.

You suggest to your wife that it might be a good idea to cool the conversations with him, but she surprises you by being strongly opposed to any such action and says that what Charlie and Jude do is their business, and this should not affect how she behaves.

The next day your wife spends even more time talking with Charlie, and Jude finally complains openly. But he simply brushes her off and tells her to grow up.

- What are you feeling?

- What do you think of your wife's behavior?

- What sort of guy do you think Charlie is?

The next day the tension is even worse on the yacht.

- What would you do then? Why?

- What would happen if you did nothing and let the situation run its course?

WHAT DID HE TELL YOU?

Did the dynamic in this scenario threaten your man? Was he protective? Is he ever jealous? Why? Is he threatened by intellect? How much difference does he think it would have made if he and Jude had found things in common to talk about? What about you? If you were the wife and getting along famously with Charlie, do you think a conflict could arise between you and Jude? If the situation were reversed—if your man was getting along famously with Jude, and you had nothing in common with Charlie—would you feel threatened or jealous?

The Writer and Your Wife brings up issues about consideration, loyalty, security, and understanding. This scenario might seem familiar to you both, and it can be a good pointer as to how safe you feel in your relationship. If you know each other very well and feel secure, then you'll both probably not perceive any problem. Your only concern would be the conflict between Charlie and Jude. They're the couple with the real problem, after all. Which raises another question. How do either of you react when witnessing another couple having a conflict? Under what circumstances would you ignore it or try to intervene?

If your man felt that his wife in the story was being inconsiderate, and that he had every reason to feel threatened, then what did he think he could have done about it at the time? What about later? Would he talk to her about it, and what would he say? If he didn't reach a satisfactory resolution, would he discuss it with someone else? Who would that person be?

What sources of help has he used in the past when a relationship (business, family, romantic) was looking unstable? Did he make efforts to restore its equilibrium, or did he leave it to the other party? If he's resorted to outside help, whether in the form of friends, family, books, or counseling, then it's a sign that he's prepared to be proactive and put time and effort into becoming a better person and building a successful relationship. If he hasn't, then maybe the discussions that follow these scenarios will enable him to become more aware of the emotional baggage that is brought into a relationship.

703.

JASPER AND THE NANNY

IN THIS EXERCISE, HE HAS THE OPPORTUNITY TO CONVINCE
A PROSPECTIVE NANNY THAT HIS NEPHEW IS AN ANGELIC
CHILD. MAKE THIS FUN BY PUTTING ON YOUR BEST SCHOOL
NURSE VOICE.

ASK HIM THIS: "Have you done much babysitting? I'm going to read you a scenario, and I want you to complete the unfinished statements or answer any questions as quickly as possible."

You're babysitting your four-year-old nephew, Jasper, at his home. Your sister has had a crisis at her work and had to take off suddenly, so you're left in charge.

There is a problem, however. Your sister was expecting to have a visit from a prospective nanny, Mrs. Rogers, whom she wants to hire. But she's been unable to get ahold of her. So, when the nanny turns up, you're supposed to postpone the interview until a more convenient time.

But the nanny says, "Well, I'm here now. So I might as well at least meet the little fellow."

Now, Jasper is a piece of work, and you know you'll have a job trying to convince the nanny that he's an adorable little boy. But you don't have any choice. So you call Jasper into the living room.

Jasper comes screaming in and jumps onto one of the chairs.

"My, what an energetic little boy he is," says the nanny, and you say…

Then she asks: "Is he always like this?" You say...

"And what are his interests, do you know?" she asks.

Then you ask Jasper to come over and say hello to Mrs. Rogers, the nanny. But Jasper just pokes his tongue out.

Mrs. Rogers says, "Isn't that just like a boy?" And you say...

Then Jasper gives you the bird and Mrs. Rogers gasps, "Goodness, that's not very nice. Or was he pointing at something?" You say...

Thankfully, Jasper settles down momentarily and even sits on her lap when invited. But you should have guessed this idyllic scene wouldn't last long. Pretty soon he begins to grab at the nanny's clothes and tries to look down her blouse.

"He's quite forward, isn't he? What do you think he's trying to do?" You say...

Then she asks: "How's his speech? I haven't heard him talk yet."

Jasper takes this opportunity to let fly with a string of obscenities. You say...

Then Mrs. Rogers says: "Your sister tells me that young Jasper here is very bright. She says he's well above average." However, just before you can add your own observations, you notice that Jasper, having jumped off her lap, is now leaning over a small lamp stand trying to fit the light bulb into his mouth. You say...

The nanny is clearly not impressed and prepares to leave. So you try to stall her by asking what else your sister has said about Jasper. She says: "Well, she did say that he is very gentle and very fond of animals." Remembering how he once killed a pet rabbit by placing it under a cushion and then sitting on it, you say...

"And isn't he supposed to be very artistic? What sort of things does he like to do?" asks Mrs. Rogers. The vision of Jasper smearing doo doo all over his bedroom walls comes to mind, and you say...

"And what about food?" she asks. "Is he a fussy eater? Personally," says Mrs. Rogers, "I think children should eat only the most natural of foods." You say...

"And what about his sleeping patterns? Does he still have an afternoon nap? Or is he go, go, go? I must say, I like a little boy with energy. Sleeping in the afternoon creates bad habits. Too much time for little hands to explore under the sheets. Don't you think?" You say...

"And is he properly toilet trained?" Noticing that Jasper has escaped outside and is now peeing on the nanny's car parked in the driveway, you say...

"You've described Jasper in such loving terms, and I commend you for that. But if you had to target one problem area that he has, what would that be?" You say...

Mrs. Rogers then says: "It's such a shame your sister couldn't be here. Tell me about her. What's she like as a mother? What's her parenting style like?" You say...

"It's just that when I talked to her she sounded...how can I put this? She sounded somewhat desperate. You wouldn't be trying to pull the wool over my eyes, would you? Is there something about Jasper you haven't told me?" You say...

Mrs. Rogers then sits back in her chair, smiles at you sweetly, and asks: "So, what would you like to know about me?" To which you say...

"Is there anything else you'd like to know?" (Keep asking this until he runs out of questions.)

Later that day when your sister returns home, you tell her that the nanny did turn up and wanted to meet Jasper.

"So how did it go?" asks your sister. "What did you think of her?" You say...

WHAT DID HE TELL YOU?

How convincing was he? How diplomatic was he? How probing was he when he had the chance to ask the nanny questions? How quickly and easily was he able to smooth over a situation or cover his tracks? How hard did he go to bat for his sister?

On the surface, this scenario might seem to be exposing his ability to lie.* But on a deeper level, it's more about loyalty, responsibility, and judgment. The sister really wants to employ this nanny, and while your man wasn't supposed to be involved, he's become implicated by circumstance. So how in control of the interview he was will give you a good idea of how confidently he can conduct himself in trying situations.

What he thought of the nanny should be revealed by how he answers his sister's questions at the end. What if Mrs. Rogers was a sly old bird who was trying to bluff him and get to the truth by appearing to be either slightly naive or puritanical? Did he suggest this as a possibility, or did he write her off because he thought she was those things? If he did think she could have been bluffing, then he is either very perceptive or possibly paranoid.

This scenario raises one more important question—how much does he actually know about child rearing? Did he think Jasper was just plain naughty, or did he figure there was a link between Jasper's behavior and his sister's parenting style? If so, did he discuss her style in a rational manner or instead take the opportunity to dump on her personality? If he did, this may suggest he has issues with the way women are with boys. If he didn't think his sister was to blame for Jasper's behavior, did he ask Mrs. Rogers how she planned to handle it? Did he take the opportunity to ask her to justify some of her opinions? Did he ask anything about her background, and if so, how perceptive did he show himself to be? His line of questioning here might reveal his own attitudes to parenting and his attitudes to children in general.

* You might like to consider whether his responses to the nanny's questions constituted outright lies or whether they should be defined as acts of diplomacy. Where do you draw the line between diplomacy and dishonesty?

704.

THE DOG, THE POOL, AND THE WHISTLE

THIS IS ANOTHER SCENARIO DESIGNED TO GAUGE HOW HE HANDLES A DICEY SITUATION. THERE'S QUITE A LOT OF INFORMATION IN THE FIRST PART OF THE EXERCISE, SO SPEAK CLEARLY, AND BE PREPARED TO GO OVER IT AGAIN IF YOU FEEL HE HASN'T TAKEN IT ALL IN.

ASK HIM THIS: "What are you like as a salesman? I'm going to pretend to be someone coming to buy your house, and I want you to answer my questions."

First, I'm going to give you some background information. You've had your house on the market for more than ten months, and finally it looks as though you have a buyer. There is a problem with the house that is pretty obvious, but because you're desperate to sell you've made an attempt to cover it up. The bank beside the swimming pool has slumped, leaving a large crack in the lawn that threatens the stability of the pool itself. It will cost thousands in concrete reinforcing to fix, and you haven't risked filling the pool for months. You've filled some of the crack in with soil and planted shrubs, and on the worst part you've put a child's paddling pool over the top to hide it.

Your neighbor's dog is another reason why you want to sell. It barks incessantly and gets through the hedge and digs up your garden. The neighbor himself is a nosy know-it-all who doesn't work and who whistles tunelessly all day long. Thankfully, on this day the neighbor is out and his dog is with him. The buyer arrives for a third visit, and after showing her through the house you end up talking to her in the garden. Here are her questions.

"What a lovely garden. It's so peaceful, isn't it?"
    You say...

"And the pool. It must look beautiful when it's filled."
    You say...

"And tell me again why it is that you don't have it filled?"
    You say...

"But I see you have this child's paddling pool filled up here. Why is that?"
    You say...

"These seem to be new shrubs here that go across the lawn in a kind of line. Why did you plant them like that?"
    You say...

"Over here by your neighbor's hedge there are these depressions like some animal has been digging. Do you have a dog?"
    You say...

"Does your neighbor have a dog?"
    You say...

"So tell me about your neighbor."
    You say...

"Well, I really like the pool, but it may surprise you to know that if I buy the place I plan to get rid of it, reinforce this whole

area, and build a large conservatory for my palm collection. What do you think of that idea?"
　　You say…

"I'd like to take just one more look inside before I leave, but what's that whistling sound I can hear now?"
　　You say…

WHAT DID HE TELL YOU?

If you hadn't known the truth, would he have convinced you with his explanations? Did he actually lie, or did he tell the truth? If he lied, was he really uncomfortable stringing you along? What was his reaction to your telling him that you planned to get rid of the pool? Did he feel relieved and blurt out the truth, or did he play it cool?

How did you feel about his lying? Did it make you feel uncomfortable, or were you proud of his ability to think on his feet?

Remember, you didn't tell him to lie in the instructions. So if he did, he may have misread the situation and thought that his salesmanship was being tested, nothing else. The word *salesman* might also have a negative connotation for him, which he may automatically define as lying.

Maybe you could ask him that if he did feel bad about lying, why didn't he simply tell the truth? And how would it make him feel later on, knowing that he may have sold a house to someone who'd inherit all his problems?

Finally, a question for both of you: Is it okay to lie in certain situations, such as dealing with the tax department, a realtor, or a used car dealer, based on the opinion that deception is almost expected and is part of the game?

AN AFFAIR OF TWO HALVES

F OR MANY COUPLES, PARTICIPATING IN THIS SCENARIO IS A VERY UNCOMFORTABLE EXPERIENCE. IT BRINGS UP PAST HURT AND POSSIBLY EVEN CURRENT FEARS AND INSECURITIES. F OR INSTANCE, SOME WOMEN HAVE REPORTED THAT IN ATTEMPTING TO EXPLAIN A CHOICE, THEIR MEN HAVE INADVERTENTLY GIVEN EXAMPLES FROM THEIR PAST, AND THIS HAS LED TO AN ADMISSION OF AN AFFAIR THEY'VE HAD WHILE IN A PREVIOUS RELATIONSHIP, OR EVEN WHILE IN THEIR CURRENT ONE. S O TREAD CAREFULLY. G IVE HIM TIME TO ANSWER EACH QUESTION, AND ASK HIM WHY HE'S MADE HIS CHOICES. T RY THIS SCENARIO OUT YOURSELF TOO.

ASK HIM THIS: "If your wife was having an affair, what would you most want to know? You've hired a private detective to find out if your wife's having an affair, and you've agreed on a fee. But when the detective reports back and confirms your worst fears, you're strapped for cash and can only give him half the money. So he says he'll only give you half the information that he's gathered. He's been very thorough, and tells you that he's even surreptitiously gleaned facts from one of your wife's friends. He then gives you a series of choices.

I'm going to read you these choices and you have to decide which piece of information you'd rather hear and why."

- He says: "Do you want to know how old your wife's lover is, or what he does?"

- "Do you want to know if the lover is married, or if is he physically stronger than you?"

- "Would you rather know what sort of suburb or district he lives in, or what sort of car he drives?"

- "Would you rather know his address, or his telephone number?"

- "Would you rather know if she's in love with him, or if he's in love with her?"

- "Would you rather know what nationality the lover is, or what political persuasion he is?"

- "Would you rather know how long the affair has been going on, or why it started in the first place?"

- "Do you want to know whether they practice safe sex, or whether they do stuff that she doesn't do with you?"

- "Do you want to know where they meet, or how often they meet?"

- "Do you want to know whether the relationship is based on sex or intellect, or whether she's really happy?"

- "Do you want to know whether he's well endowed physically, or whether he's a better lover than you?"

- "Would you rather know who else knows about the affair, or whether the affair is simply a fling?"

- "Do you want to know whether she's ever brought him back to your place, or whether she's been out with him publicly?"

- "Do you want to know whether they share special rituals together, or if he has introduced her to his family and friends?"

- "Would you rather know what her best friend has advised her to do, or find out if she's ever had other affairs?"

- "Which would you rather know: what he says to her that makes her cry, or what he says that makes her laugh?"

- "Would you rather know what he's giving her that you aren't, or what she's giving him that she doesn't give to you?"

Having received all this information, your next course of action would be to…

And then you would…

WHAT DID HE TELL YOU?

What was most important to him—keeping his self-esteem intact, or trying to find out what had happened in the relationship to make room for an affair in the first place? Was he more interested in laying blame, or seeking information for more understanding and possibly stopping the affair from going any further? If the roles had been reversed, would you have made the same choices as your man?

An Affair of Two Halves* will tell you what's more important to him—the relationship or what it makes him look like. It will also tell you what he thinks he might lack, or what he could do to improve the relationship. You in turn will find out how much an affair would hurt him, and therefore be able to define your responsibility toward him and your relationship. By sharing how you would have answered the questions, you'll also be able to let him know how an affair would affect you.

While this exercise would appear to be asking him to list his priorities, there are actually some other factors that should be of equal if not more importance. For instance, what's the main theme of his curiosity—is he mostly concerned about what effect the affair will have on him, on the wife, or on their future together? Does he demonstrate any empathy or understanding of the wife's plight, or does he ride the moral high ground and wash his hands of any responsibility?

As with all of the scenarios in this book, *An Affair of Two Halves* is not designed to pass judgment on his behavior or opinions. Rather, it's an opportunity for you to understand him better. So whatever his question choices are, he will have his reasons. It will be exposing either his fears, his trust, his ability to forgive, and what he's learned from his past experiences. That's why asking him to explain his choices will give you a better idea of where he's coming from. And telling him how you'd respond will give him a better understanding of how you feel and what insights you've gained from your past.

---

* Some men find this scenario particularly frustrating because they want to know all the information so that they can regain a sense of control. One woman reported to us that her man, on being asked what he'd do next, replied that he'd arrange a loan at his bank so that he could pay the detective in total, and therefore get the other half of the story.

706.

THE INVISIBLE MAN

THIS ONE IS ALL ABOUT ULTIMATE POWERS AND WHAT HE'D
DO WITH THEM. YOU MAY NEED TO ALLOW A BIT OF TIME
FOR THIS ONE BECAUSE IT'S A SUBJECT QUITE A FEW MEN
DELIGHT IN EXPLORING.

ASK HIM THIS: "What do you dream about? I'm going to ask you a
few questions, and I want you to answer them as quickly as possible."

- If you could have an exceptional talent, what would it be
  and what would you do with it?

- If you could enhance one of your physical attributes, what
  would it be and what would you do with it?

- If you could make yourself invisible, what would you do?

- If you could defy gravity and fly unassisted, what would
  you do?

- If you became the ruler of the world, what's the first thing
  you'd do?

- If you could travel back to a time before you were born,
  where would you go?

- If you could predict the future, what would you do?

- If you could go back into the past and bring someone back with you, who would you bring?

- Who would you like to be in history?

- If you could go back in your own lifetime and change something, what would you change?

WHAT DID HE TELL YOU?

How did he use his power—for the good of mankind, for his family, or for his own purposes? Did he seek recognition for his feats, or were they entirely selfless? What were the things he chose to do, and why did he think they were worth doing?

As gender roles merge, the drive to find a male identity and prove self-worth through independent performance has never been stronger. For this reason, many of us indulge in power-based fantasies. But we seldom, if ever, divulge them. However, his responses in this exercise may possibly give you an inkling of what they are and how pressured he feels to achieve personal power and a lasting significance. In these scenarios, the more he concentrated on how things would feel—in other words, concentrating on the process as opposed to the effect they would have in the wider world—the more secure and grounded we think he will be. However, the more waves he hoped to make, the greater his need will be for recognition and the less comfortable he'll be within himself.

For example, was being invisible an exciting prospect for him because he could feel people walking right through him, or because he would be able to infiltrate a top-level political meeting and receive widespread attention for exposing corruption?

707.

THE CONFESSION

WHO SAID THAT IF YOU REALLY LOVE SOMEONE YOU
SHOULD BE ABLE TO LET THEM GO? OBVIOUSLY, SOMEONE
WHO HASN'T HAD TO DO IT. IN *THE CONFESSION*,
YOUR MAN IS FACED WITH JUST SUCH A DILEMMA.
SO TREAD LIGHTLY.

ASK HIM THIS: "How good are you at giving advice? I'm going to read you a story line, and I want you to answer the questions at the end, giving as much detail as possible."

Your wife confesses to you that she's become very attracted to someone else. She's been plagued by guilt for weeks now, and although nothing has happened, she just can't stop thinking about him. Even when she's making love to you, she is thinking about him. She is terribly confused because she still loves you and wonders why she should even have room in her heart for someone else. She asks you for advice.

- You ask her a number of questions, the first of which would be…

- What other questions do you ask her?

- Why would you want to know all these facts?

- What would your advice to her be?

WHAT DID HE TELL YOU?

How many questions did he ask the wife? How quick was he in giving advice, and was the advice constructive, or did he become angry or defensive? Did he try to understand what the wife might have been going through? In other words, did he ask questions relating to her feelings rather than factual ones? Did he ask whether the third party was aware of her interest, and if so, was he reciprocating her feelings?

This scenario is not an attempt to judge your man, merely to find out how he might react. It's also an opportunity for you to see his point of view.* There are different approaches that he could take here, all of which may be valid and reasonable. He may, for instance, become hostile and resistant to helpful dialogue. This is understandable, as he will be feeling hurt and rejected.

He may tell the wife that if she is so obsessed about this man, she should just go off and get it out of her system, and that he'll wait for her. This is a very noble approach but fraught with problems. It may subconsciously be saying that he doesn't care, and it may lead to a precedent that places him in a very weak position, which in turn might make the wife think less of him.

A third approach would be for him to see the other man as a symptom, a signpost that things are not right in the relationship, and that he and the wife should both examine where they are and where they think they're going together.

---

* You could reverse the exercise and get your man to question you. It might allow you to both compare your respective priorities and approaches.

708.

THE BEAUTIFUL DENTIST

THE BEAUTIFUL DENTIST WILL BRING UP A RAFT OF
DIFFERENT ISSUES FOR BOTH YOU AND YOUR MAN TO
CONSIDER. THERE IS A LOT OF INFORMATION IN THE FIRST
PART OF THE SCENARIO, SO READ IT SLOWLY AND CLEARLY.

ASK HIM THIS: "What are you like at judging character? I'm going to read you a story, and then I'll ask you some questions."

Alan meets a beautiful woman at a party and has a brief but fascinating conversation with her before she has to leave. A good friend of his who is also at the party and who knows the woman well tells him that the woman is in the throes of a messy breakup and is very vulnerable and he should definitely not consider trying to contact her at the moment. His friend refuses to tell him anymore.

As the days go by, Alan can't stop thinking about her and persuades his friend to at least say what line of work the woman is in. He's told, as long as he promises to take it no further. It turns out that the woman is a dentist, and armed with her name it doesn't take him long to call around and find her place of work. Two days later he goes around and waits outside her surgery. When she emerges, he "accidentally" bumps into her and suggests they go for coffee. She agrees. Over coffee she asks him if he really just bumped into her by chance or whether he actually set it up. Alan says it was completely by chance.

I'm going to ask you some questions now, but if at any stage you'd like me to read the story or part of it again, just ask.

- I want you to think of a name for Alan's friend.

- What do you think Alan did that was right?

- What do you think Alan did that was wrong?

- What do you think Alan's friend did that was right?

- What do you think Alan's friend did that was wrong?

- What do you think the woman did that was right?

- What do you think the woman did that was wrong?

What Did He Tell You?

What his answers will tell you is how much he understands his own and others' needs and the degree to which he can balance them against each other. There will be any number of possible answers to the questions. Here are some points worth considering:

Did he think Alan's friend was a male or a female? This is important. It's possible that in his experience it would be more likely for a woman to give Alan advice. He may feel a woman's advice would be more genuine, and that her disapproval would be more unpalatable than a man's if he chose to ignore this advice. He might also suspect the motives of a man. He might see him as competition, and that warning him off was a none-too-subtle way of keeping the woman for himself.

What did he think Alan did that was right? Admittedly, Alan showed initiative and resourcefulness, and he followed his heart. But these are merely attributes. Did he actually do anything that was right?

What did he think Alan did that was wrong? On the surface, Alan ignored his friend's advice and was willing to take advantage of the dentist's vulnerability. He also lied to her about their chance meeting. But it could be argued that Alan only had the friend's word for the woman's situation. Regardless, what right did the friend have for trying to protect the woman in the first place? Maybe Alan could have been just what the woman needed.

What about the friend? What did she or he do that was right? The friend was trying to protect the woman and could have been trying to protect Alan. What did the friend do that was wrong? Relenting to pressure and giving the woman's occupation is fairly obvious. But should the friend be playing God? It's fine to tell Alan about the woman's circumstances, but should he or she warn him off? Isn't that inferring a lack of trust in Alan's judgment or morals?

Finally, the woman. What did she do right? Questioning the randomness of her meeting with Alan was astute, but neither right nor wrong. And what did she do that was wrong? Well, if she was dubious about the fact that he just happened to be outside her workplace, why would she agree to have coffee with him? Again, though, we only have the friend's word that she is in an unsettled place after her breakup. Maybe she's stronger than the friend gives her credit for.

709.

THE BURGLARY

THIS SCENARIO ALWAYS PROVOKES A LOT OF DISCUSSION.
IT'S ALSO AN OPPORTUNITY FOR YOU TO BOTH GET INTO
YOUR ROLES AND PLAY AN ADULT VERSION OF COPS AND
ROBBERS.

ASK HIM THIS: "Have you ever witnessed a crime? I'm going to read you a story, and then I want you to answer any questions that I give you as quickly as possible."

You're walking home from a party at 2:00 a.m. when you hear a security alarm and see a man running out of a house carrying a bag. He's wearing a black jacket and trousers, black gloves, and black sneakers. There have been a lot of robberies in the neighborhood lately, and you realize that this must be the culprit.

As he rushes past, you trip him up and he falls heavily. You wrestle the bag off him and only then do you realize that you know him. It's one of your neighbors, Bob Smith. He confesses to the burglaries but explains that his wife is dying of cancer and this is the only way he can raise the necessary funds for a cure.

You know his wife, and one of her three daughters is in your son's class at elementary school. She is a lovely woman and does a lot of good work in the community, and her illness is viewed as a great tragedy. On reflection you decide to give him back the bag and let him go. You promise that you won't tell anyone. He thanks you profusely and says he'll make it up to you someday. He tucks the bag under his arm and disappears into the night.

Just after Smith has run off, a squad car attracted by the alarm arrives, and the police ask you if you've seen anyone in the area. You can't tell if anybody else saw you with your neighbor or not, so you decide to give a brief and vague description of someone you didn't recognize who was running away, wearing a black jacket and carrying a black bag.

The next day the police come to your house and go through your statement again, asking you for more details. One of the officers reads out each point from a notebook.

He says: "You said last night that you were walking home. Why were you walking?"
    You say...

"And you said that you saw a man running from a house. Is that right?"
    You say...

"You told us he was wearing a black jacket. Is that right?"
    You say...'

"Is it possible that his jacket was actually dark green?"
    You say...

"It says here that you told us last night that he was carrying a black bag. Is this correct?"

You say...

"Would you say it looked heavy?"

You say...

"You said that he ran right past you, but you didn't see his face. Is that right?"

You say...

"So you wouldn't recognize him if you saw him again. Is that right?"

You say...

"Well sir, I have to tell you that we also talked to another man in the area last night by the name of Bob Smith. We know that Mr. Smith is a neighbor of yours. Is that right?"

You say...

"How well do you know him or his family?"

You say...

"So if you'd seen Mr. Smith last night, you'd have recognized him."

You say...

"Well, he told us that he saw you running out of the house in question carrying a black bag. We found the bag, and it contains items of jewelry. We want to take you down to the precinct for fingerprinting."

You say...

WHAT DID HE TELL YOU?

In the face of being ratted on by his neighbor, does he spill the beans to protect himself, or does he stick to his original story and keep his promise? Did he immediately change his story, or did he stall for time while he considered the implications? If he changed his story in the belief that Smith had turned on him, he may not be versed in police questioning techniques. How does he know that Smith really has implicated him? He's only got the police's word for it. If the police suspected that he was covering for Smith, they may well have fabricated the allegation to get him to squeal.

It's quite usual for people to immediately rat on Smith once they're told he's actually accused them. Self-protection comes rapidly to the front while loyalty to someone they've made a promise to goes straight out the door. Many of us don't mind protecting another human being as long as we're not going to lose something ourselves. But it's also reassuring to know that there are people out there, although admittedly very few, who are strong and independent enough to carefully consider all the options in the face of their own betrayal.

Of course some men won't let Smith go, or they immediately tell the police so as not to become an accessory to the crime. Whether they do this because, in principle, to do otherwise would be to break the law or whether they do it to protect themselves from becoming an accessory to the crime is a moot point. In this case, you'd want to know whether they've considered what effect ratting on Smith will have on his sick wife and dependent family.

Because of the way their brains are structured, men and women often take different approaches to moral questions. With more connections between their brain's emotion centers, women are better equipped to base their moral thinking on empathy with others while men, whose brains are more impulse directed, tend to rely on a predetermined set of guiding principles rather than on personal feelings.

710.

FANTASY FOLLIES

IN *FANTASY FOLLIES*, YOUR MAN WILL REVEAL HOW
IMAGINATIVE HE IS, AND WHETHER HE'S ABLE TO SHOW
A MIX OF HONESTY AND DIPLOMACY WHEN CAUGHT RED-
HANDED IN WHAT IS NOTHING MORE THAN A FICTITIOUS
SETUP.

ASK HIM THIS: "Have you ever had a dream girl? I'm going to read you a scenario, and I want you to answer any questions that I put to you as we go along."

You are fantasizing about a beautiful woman whom you talked to recently at a party. Your eyes are shut and you are smiling. So I want you to do this now. Close your eyes and think about this woman.

Now your girlfriend comes into the room and says: "You look very happy. What are you thinking about?"
    You say…

She says: "What made you think of that?"
    You say…

"So, why were you so pleased?"

350

"When did you last think about this?"

"How important is it to you?"

"What sort of other thoughts do you have like this?"

"Tell me more about what you were first thinking."

"You seem uneasy. What are you trying to hide?"

"You were looking kind of aroused. How come?"

"Do you really expect me to believe that?"

"Have you ever lied to me before?"

"So why are you lying to me now?"

(At this point if he's been telling the truth, congratulate him on his honesty, and stop the exercise. If, however, he's continued spinning you a line, ask him the last question.)

"Why don't you just admit you were thinking about that woman you met the other night at the party?"

WHAT DID HE TELL YOU?

In spite of knowing that you knew what he was thinking about, did he still lie? Do you think he was trying to protect you or himself? Or was he just enjoying himself and playing along with the story? How plausible were his answers? Did it make you wonder about the truthfulness of things he's told you in the past?

If he has lied in this scenario, the inference is that he may also lie in the real world, both to you and to others. But only you will know for sure. However, you shouldn't automatically conclude that this is a bad thing. People often lie in a relationship to protect the other person, and it can be regarded as an act of loyalty. But if your man is to lie, would you want him to do it in order to protect you or others? Or does he have the right to protect himself, especially from you?

This scenario often leads to a host of questions about honesty. Here are a few issues you might not have thought of:

Is lying always bad? Is there a place for lying in a relationship? Should you lie to protect your relationship? For instance, if your husband/boyfriend has committed a crime, would you lie to protect him? Would you ask him to lie for you? Under what circumstances *would* you agree to lie for your husband? Should we always be honest about our private thoughts? Are there secrets you think you should never divulge in a relationship because the other person would never really be able to understand or forget what you told them?

Do you have a right to know every single thing your partner is thinking about? What do you do if you suspect your partner is lying about his/her faithfulness? What have you lied about with previous partners? Has someone ever come to you and admitted that they've been lying to you? Have you ever admitted being dishonest?

What's the biggest lie you ever told your parents? What did they do if they caught you lying? How has this affected your attitude toward lying?

Would you hide information about yourself if you thought that divulging it would mean missing out on a relationship or a job? And what about lying to protect your country? Do you think there are circumstances in which politicians should lie?

Telling a lie is one thing, but what about living a lie? What would that involve? Do you know anybody who does that?

711.

A WEEKEND AWAY

THIS SCENARIO WILL PLUNGE YOUR MAN INTO THE REALMS
OF FANTASY, SO TRY TO HELP HIM STAY IN HIS ROLE BY
KEEPING YOUR DELIVERY LIVELY AND COLORFUL.

ASK HIM THIS: "Have you ever been to a conference at a resort hotel? I'm going to read you a story, and I want you to fill in the gaps as quickly as possible."

You're at a weekend conference at a coastal resort. You've only just checked in at reception and registration. You enter the elevator to go up to your room. Also in the elevator is a woman who, you know by the name tag on the lapel of her jacket, is also attending the conference. She looks up at you and...

She seems a little tired but still she...

It turns out that she's on the same floor as you, and as she walks up the corridor to her room you...

The first official item of the conference is a cocktail party, so after having a brief nap and freshening up, you head back to the elevator. As luck would have it, the woman is walking back down the corridor too, and whatever she'd done in the interim, the transformation is stunning. Despite yourself you say...

She smiles and compliments you on your appearance. You can't help but notice that she's…

Her face is all…

Her voice is…

Her hair smells of…

And she moves like a…

Once in the function room you offer to get her a drink. She asks for a…

As you talk to her, you realize that…

Somehow she has a way of making you…

And by the time you've finished your drinks, you are thinking that…

You ask her if she wants another drink and she says yes. But when you return, she's with another man. If you were asked later to describe him, you would say that he was…

The man looks at you as if…

It's at this point that she introduces the man as her husband. You say…

But you think…

What Did He Tell You?

As in most of these scenarios, there are no right or wrong responses.
They are merely indicators. So if your man plays along with the idea
of a romantic interlude, it could mean several things. On one hand, it
could show he's still a red-blooded male who's not averse to flirting
when the opportunity arises. It can be an almost automatic response*
and a way of proving to himself that he still has what it takes—and
it doesn't necessarily mean that he'll take it any further. Though if
you want to judge how immersed he became in his role, note his
reaction when he meets the husband. Does he appear guilty or simply
amused? On the other hand, by playing along he could be taking the
opportunity to tease you. Or perhaps he's just doing what he thinks is
expected of him as a real man.

What does it say about him if he doesn't see the woman as a potential
pickup? Again, this could mean different things. He could have a
genuinely healthy attitude toward women. He could have imagined
her as being unattractive. Or he could be reflecting how he feels about
you, and so it doesn't occur to him to play the romantic line with
the woman in the scenario because you're everything in his life at the
moment. Alternatively, he may just be terrified of your reaction.

---

* It's not just men who are wired to react to certain biological signals. A
New Mexico University team found that when women are at the most fertile
period of their menstrual cycle, they prefer the aroma of dominant men and
are attracted to men with symmetrical bodies. Researchers found that even
ovulating women in stable relationships were attracted to symmetrically
shaped men if their husbands had asymmetrical bodies. Genetic studies have
confirmed that a female will often mate with a good provider but then sleep
around with better genetic stock in order to pass on superior genes to her
offspring. This makes good biological sense as she will produce strong, healthy
children who will be well looked after.

712.

THE SETUP

THERE'S A SAYING THAT GOES: "THE END JUSTIFIES THE MEANS." BUT DOES IT? *THE SETUP* SHOULD ENLIGHTEN YOU.

ASK HIM THIS: "What lengths would you go to in order to contrive an "accidental" meeting with someone? I'm going to read you a series of scenarios, and I want you to answer a question after each one."

Patrick is attracted to one of the women at his workplace and decides to devise an elaborate plan to hook up with her. She is in upper management and he wouldn't normally have any contact with her, so he needs to find a way of meeting her "accidentally."

He rents a car identical to hers, and then before she leaves work one evening he finds her car and lets the air out of three of the tires. He then makes sure he is driving past her just as she gets to her car. He offers to give her his spare, plus he'll take one of his wheels off his car so that she can get home. But would she mind giving him a ride to the subway? She may decide to simply ride with him to the subway in his car. But either way he'll get to talk with her and show his concern.

- What do you think of his plan?

In the second scenario, Carl is trying to set up an accidental meeting with a woman named Margaret. He knows where she lives and so sends her a dozen red roses. The next day he turns up at her place and asks her if she received some flowers the previous day. She says yes, and then he tells her that the florist got the wrong address, sending them to Carlow Crescent instead of Carlow Street where his girlfriend lives. He explains that they were a peace offering. It was her birthday yesterday, and he was trying to patch up a rift that had developed between them. But she had dumped him anyway. Carl seems suitably upset, so Margaret invites him in for coffee. And so it begins.

• What do you think about Carl's ruse?

In the third scenario, Beth often notices a man walking his black standard poodle in the park near where she lives. She is very attracted to him. So she hires her own standard poodle for the day and contrives to be out walking it at the same time as the man is walking his dog.

Naturally, when the man sees Beth with an identical dog, he stops and strikes up a conversation. She learns that his name is David and he seems every bit as interesting as she hoped he'd be. They talk at length about their dogs, how long they'd had them, their particular quirks, and so on, and then they say they'll probably bump into each other tomorrow.

Beth takes the poodle back and the next day is sitting forlornly on a park bench when David comes by with his dog. He enquires where her poodle is and she says that it was run over and killed that very morning. He is very upset and sympathetic for her, and offers to take her for a drink at a local café.

• So what do you think of Beth's scheme?

- Finally, if all three of these relationships were to develop, do you think that Patrick, Carl, and Beth should own up to their ruses?

What Did He Tell You?

Did your man's opinion differ depending whether the setup was perpetrated by a woman or a man? If so, why? Does he think any of these three setups are acceptable, or does he think they're all too manipulative? Did he consider the implications if the relationships were to develop, given that they would be based on deception? And what about you? What's your take on setups?

Some people think that any setup is unnatural and goes against fate. They say that whatever contrivance you use to assist with a meeting is a deceit and even if you admit to it later, the relationship will be soured. What do you both think about that?

These scenarios should tell you plenty about his values. You could also ask him if he's ever set up similar "accidental" meetings with prospective partners. Our examples may pale in comparison.

713.

DADS AND DAUGHTERS

DADS AND DAUGHTERS IS AN ETHICAL DILEMMA THAT MAY
GIVE YOU AN INKLING INTO THE WAY HE CAN REACT WHEN
SUDDENLY FACED WITH A DIFFICULT SITUATION. TRY TO
KEEP HIM INVOLVED IN THE STORY, BUT IF HE CONTRIVES
TO BAIL OUT, THE EXERCISE IS CONCLUDED.

ASK HIM THIS: "Do you remember the first time you met the in-laws? I'm going to read you a scenario, and I want you to complete the unfinished sentences."

You go for the weekend with your girlfriend, Liz, who is the love of your life, to her parents' home in another city. You've never met them before. You're planning on telling them that Liz is pregnant, and that you're going to get married. It's been a whirlwind romance, so it will take everyone by surprise.

Right from the start you like her parents, especially the father, who seems to have taken a particular shine to you and because you have many things in common. It's going well and you're all having a good time. But before you can break the news, your girlfriend's sister, Annie, arrives with her five-year-old son. You immediately recognize her as someone you had a one-night stand with years ago. Seeing her makes you want to...

You manage to find a moment alone with the sister, and you say to her…

Annie, however, now tells you that this one-night stand resulted in her becoming pregnant, and that you are the father of her five-year-old son.

But your conversation is interrupted by the father, who's arranged for you to have a game of golf at his club. Driving to the golf club, you begin to wonder what the three women back at home are talking about. You think they…

You're out on the course, and even though you're actually a good player, your game has gone to pieces. But as the game progresses you calm down somewhat, and while you still play poorly, you admire the father's play. He starts talking about Liz and Annie, telling you how lucky he is to have two such beautiful daughters, and that if he was your age he wouldn't know which of them to choose.

At the bar after the game, the father introduces you to one of his friends, Sam. Sam says: "You remind me of someone. Oh, I know, it's because you look a bit like Annie's son."

On the way home the father says: "It's strange how people can look so similar and yet not be related. You may have noticed how much Liz looks like me and yet I'm not actually her father." Liz had already told you that she was the result of a brief affair her mother had.

When you get home, you find the mother in the kitchen preparing dinner. She tells you that the girls are in their rooms.

• What do you do?

What Did He Tell You?

Was he able to comprehensively outline the dynamics of the situation, and resolve it with compassion, maturity, and responsibility? Did he bail out, or did he treat the whole thing as a joke and fail to see the implications for all concerned?

If his initial reaction was to bail out, what reasons did he give? Perhaps he was so shocked that he instinctively put it in the too-hard-to-handle basket. But if he wanted to quit the scene after considering the implications, then he would seem to be lacking in empathy or responsibility. Maybe he forgot that in the scenario he was in love with his girlfriend, and if the situation were real it would be highly unlikely for him to contemplate running off. Also, given that his girlfriend is pregnant, he would be failing in his duty as a loving partner and future husband.

If he didn't bail out, did he try to handle the situation on his own, or did he enlist the assistance of the parents? How did he do this? Did he approach both the parents, or just one of them? Which one, and why? Or did he approach the sisters first, and if so, which one, and why? And what did he say to them?

Did he consider how everybody would be affected, including the five-year-old son? Did he consider how *he* would feel if he suddenly met a son he didn't know he had? What would he say to him?

Did he take into account his own shock and realize that this would affect his thinking and behavior? Has he ever been in a situation in which he's had to make these kinds of decisions or considerations?

How would you have handled the situation if you were his future wife? What if you were the sister? And last, how would you have liked him to handle the situation?

DREAMS ARE MADE OF THIS

WHETHER YOU DREAM OR NOT, THIS SCENARIO OPENS THE
DOOR ON A RICH DREAM LIFE FOR YOU AND YOUR MAN TO
SHARE. YOU'RE BOUND TO BE SURPRISED AT WHAT'S THERE
TO BE DISCOVERED.

ASK HIM THIS: "Do you remember your dreams? No one is quite
sure what dreams are all about. Some think they're full of symbolism
while others believe they are our entrance into a parallel universe.
I'm going to read you a few simple dream events, and I want you to
imagine that these were part of a recent dream you had. Then I'm
going to ask you to tell me what you think the things in the dream
might symbolize and what the dream might mean. After that, I want
you to try one on me."

In the first dream you're walking beside a beautiful, slow-flowing
river. The sun is shining and you feel at peace with the world.
Standing on one leg in the middle of the river is a white heron
peering into the water. For some reason you suddenly feel very
afraid. Just then a huge crocodile leaps out of the river and devours
the heron with one snap of its jaws. You wake up in a sweat.

• What do you think the river could be a symbol for?

- What could the heron be a symbol for?

- What does the crocodile represent?

- What do you think the meaning of the dream could be?

In the second dream you are lost in a maze of narrow streets in an unfamiliar city, and to make matters worse you can't understand the language. A beautiful young woman in a red dress takes you by the hand and leads you out of the city to a castle with a balcony high above a lake. As you stand on the balcony looking out at the view, she approaches with a drink trolley. You suddenly feel a wave of joy, which just as quickly turns to horror as she pushes it into you. The last thing you remember before you wake up is falling toward the lake below.

- What do you think the city could be a symbol for?

- What could the woman in the red dress be a symbol for?

- What could the castle represent?

- What do you think the drinks trolley could be a symbol for?

- And the lake? Could that be a symbol for anything?

- What do you think the meaning of the dream could be?

In the third dream you are sitting at a large table in a basement. There are men dressed in suits sitting around the table. You are showing them a small mechanical device, which you have taken out of a box. You are very nervous. One of the men takes the device and later you find it in the urinal. You are disgusted.

Suddenly, the men come in to the urinal and are all very friendly toward you. At this point you wake up.

- What do you think the table could be a symbol for?

- What does the basement represent?

- What are the men in suits symbolic of?

- What is the mechanical device a symbol for?

- What does the urinal stand for?

- What do you think the meaning of the dream could be?

In the fourth dream you are climbing a ladder that's leaning against a very high tower. On your back is a baby in a sling. It is crying, and you are worried that the ladder may fall over before you get to the top. But you do arrive safely, and a large bear takes the baby, which has now changed into a one-legged pig, and puts it into a glass cot. The bear becomes a white horse. You mount it and gallop off. You feel a strong sense of freedom. At this point you wake up.

- What could the tower be a symbol for?

- What could the ladder represent?

- What is the baby symbolic of?

- What is the pig a symbol for?

- What does the bear represent?

- What about the cot? What is that a symbol for?

- What is the white horse a symbol for?

- What do you think the meaning of the dream could be?

What Did He Tell You?

A person who believes that dreams are full of symbols would have a field day here. A crocodile might represent primordial fear while a bear could signify victory over enemies. Horses are often said to be associated with riches and wealth and dreaming about pigs, they say, denotes future prosperity. Whatever is the truth of these notions, they have no relevance to us here.

What is of interest is how you and your man interpreted the things in the dreams as areas of relevance in your lives. Attempting to make all the elements come together in a credible way, by thinking of things that the dream might mean, can be a fascinating way of exploring yourselves and your situation.

This sort of scenario is never going to be definitive, but it can give you new and interesting ways of looking at your lives that you may not have considered before. For example, you could have said that the river in the first dream represented the passage of your life. You might have decided that the heron represented some insecurity about your love life because it was standing on one leg. The crocodile could then be any event, habit, or person that impacted negatively on your love life. And that might have made you consider who or what that might be, which might have led to a new insight. On the other hand, if you saw the heron as an evil presence, the crocodile could be your savior.

There are any number of possible interpretations, and they can all make for interesting speculations, which in turn can lead to new perceptions and a greater understanding of each other. If you've found this scenario helpful, you can continue it by discussing your real dreams and sharing what you think they might mean.

715.

THE MAN IN THE WHITE SUIT

THIS SCENARIO AND THE DISCUSSION IT'S LIKELY TO PROMOTE WILL UNDOUBTEDLY REVEAL A LOT ABOUT YOUR RESPECTIVE FEELINGS ON HONESTY, PRIVACY, AND FLEXIBILITY WITHIN A RELATIONSHIP. IT MAY TAKE A WHILE, SO MAKE SURE YOU HAVE PLENTY OF TIME.

ASK HIM THIS: "Have you ever fallen in love at first sight? I'm going to read you a scenario about people falling in love, and I want you to answer some questions along the way."

Marie is dining at a restaurant with her husband, Claude. Halfway through the main course, Claude excuses himself to go to the bathroom. While he's away, a waiter approaches and discreetly slips Marie a handwritten note.

It reads:
"Please forgive me for intruding on your privacy, but I don't know what else to do. From the moment I saw you enter the restaurant, I fell deeply in love. This has never happened to me before. If you see me, maybe you will have the same feeling. I am the man in the white suit at the table by the window. If you feel anything, let me know with some gesture. I will find a way to contact you later."

Marie cannot help herself. She glances furtively to her left, peers between some other diners and sees a man in a white suit who is sitting alone by the window. He is the most handsome man she has ever seen!

- Is what the man in the white suit did okay? What should Marie do?

This is what happens next. A few moments later Claude comes back and takes his seat. Marie smiles up at Claude and pretends to adjust her dress while slipping the note surreptitiously underneath her, hoping that he hasn't seen. She blushes. She is not herself anymore. She is intrigued, confused, and very excited all at the same time. She and Claude have lived together for ten years in a comfortable relationship that has become uneventful and boring. But they are married and Marie has always known that she will be faithful. In fact, she told him as much a few days ago when he seemed distracted and insecure about her fidelity.

But now, as she steals another look at this beautiful dark-haired man, a tiny finger of doubt slips into her heart and then another and another until a whole hand grips her with a passion she has never known before. As calmly as she can, Marie takes her red napkin, touches it to her mouth, and then shakes it in his direction, as if flicking crumbs from it before restoring it to her lap.

- How do you feel about the way Marie has reacted?

This is what happens next. As Marie returns the napkin to her lap, Claude leans forward and says, "Why were you waving to that man?"

"What man? What are you talking about?" says a very startled Marie.

"That man by the window. You looked as if you were waving at him. Do you know him?"

"Don't be silly, Claude, you're being paranoid again. I was just flicking crumbs from my napkin. I've never seen that man before!" But as she glances over to the table by the window, the man looks up for a moment and seems to smile at her.

> • How do you feel about Marie's behavior now? How do you feel about the man's behavior? And what about Claude's behavior?

This is what happens next: Claude leans back in his chair and says, "Marie, is there something you want to tell me? Something you *should* tell me?"

"This is ridiculous, Claude! I don't understand what's gotten into you!" says Marie.

"Look Marie, I'm your husband. Why won't you be honest with me?"

"I *am* being honest with you!" says Marie. "I don't know that man. I've never seen him before! It's you I love, why won't you believe me?"

"Because I think you're hiding something from me," says Claude, leaning forward.

"I'm hiding nothing, nothing at all!" cries Marie.

"Well, let's see," says Claude, standing up and moving to her side of the table. "When I came back from the bathroom, I saw you reading something, and then you hid it when I reached the table. What was it?"

"You must have been mistaken. I wasn't reading anything."

"Okay, then. Prove it. Stand up."

"What?"

"Stand up. I think you're sitting on something."

Ashen faced, Marie slowly stands up. For a moment the note remains hidden in the folds of her dress. Then it flutters to the floor. Claude bends down, picks it up, and reads it.

- What do you think Claude should do now, and what should Marie do?

This is what happens next: Claude pockets the note and says, "I'll get the bill." With that he turns on his heel and heads for the lobby. Marie stands staring ahead as if transfixed, then with tears beginning to well in her eyes, she sits down again. She doesn't know what to do.

As his credit card is being processed, Claude beckons to the waiter, slips him a fifty-dollar bill, and says, "Thank you for writing the note for me and delivering it so perfectly. It's a little game we like to play."

"It was my pleasure, sir," says the young waiter.

Claude then comes back to the table, gets his jacket, and snorts at Marie:

"I'm going to get the car. I'll see you out front," and he walks out of the restaurant.

Marie stands awkwardly, still feeling stunned. She gathers up her pocketbook and is about to follow Claude outside. But she can't resist taking one last look at the man in the white suit. At that precise moment, he looks up and once again he smiles at her. The effect is mesmerizing, and before she knows what's happening she finds herself walking slowly and very deliberately toward his table.

- What do you think happens next?

- What do you think of Claude's ruse?

- What would have happened if Marie had confessed right away to having been given a note? And what if she had then told Claude to approach the man in the white suit to ask him what he was up to? What would Claude do then?

- Would it be all right to set up your partner if you thought that she either was wanting to have an affair, or was already having one? Would this be any different from hiring a private detective?

WHAT DID HE TELL YOU?

Like many of the scenarios in this book, *The Man in the White Suit* has been designed to promote discussion. While we don't wish to preempt this to any great degree, there are a few things you may like to consider. For example, how clearly could your man see a motivation for Marie and Claude's behavior? Was he able to change his mind about Claude's behavior when he realized it was a setup? How understanding was he of Marie's behavior? Did he feel Claude's actions were justified? Did he think the waiter should have agreed to Claude's request to write and deliver the note? Did he have any thoughts about the future of Claude and Marie's relationship? Did he question the wisdom of Claude's tactics? After all, he's ignited something in Marie that he will have no control over. And what about Marie? Did your man have any thoughts about what would happen between her and the man in the white suit? What did you think would happen when Marie walked up to him? What did you want to happen?

What if you think your man is having an affair? Would it be fair to set a trap for him? What if you think he might be tempted to have one? Is it okay to test him? Did the ending of the scenario take you by surprise, or did you see it coming? Did he? Can you imagine yourself acting like Marie? Can you imagine circumstances where your man might act like Claude?

SCENARIO INDEX

Numbers refer to scenarios

We welcome your feedback.
Please visit the website for more scenarios and to share your thoughts and experiences with other readers:

www.everythinghehasnttoldyouyet.com